contents

Introduction 3

1. The employment law system 8

Employment tribunals 8
Employment Appeal Tribunal 17
Other courts 17
Compromise agreements 18
Binding arbitration 19
Settling cases through Acas 19

2. Categories of worker 20

Employed or self-employed 20
Young workers 23
Apprentices 24
Children 24
Part-time workers 25
Temporary employees 27
Agency workers 30
Homeworkers 31
Public sector workers 32
Working outside the UK 32

3. Starting work and the employment contract 34

References and employer checks 34
Previous criminal convictions 36
Written contracts 37
What makes a contract 39
Implied terms 41
Contract changes 49

4. Rights to pay and conditions 55

National minimum wage 55
Pay slips and pay intervals 56
Deductions and underpayments 57
Overpayments 60
Guarantee pay 61
Medical suspension pay 61
Equal pay 62
Working hours and breaks 70
Holidays 72
Time off for public duties 75

5. Union and collective organisation 77

The right to recognition 77
Membership rights 81
Rights to time off 86
Rights to information 88
Employee reps and European works councils 89
Internal union matters 90

6. Discrimination 92

Types of unlawful discrimination 92
Direct and indirect discrimination 95
Harassment 100
Victimisation 103

Proving and inferring discrimination 104
Positive action 106
Disability discrimination 107
Taking a discrimination claim 115
The Commissions 118

7. Sick pay and sickness absence 121

Statutory sick pay 121
Dismissal while sick 123
Medical reports 128

8. Leave for working parents 129

Antenatal care 129
Maternity leave 130
Maternity pay 131
Returning to work 133
Appointment and dismissal 134
Paternity leave 136
Adoption leave 136
Parental and dependency leave 137
Flexible working 138

9. Industrial action 140

The legal position 140
Workplace reps 143
"Official" or "unofficial" action 143
Balloting 144
Requirements to notify employers 148
Picketing 150
Supporting other workers 151
How the law aids employers 151
State benefits for strikers 154

10. Dismissal 157

What is a dismissal? 157
Termination with/without notice 158
Non-renewal of a fixed-term contract 160
Constructive dismissal 160
Other types of dismissal 162
Fair dismissal 162
Disciplinary procedures 167
Qualifying for unfair dismissal rights 171
Employer's reasons for dismissal 174
Dismissal while on strike 176
Automatically unfair dismissals 177
Successful claims 182
Wrongful dismissal 189
Injunction 189
Date of dismissal 190

11. Redundancy 192

What is redundancy? 192
Consultation 193
Selection for redundancy 199
Alternative work 201
Looking for work 203
Qualifying for redundancy pay 203
State benefits 207

12. Business transfers and contracting out 208

Relevant transfers 209
Collective agreements and consultation 213
Protecting employment rights 215
Protection against dismissal 220
Contracting out of public services 222

Further information 224

Introduction

Since the last edition of *Law at work* was published in June 2004 there have been a number of important developments affecting employment rights. Some are the result of changes to the law through new legislation, while others have come about as a result of court rulings interpreting previous law. Most of the provisions of the *Employment Relations Act 2004* are now in force. These offer important **new collective rights**, including those on the right to **recognition** and on protection from **dismissal while taking industrial action**.

But not all of the legislative developments over the last 12 months have been positive for workers. In **October 2004**, new legislation came into force making it **more difficult for workers to take claims directly to tribunals**. The changes, which came about as a result of the *Employment Act 2002*, make it more important than ever that workplace representatives understand the law, as increasingly they will have to rely on their ability to resolve issues in the workplace itself.

Landmark court rulings over the last year include those from the House of Lords in the conjoined *Eastwood* and *McCabe* cases, which held that unfairly dismissed employees could claim compensation based on their employer's conduct prior to dismissal (see Chapter 3); the *Redcar* case on holiday pay (see Chapter 4) and the European Court of Justice decision in the *Junk* case that ruled on the obligation to consult on redundancies (see Chapter 11). As well as providing a comprehensive, up-to-date guide to employment legislation in force in April 2005, *Law at work 2005* explains how any new laws will affect existing employment rights. It is a unique guide to the law as, unlike most other publications on employment law, it examines the law from the perspective of workers and trade unions.

Law at work provides the **basic information** to help representatives and individuals decide whether there is a legal claim. It is not intended that this booklet on its own should enable a representative to take a claim through the legal procedures, but it will show where the relevant law can be found and give examples of the areas that are covered. The LRD booklet, *Case law at work*, should be read in conjunction with this booklet. It provides more detailed information on many of the cases referred to in the *Law at work 2005.*

Most trade unions offer their members a comprehensive legal service and any member or representative contemplating taking a legal case should contact the union first. In many unions, tribunal cases will be handled internally at district, regional or even head office level.

The main legislation

Statutory law covers most of the rights dealt with in this booklet. Anyone taking a tribunal case should acquaint themselves thoroughly with the appropriate sections of the statutes, which are always given. Where, for example, the booklet mentions *"section 1 RRA"* it means that the relevant law is to be found in the first section of the *Race Relations Act 1976.* (See the Further information section for where to get hold of copies of the statutes).

Relying on the **exact wording of the statute** and showing its relevance to your argument is the key to success, particularly at employment tribunals. The legal cases quoted in the booklet are examples of how the judges have previously interpreted the law.

The volume of legislation governing employment relationships has grown dramatically over the last 20 years or so. This led to demands from employers for a more **orderly system of changes**. Effective from 2004, the government has decided that **changes to statutory employment law** will only come into force on two dates in the year. These are 6 April and 1 October. However, legislation originating from European Union (EU) law will continue, for the time being, to be brought into force on the dates that are closest to the latest dates for transposition of the EU law into UK law.

Case law

The law also changes constantly as a result of decisions made by the judges. Decisions from previous legal claims, known as "case law", are referred to throughout this booklet. In each instance, the case reference is given, usually in brackets after the relevant point. The reference consists of the name of the individual or body bringing the claim to the Court and that of the individual or body against whom it is being made (see below).

Reading a case reference

"*Gibson v East Riding of Yorkshire Council [2000] IRLR 598*" tells you that the claimant (usually the employee) was called Gibson, that the case was brought against East Riding of Yorkshire Council and that the judgement was reported in the law reports for 2000. The letters *IRLR* stand for *Industrial Relations Law Reports* and the case was reported on page 598. Employment cases are also reported in *Industrial Cases Reports*, shown as *ICR*. Law reports can usually be found in large public libraries or in specialist law libraries. Where the case is not to be found in the official law reports, sometimes because it is too new to be included, it will usually have a case reference number, which follows the case name. You can then search for the text of the case yourself (see Further information).

European law

UK employment law is now heavily influenced by European law particularly, although not exclusively, in the areas of **discrimination** and **business transfers**. Judgements from the European Court of Justice (ECJ), even where the case is brought from another EU state, bind the UK courts.

Public sector workers, including those in the former public industries like gas and water, can take claims in the UK based on EU law. This process is known as "direct effect" and gives direct access to the benefit laid down in European law. To claim direct effect, however, the right under EU law has to be **precise**.

In the case of *Gibson v East Riding of Yorkshire Council [2000] IRLR 598,* the Court of Appeal held that Mr Gibson could not get the right to four weeks' holiday, as provided under the EU *Working Time Directive.* At the time, the UK government had not implemented the directive within the time limits laid down. However, the wording of the directive was not sufficiently precise about the situations when the right would apply. This meant that the UK courts could not rule that the right under the directive was automatically incorporated into his employment contract.

The ruling of the European Court in *Francovich v Italian Republic [1992] IRLR 84* gave individuals working in the **private sector** the right to sue their own state where it has failed to properly implement

European law. However, in the UK these cases must be initiated in the High Court, not the employment tribunals. The claim would be for damages for the state's failure to introduce the right under European law, rather than a claim for the right itself.

Civil liberties and employment law

The *Human Rights Act 1998* gives citizens the right to challenge **public authorities** where they act in conflict with human rights, including the right to freedom of association, expression and assembly, the right to a private life and the right to a fair trial. Claims that a public authority has infringed human rights can be taken in the UK courts. It should also be possible to use the Act to challenge the actions of public sector employers where these infringe human rights principles.

So far there have been few employment law cases using the Act, and the following attempt was unsuccessful.

Mr Whitefield, a doctor, argued that a requirement imposed by his professional organisation that he refrain from alcohol and attend meetings of Alcoholics Anonymous breached his human rights. He said that the ban prevented him from entering public houses and therefore deprived him of his right to a social, **private life**, a right guaranteed under the Act. The court rejected his claim, saying that there was nothing to stop him from going into a bar, as long as he refrained from consuming alcohol *(Whitefield v GMC [2003] IRLR 39)*.

In the case of *O'Flynn v Airlinks EAT/0269/01*, the EAT held that a company policy of **zero tolerance on alcohol and drugs** that made it clear it would randomly test employees and dismiss anyone who failed the test was **unlikely to be a breach** of the *Human Rights Act*. The policy was reasonable, taking account of the employer's legitimate safety concerns. And, in the case of *X v Y [2003] IRLR 561*, the EAT held that a person who was dismissed for failing to inform his employers that he had been charged with gross indecency did not have the right to protection under the *Human Rights Act 1998*. The activities for which he had been charged had occurred in a public place and his dismissal due to the charge could not be said to have breached his right to a private life. In addition, all legislation in the UK has to be interpreted in a way that is compatible with the European Convention on Human Rights, as far as is practicable.

The **EU Charter of Fundamental Rights**, although not legally binding, has been adopted by EU member states, including the UK. It recommends that member states guarantee the right to equality and non-discrimination and the right to freedom of thought and expression, including the right to take strike action. **Whistleblowing** is another issue of civil rights that affects employment relationships (see chapter 10 – Automatically unfair dismissals).

The *Regulation of Investigatory Powers Act 2000* places limits on the extent of employers' rights to intercept **employee e-mails, faxes and phone calls**. Regulations accompanying the Act state that the right to intercept messages only exists where consent has been given, where there is a legitimate business interest, or in cases where the employee is off work either sick or on holiday. A code of practice covering monitoring of electronic communications at work, published by the Information Commissioner, sets out guidance and recommendations on the steps that employers should take to comply with the legislation.

Employees also have rights under the *Data Protection Act 1998* that cover both information stored in electronic form and paper files or documents. Employees can ask to see any **stored personal information** held by the employer. You may see copies of your job application, references, bonus assessments, sickness and other attendance records and any e-mail communications referring to you individually. Employers can charge a fee for access, which is currently set at a maximum of £10 for each request.

The employer must abide by certain **data principles** designed to ensure that the information stored is not excessive and that it is kept securely. The Information Commissioner has published a Data Protection Code which sets out what your employer should do to comply with the Data Protection Act 1998. Part 4 of the Code was published at the end of last year. It deals with how employers should keep information on workers' health.

More information: LRD booklet, *Monitoring and surveillance – a guide to privacy at work £4.00).* Each month the LRD magazines, *Labour Research* and *Workplace Report*, update readers on legal changes. LRD also publishes booklets that look at specific areas of the law in more detail (see Further information). Relevant publications are highlighted at the end of each chapter.

1. The employment law system

There are two systems of law in the UK. **Statutory law** is the law enacted by Parliament. Statutory law provides the framework for most current employment legislation. **Common law** is law developed over the years by judges when giving their rulings in the courts and, in employment law matters, claims taken to the Employment Appeal Tribunal (EAT) make up the bulk of case law.

Employment tribunals

Employment tribunals deal with most cases taken under employment legislation. They consist of a **legally appointed chairperson** and two **lay members**, one representing employers (drawn from a panel of employer representatives) and one representing employees (drawn from a panel of employees representatives). The secretary of state appoints lay members, after consultation with employer and employee organisations. Individuals can also apply directly to be appointed.

The tribunals, like all other judicial bodies have to, where possible, interpret the law to give effect to the *Human Rights Act 1998* (see Introduction – Civil liberties and employment law). They are also bound by the rules of **natural justice**. This means they have to demonstrate an **absence of bias**, give the **right to a hearing** and give individuals the **right to state their case**. The EAT, in the case of *Skelton v Salvesen Logistics EAT/151/02*, has held that a casual relationship between tribunal members and one side's representative would not by itself indicate the presence of bias. Individuals also have the right to notice of any allegations against them and the right to challenge any charges made.

This obligation to comply with the rules of natural justice does not mean that the tribunal has to bring cases to the attention of the parties if they have not raised them. It is the obligation of each of the parties and their advisors to bring all of the relevant case law to the attention of the tribunal (*Stanley Cole (Wainfleet) v Sheridan [2003] IRLR 885*).

Claims of unfair dismissal and those connected with trade union rights, redundancy, minimum pay, equal pay, parental rights, the right to request flexible work and all forms of unlawful discrimination go to the employment tribunals which have the power to award compensation and, in some cases, reinstatement, re-engagement or equal pay.

The tribunals can also hear **breach of contract** claims (see chapter 3 – Contract changes), provided they are taken at **termination of employment**. A breach of contract claim should not be lodged with the tribunal until employment has ended. Otherwise it goes to the County or High Court. The advantage of the tribunals over the ordinary courts is that they are cheaper and relatively speedy. The disadvantage is the **shorter time limit** for presenting a claim — usually three months, rather than the six years for breach of contract claims in the ordinary civil courts. The maximum award that a tribunal can make in a breach of contract claim is £25,000. Anyone who has been **declared bankrupt** can only take a claim if approved by the trustee in bankruptcy.

As a result of changes introduced under the *Employment Act 2002*, in force from 1 October 2004, in most cases, if you are an employee (rather than a "worker" — see Chapter 2), you **cannot lodge a tribunal claim until you have followed the internal workplace disciplinary or grievance machinery** that all employers must have. A grievance is defined as "a complaint by an employee about action, which his employer has taken or is contemplating taking in relation to him". You have to set out your grievance to your employer in writing, leaving at least 28 days for a reply. If the 28 days pass and either it has not been possible to resolve the dispute or your employer has not responded, you can then submit your tribunal claim.

If these statutory procedures are not followed, compensation will be increased (if the employer is at fault) or reduced (if the fault lies with the employee).

To pursue a tribunal claim you need to submit an application to the relevant employment tribunal office. This is decided by the postcode of your normal workplace. If you are unsure where to send it, phone: 0845 795 9775 or check the Employment Tribunal website: www.employmenttribunals.gov.uk. The *2002 Act* also introduced **new forms** replacing the previous ET1 and ET3 forms. You make your application using the "Claim to an employment tribunal" form. The form can be obtained from job centres, most advice agencies and benefit offices. At present, you can still make an application without using the new form, but from 1 October 2005 you will no **longer be able to submit a claim without the right form**.

You will need to **complete all of the form**, providing answers to all of the questions it asks. Include any information on which you think your claim will be based because it is difficult to add new information later, should other issues emerge following your submission of the application.

Time limits

The application must be submitted within the **time limits** laid down for each piece of employment legislation. If a claim is based on an employer's decision taken over a period, the time limit runs from when the decision was completed. A large number of cases fail because they are out of time.

In the case of *Consignia v Sealy [2002] IRLR 624*, the Court of Appeal refused to extend the time limit in a case involving a postal worker who posted his application a day before the time limit expired. The court said that he, above all, should not have relied on next day delivery, knowing that the Royal Mail does not guarantee that all first class post will be delivered the next day. Time limits are strictly enforced — in one case, where the application faxed to the tribunal office just 11 minutes after the deadline had passed was out of time.

However, the EAT has held that provided a faxed application had been transmitted within the time limit, the fact that it did not arrive at the tribunal office fax until a few minutes later did not make it out of time (*Midland Packaging v Clark EATPA/1146/04*).

If you deliver the application in person to the tribunal office and post it through its letter box it will be held to be properly submitted, provided this is done before the expiry of the time limit for submitting the claim.

However, you should always check that the application has been received. In one case the form was posted within five weeks of the deadline but **never reached the tribunal**. Neither the claimant nor her solicitor took steps to follow it up until well past the three-month deadline. The EAT ruled that the application was out of time *(Capital Foods v Corrigan [1993] IRLR 430)*.

Union representatives need to be very aware of time limits. In unfair dismissal cases, the time limits will not be extended unless there are real reasons to show why it was **not reasonably practicable** to present the claim in time. In one case the reason given was that the fax machine had not worked first time. The EAT held that to be a relatively common occurrence and was not enough to make it not reasonably practicable to comply with the time limit (*Fishley v Working Men's College EAT/0485/04*). Although they have a power to **extend time limits**, the tribunals will not do this without very good reasons, as the case below also demonstrates.

Mr Birch submitted his application late. He argued that this was because he was suffering from a medical condition. The EAT refused to extend the time limit. When he eventually did submit the application he was still suffering from the same medical condition. In the view of the EAT, if his condition did not bar him from submitting it late, it could not have prevented him from submitting it on time *(Scottish & Southern Energy v Birch EAT/325/01).*

If you are advising or representing members and fail to alert them to the need to submit the claim in time, a tribunal could refuse to extend the time limit. In one case *(Opare-Addo v Wandsworth BC EAT/0740/01)* the fact that the claimant was represented by her union was one of the reasons why the tribunal thought it was reasonably practicable for her to have lodged the claim in time. In general, claimants who are represented are less likely to have late applications accepted. However, in another case (*Royal Mail v Spence EAT/0992/03*) where the claimant was late in lodging a tribunal claim, the fact that he had received some advice from the union did not put him outside the time limits since he had not been formally represented by the union, If a claimant is late submitting a claim because their solicitor has been negligent, for example by failing to tell them about the time limits, this is not grounds for a tribunal to extend the time limit (thought the claimant could have a claim against their solicitor).

However, it is not necessarily the case if legal advice was sought from a CAB advisor, as the Court of Appeal found in the case of *Marks & Spencer v Williams-Ryan (A1/2004/2070).* This decision contains a review of the authorities relating to extension of time. But the Court of Appeal was heavily influenced by the fact that the delay in submitting her claim was largely because Marks & Spencer had taken so long to go through their internal appeal procedure.

In a case of discrimination, a tribunal can consider a claim that was submitted outside the time limit if they consider it is **just and equitable** to do so. In the case of *Chohan v Derby Law Centre [2004] IRLR 685*, the EAT suggested that wrong advice could be regarded as a valid excuse for submitting a late application.

If you are outside the time limits through **no fault of your own**, there may be circumstances where the tribunal will consider the claim.

In the case of *Langley-Di Guiseppe v Yamaichi (Europe) International EAT/248/99*, the EAT allowed a claim which was out of time because the employee was on maternity leave, her baby was very ill and she did not know she had grounds for a claim. As soon as she was alerted to the fact, she lodged her claim.

Similarly, you may be able to **amend the basis** on which you are making an application, even if the time limit has passed.

Mr Childs was dismissed by his employers shortly after reporting them to the Vehicle Inspectorate. Childs was told by various agencies that he could not bring an unfair dismissal claim because he had not worked for a year. It was only later that he discovered that if he had been dismissed for "blowing the whistle", he did not need the year's service. The EAT held that it would be appropriate for his claim to be heard by a tribunal, even though it was presented outside the three-month time limit *(Childs v Pegasus Engineers EAT/57/02)*.

Ignorance of the time limit is not in itself enough to get an extension, unless the ignorance or mistaken belief itself was reasonable. Also take additional care if you are pursuing a breach of contract claim. If a tribunal rules it out because you have missed the time limit, the employer could still counter-claim a breach of contract. This counter-claim would be within the time limits.

Pre-hearings and deposits

Prior to the hearing the tribunal can ask you to provide a written answer to any questions, if this is considered helpful in clarifying the issues.

There may be cases where the employer tries to argue right at the start that there is **no case to answer** and asks the tribunal to dismiss the claim without a hearing. The Court of Appeal has held that, except in the rarest of cases, the tribunal should hear the evidence first and then decide whether there is a case to answer (*Logan v Commissioners of Customs & Excise [2004] IRLR 63)*.

Tribunals may order a **pre-hearing review**, during which they can ask you or your employer to pay a **deposit** of up to £500. When deciding whether to do so, the tribunal can take account of your ability to pay. If ordered, it has to be paid within 21 days or the tribunal can strike out the case. Tribunals have the right, even before hearing the evidence, to **strike out** claims they consider "ill-founded" or where the tribunal has formed the view that there is no reasonable prospect of success. They can also do this if they believe that one side is conducting the case so as to cause the other side to incur high costs (*Renwick v Scottish Widows Services EAT/1225/02*). The deposit is refunded unless the claim is lost and the tribunal makes a costs award (see below – Costs and other orders). Tribunals can throw out **weak cases** at a pre-hearing (see below – Proposed changes).

Before the tribunal hearing takes place you will be given a **set period for Acas conciliation**, with the aim of encouraging you and your employer to settle. There are two set periods. The **"short"** period (lasting for seven weeks and applying in cases involving unauthorised pay deductions, breaches of contract, redundancy, guarantee and medical suspension pay), or the **"standard"** period (lasting up to 13 weeks, which can be extended at the discretion of Acas, for all other types of tribunal claim other than discrimination, equal pay or public interest disclosure). Tribunals also can decide on cases without having a hearing, provided that both sides consent.

The hearing

If the claim clears all the hurdles above, a **full tribunal hearing** will take place, usually within three months of the original application. The length of delay can vary depending on the backlog of cases the tribunal is dealing with. If there are very long delays, claimants may be able to show that the right to a fair trial, as guaranteed under the *Human Rights Act 1998,* has been breached, according to the European Court of Human Rights in the case of *Somjee v UK [2002] IRLR 886.*

The hearing is normally **in public**. Certain claims may now be dealt with by the chair sitting alone, but not when the facts are in dispute. At the hearing it is important to present all of the case law that could be relevant, as well as relying on the words of the law itself. If the tribunal itself is aware of case law must ask both parties to make representations on it before coming to its decision *(Albion Hotel v Maia e Silva [2002] IRLR 200)*. If you submit a claim to a tribunal and then fail to attend the hearing you could have a costs order made against you (see below) unless you have very good reasons and have given them to the tribunal in advance.

You have the **right to be represented by an individual of your choice** *(Bache v Essex CC [2000] IRLR 251)* or you can represent yourself. You can call **witnesses** in support of your claim and can ask the tribunal to issue a "witness order" compelling them to attend. Once an order has been issued, an employer has to concede the time off. A tribunal can decide not to grant a witness order where, for example, the claimant asks for an excessive or unnecessary number of witnesses *(Noorani v Merseyside TEC [1999] IRLR 184)*. If you are suffering from stress or anxiety you may be able to have the **case adjourned**, although you will need to produce evidence of your medical condition.

Costs and other orders

In some cases the tribunal can award **costs** against you where it decides that you have acted vexatiously, abusively or disruptively in pursuing your claim or where, in the view of the tribunal, there was no reasonable prospect of success. A claimant who insists on continuing with a claim, despite strong legal advice from their legal advisor to withdraw, risks a costs order as does one who withdraws a claim at a very late stage (*McPherson v BNP Paribas (London Branch) [2004] IRLR 558*). The tribunal can now also issue a wasted costs order against a representative for improper, unreasonable or negligent acts.

Costs can also be ordered where **representatives** have, in the view of the tribunal, **"acted unreasonably" in** the way that they have conducted the case, rather than the fact that they have taken a case which appears to have little prospect of success (*Hosie v North Ayrshire Leisure EATS/0013/03*). Costs are awarded only for those incurred after the tribunal claim has been lodged.

A ruling of the Court of Appeal makes it clear that costs awards should not be threatened unless there is a real risk that the tribunal will impose one *(Gee v Shell [2003] IRLR 82)*, nor are they intended to be punitive (*Khan v The University of Warwick EAT/1223/02*).

In the case of *Beynon v Scadden [1999] IRLR 700,* the tribunal imposed a costs award on the grounds that the claimant's union had supported the case even though it had known that there was no prospect of success.

Tribunals also have the power to include the other side's non-legal costs in the costs award. In cases where claimants are unsuccessful it could include the cost of the time that the employer said it took to prepare the case. A Department of Trade and Industry survey put this at an average of 64 hours, with larger organisations claiming they spent more time on each case. However, the tribunals have an obligation to take account of the individual's ability to pay costs.

Claimants also have the right (known as **discovery rights**) to get from the other side documents necessary to support the claim. Some documents, primarily written communications between respective lawyers and their own clients, are "privileged" and do not have to be disclosed to the other side. But this does not extend to reports prepared by a consultant for the employer *(New Victoria Hospital v Ryan [1993] IRLR 202).*

In cases of alleged sexual offences the tribunal may issue a **restricted reporting order** to prevent identification of the party or parties. In sexual misconduct cases (sexual harassment, for example) the restriction applies up to the date of the decision. In some cases involving sexual offences the restriction is permanent (see also chapter 6 – Harassment).

Once the case has been heard, the tribunal will issue its decision and must give reasons. It will do this either at the end of the hearing or later, in which case it will issue a **reserved judgement**. The tribunal will normally deliver its judgement within three months of the end of the hearing (*Kwamin v Abbey National [2004] IRLR 516*).

There is **no right to legal aid** for employment tribunal cases, although legal aid is available for cases going to the Employment Appeal Tribunal, provided the individual qualifies under the income rules. Claimants, witnesses and volunteer representatives at employment tribunals can, however, **claim travel and other expenses**, including some loss of pay. These amount to £81 a night in central London and £71 elsewhere. If lodging with relatives, £21 a night can be claimed.

Loss of earnings of up to £45 a day can also be claimed, together with child and adult care allowances of up to £5 an hour.

Employment Appeal Tribunal

Either side can appeal against a tribunal decision, but usually only if there has been a mistake of law or the decision was "perverse" — that is, no reasonable tribunal could have come to that decision. Appeals from employment tribunals go to the Employment Appeal Tribunal (EAT) in England, Wales and Scotland and to the Court of Appeal in Northern Ireland. The appeal must be **lodged within 42 days** of the tribunal sending out its decision, not the date when you received it (*Gdynia American Shipping Lines v Chelminski [2004] IRLR 725*). In February 2005, the President of the EAT handed down a **Practice Statement** stating which documents must be lodged with the notice of appeal. If you are making an appeal you must make sure that your representative has complied with the requirements in the Practice Statement. The EAT has a discretion to extend the time limit but it is exercised only in rare and exceptional cases *(Aziz v Bethnal Green City Challenge [2000] IRLR 111)*. If you have submitted an appeal and not had it acknowledged it is important to check that it has been received. You should **contact the EAT** office to make sure. An appeal should never be contemplated without first seeking legal advice.

Appeals cannot usually be made on the basis of new evidence, particularly in cases where the claimant has been legally represented at the initial tribunal hearing *(Glennie v Independent Magazines [1999] IRLR 719)*. It is not the function of the EAT to reverse the tribunal's ruling by reinterpreting the facts, unless it is clear that the tribunal's decision on the known facts was "perverse".

Other courts

Some cases go to the **ordinary courts** rather than to the tribunals. Police prosecutions for offences to do with **picketing**, for example (see chapter 9), go to either the **Magistrates' Court** or the **Crown Court**, depending on the severity of the charge. Claims for breach of the employment contract, except on termination, usually go to the **County Court** or the **High Court**.

It is normally the case that if you take a claim to one court you cannot then take the same claim to another. However, in the case of *Sajid v Sussex Muslim Society [2002] IRLR 113*, the Court of Appeal held that the High Court could hear a claim that initially had been lodged with an employment tribunal. If the claimant makes it clear that the case is being withdrawn from the tribunal, with the aim of pursing it in the ordinary civil courts, that claim can proceed *(Ako v Rothschild Asset Management [2002] IRLR 348).*

Compromise agreements

Legally binding settlements in which the parties refrain from issuing or continuing proceedings, can be agreed before a case reaches a tribunal. However, this can only happen either where an Acas conciliation officer has taken action in accordance with her/his statutory duty on conciliation (for information on Acas and its role see below) or where a compromise agreement has been reached after advice from relevant independent advisors, such as lawyers, union officials and advice workers. If an advice centre worker is providing the advice there must have been no payment for it.

Compromised claims can include present and future claims, where these are or could have been contemplated at the time of the agreement (*Byrnell v BT EAT/0383/04*). If employees sign a compromise agreement they are **barred from presenting further claims** to employment tribunals on the same issue. In effect, by signing a compromise agreement employees waive the right to pursue a tribunal claim. In one case, *Byrnell v BT EAT/0383/04*, the EAT held that an employee could not pursue a claim which he had knowledge of at the time when he had signed a compromise agreement but where the agreement did not specify the claim. In the case of *Hinton v University of East London A2/2004/2364*, the Court of Appeal held that the compromise agreement must specify the particular statutory claim being compromised. Individuals will not be bound by any compromise agreement reached between the employer and union unless they have expressly given a union official the right to draw up an agreement on their behalf *(Gloystarne v Martin [2001] IRLR 15).* If however, the settlement is reached after Acas assistance then it can have a wider scope, barring other claims.

Binding arbitration

The *Employment Rights (Disputes Resolution) Act 1998* introduced a system of **voluntary but binding** arbitration, as an alternative to taking a tribunal claim. The scheme covers unfair dismissal claims as well as claims concerning flexible working and aims to cut down the number of claims reaching the tribunals. Arbitration is seen as a more informal and cheaper way of resolving claims.

The scheme is administered by the arbitration service Acas (see below – Settling cases). Arbitration is available where a claimant is pursuing an unfair dismissal claim and where:

- the claimant has already **received independent advice** by way of a compromise agreement;
- the parties have agreed in writing to be **bound by the decision**; and
- there is a **bar on any further tribunal hearing** on the claim.

The arbitration hearing is in private and the arbitrator can award reinstatement or compensation. Arbitration may seem an attractive option for many claimants, as it should resolve the claim more quickly. But representatives need to be aware that there may be **disadvantages** in agreeing to arbitration. The **decision** of the arbitrator is **final**. There is **no appeal** to the EAT, as there is for employment tribunal claims. Most claimants still prefer to use the tribunals rather than to take the option of arbitration. While arbitration is likely to give a speedier result, the fact that its outcomes are private means that it is difficult to compare what different people achieve. One of the advantages of the tribunals system is that the outcomes are known. The other area of concern is in the fact that there is no appeal from an arbitration ruling.

Settling cases through Acas

Many claims, though initially lodged with a tribunal, end up being settled through **conciliation** using the services of the **Advisory, Conciliation and Arbitration Service (Acas).** Acas has a general duty to promote the improvement of industrial relations. It provides advice and guidance on employment issues; runs training events; provides conciliation in collective and individual disputes; and arranges arbitration in both collective and individual disputes.

Most Acas services are free. Where there is a charge, Acas must give notice in advance of its intention to do so. Acas officers may be called in to conciliate following presentation of a claim to a tribunal.

Acas is involved in conciliation in most employment tribunal claims, but with effect from 1 October 2004, must withdraw its conciliation services in the period running up the date for the tribunal hearing.

Acas also issues **codes of practice**. Although the codes are not legally binding in themselves, tribunals will take account of them when determining how the law should be applied. They can be obtained from Acas (see Further information).

More information: LRD booklet, *Disciplinary and grievance procedures (£4.20)*. LRD's *Workplace Report* has regular updates on cases concerning procedural issues.

2. Categories of worker

Employee or self-employed

An individual's status, that is whether they are an **"employee"** or a **"worker"**, is very important in establishing their statutory rights. The box below shows which rights apply to all workers and which apply to employees only. An "employee" works for an employer under a contract of employment. A "worker" also works for an employer but under a contract for services, which is more like self-employment. Most of the legal rules outlined in this guide apply only to employees.

Rights covering all workers

- National minimum wage (unless excluded on grounds of age or training)
- Protection against unlawful pay deductions
- Equal pay
- Working hours and breaks
- Holidays
- Union recognition where a majority is in favour
- Not to be refused work on grounds of union membership
- Time off for union duties and training in recognised workplaces
- Time off for union activities in recognised workplaces
- Protection against discrimination on all unlawful grounds

Rights covering employees only

- Written pay statement detailing gross and net pay and deductions
- Written statement of employment particulars
- Statutory minimum notice
- Protection from unfair dismissal
- Time off for ante natal care
- Statutory maternity pay and leave
- Statutory paternity pay and leave
- Statutory adoption pay and leave
- Parental and dependency leave
- Right to request flexible working
- Protection in business transfers (TUPE)
- Redundancy pay and redundancy selection rights

- Guarantee pay on layoffs
- Medical suspension pay

There are two fundamental tests that the courts usually use. The **"control"** test. This looks at the degree to which the individual's work is under the control and direction of the employer; where it is not, there is a presumption that there is no contract of employment. For example, a yacht skipper who exercised a level of control and freedom over how he worked and was treated as self-employed for tax and National Insurance purposes has been held not to be an employee (*Haine v Rolls Royce EATS/0028/04*).

The second fundamental test is whether there is a **"mutuality of obligations"** (*Stephenson v Delphi Diesel Systems EAT/131/01*). This means that there must be a legal obligation on one party to provide and pay for work and on the other to turn up for work and to do it. Volunteers who are not obliged to work a minimum number of weekly hours and who can withdraw their services at any time, are not employees, according to the EAT in the case of *SE Sheffield CAB v Grayson [2004] IRLR 353.* If you have the right to refuse an offer of work for any reason you are unlikely to be an employee.

Some employers will seek to argue that individuals are not employees but self-employed, either as a way of avoiding payment of National Insurance or to deprive them of their statutory rights. The courts have said that individuals will be classified as **employees** where they:

- do not provide their own equipment;
- do not have their own helpers;
- have no responsibility for investment;
- are not called upon to exercise skill and judgement; and
- run no financial risk except that of being unable to find employment *(Lee v Chung [1990] IRLR 236).*

Applying these tests, courts have ruled that an individual working on a building site did have employee status. This was despite the fact that his tax status appeared to define him as "self-employed". He had never worked for anyone else and was **never truly in business on his own account.** The Court of Appeal defined the term "employee" widely, saying that, certainly in **health and safety matters**, the interpretation had to be as wide as possible to ensure safety *(Lane v*

Shire Roofing [1995] IRLR 493). Each case will be decided on the issue of control, but the basic rules are always the same.

A recent case involved bricklayers working in a gang, one of whom took responsibility for sorting out the price for each job. The company tried to argue that as the gang leader he could not be a worker but was a self-employed **gangmaster**. The EAT disagreed. It noted that the company paid each worker directly. Had the gang leader been a gangmaster and genuinely in business on his own account, he would have been responsible for distributing pay to the gang.

Casuals

Particular problems can arise in relation to **casual workers**. Court rulings recognise that casual workers can be employed under a hybrid contract somewhere between a standard contract of employment (which denotes an employee) and a contract for services (denoting a self-employed person). Casuals whose contractual relationship with the employer is not sufficiently close for them to be defined as employees, or sufficiently distant for them to be defined as self-employed, are defined as "workers". They have limited statutory rights. However, in the case of *Carmichael v National Power [2000] IRLR 43*, the House of Lords held that casuals working as guides for National Power were self-employed because their contracts referred to them working "on a casual, as required basis". This approach was followed in the case of *Stevedoring & Haulage Services v Fuller [2001] IRLR 627*. There the Court of Appeal held that workers who had been made redundant and were then offered casual work were not employees because there were no mutual obligations to offer and to accept work. This is the **"irreducible minimum",** according to the court. Without the obligations to offer and to accept work, there is no contract of employment. An obligation merely to pay for work done does not of itself create a contract of employment.

There will also be cases where the nature of the contractual relationship does not even meet the standard for a contract for services. In the case of *South Tyneside MBC v Toulson EAT/1333/01*, the EAT held that a pool lifeguard who worked on a casual contract and would be contacted whenever work was available was not a worker and therefore had no right to statutory holiday pay.

Workers

A contract that permits an individual to **substitute** someone else to do her/his work is not a contract of employment and the individual is not an employee but more likely to be a worker, according to the Court of Appeal in the case of *Express and Echo Publications v Tanton [1999] IRLR 367*. Where there is a genuine substitute clause, a worker cannot claim statutory holidays, statutory minimum pay or any other statutory employment rights. However, it is often a **question of degree**. If the contract says that you can arrange for a substitute, but it is the employer who decides who the substitute is and how the substitute is paid, you could still be an employee *(MacFarlane v Glasgow City Council [2001] IRLR 7)*.

You should check to make sure that your employer is not inserting a clause in your contract allowing you to provide a substitute as a way of avoiding having to provide some employment rights. The list given at the beginning of this Chapter shows the rights you do have as a "worker". The Court of Appeal, in the case of *Redrow Homes (Yorkshire) v Wright [2004] IRLR 720*, has held that building workers who were paid weekly and expected to carry out the work personally were workers and were entitled to holiday pay which their employer had refused to pay, arguing that they were self-employed.

Under *section 23* of the *Employment Relations Act 1999 (ERA 99)*, the secretary of state for trade and industry has the power to extend employee rights to those currently excluded on account of their contractual status. However, these powers have not been exercised.

Young workers

The *Working Time Regulations 1998* give young workers (those under 18 but above school leaving age) the right to a **minimum 30-minute** break after four-and-a-half hours' work, in addition to a **daily break** of at least 12 hours and **at least two days off** a week. In most cases young workers are prohibited from working nights. However, where they can do so the employer has to undertake a **health assessment**.

Under the *Working Time (Amendment) Regulations 2002* the **maximum working hours** for young workers must not exceed eight hours a day or 40 hours a week. These hours cannot be averaged over a longer period and young workers cannot individually opt out of the requirements. In addition, where a young person works for more than one employer, working hours are aggregated and must be within the overall maximum.

Those aged under 18 who work with dangerous machines and substances have limited statutory protection under the *Factory Acts*. Employers are legally obliged to **take particular account of young people's inexperience** in carrying out risk assessments and deciding what work is suitable for them.

Apprentices

Apprentices cannot normally be dismissed unless their contract specifically says so. If an employer uses the term "apprentice" to describe an individual, the courts could imply that this was the legal status of the employment relationship, but it may depend on the particular facts of the case *(Wallace v CA Roofing [1996] IRLR 435)*.

Mark Whitely was employed under the Modern Apprenticeship scheme, although his contract defined him as an "employee". He was dismissed before the end of the apprenticeship and claimed damages from his employer. The EAT upheld his claim. It said that even though the employer treated him as if he was an employee, in law he was an apprentice. He therefore had the right to be employed for the whole of the apprenticeship contract (*Whitely v Marton Electrical [2003] IRLR 197)*.

Another EAT ruling, *Thorpe v Dull EAT/0630/02*, held that a **Modern Apprenticeship** (a government training scheme) was not the same as an apprenticeship in law, but was a combination of training and job experience. This meant that the employee did not have job protection rights available to apprentices.

A contract **terminable by notice** cannot be an apprenticeship contract, as these are always contracts for a fixed term *(Richardson v H Mullins EAT 996/99)*.

Children

Children **under the age of 13** cannot be employed in any capacity. **Thirteen-year-olds** can do **light work** that is not harmful to their health and safety, school attendance or other factors, and which is permitted under local authority bye-laws.

There are strict limits on the working hours of **children under 16.** Fourteen-year-olds can work up to five hours on weekdays and Saturdays during the school holidays. In all they cannot do more than 25 hours a week. Fifteen-year-olds can do up to eight hours a day and a maximum week of 35 hours, again during the school holidays.

A child under the age of 16 cannot work more than two hours on a school day or Sunday. They are totally prevented from working in industrial undertakings, including transport, street trading, merchant shipping or mining. Employers must have carried out a **risk assessment** before offering employment to a child or young person.

Children have the right to a **rest break** of at least an hour in any shift lasting more than four hours and to a two-week break from any work during school holidays.

Part-time workers

The *Part-Time Workers (Prevention of Less Favourable Treatment) Regulations 2000* define part-time workers as any worker whose hours are less than those of a full-time worker. This definition would even cover workers on "zero hours" contracts who have no fixed hours at all. Anyone defined as a part-time worker has the right to **no less favourable treatment** than full-time workers. This includes the right to holidays and other contractual benefits and is limited only by the fact that entitlement might be pro rata to the hours worked. However, if the less favourable treatment is not due to the worker being part-time there is no protection under the regulations (*Gibson v The Scottish Ambulance Service EATS/0052/04*). When considering claims of less favourable treatment, tribunals consider the following questions:

- what is the treatment complained of?
- is it less favourable than that of a full-time worker?
- is the treatment less favourable because the worker is part-time?
- is there any objective justification for the less favourable treatment?

Part-time workers can compare their terms and conditions with those of full-time workers, regardless of whether the full timers are employed on permanent or fixed-term contracts. However, the **comparison has to be with workers who are full-time**.

Ms England claimed that she was treated less favourably than full-time workers. However, although the workers whom she had identified as her comparators worked nearly twice as many hours as she did (she worked 18 hours a week while they worked 35) the employer was able to show that contractual "full-time" hours were actually 37, even though no one worked those hours (*England v The Governing Body of Turnford School EAT/438/02*).

To make a claim the part-time worker also has to be employed under the same type of contract as their comparator and be engaged in the same or broadly similar work. In the case of *Matthews & others v Kent & Midway Towns Fire Authority [2004] IRLR 697*, the Court of Appeal held that part-time firefighters, whose duties were similar to those of their full-time colleagues, but who performed a smaller range of duties could not compare their terms with those of the full-time firefighters.

Part-time workers have the right to the **same pension arrangements** as full-time workers. In the case of *Preston v Wolverhampton Healthcare NHS Trust [2004] IRLR 96*, the EAT held that excluding part-time workers from joining an occupational pension scheme was unlawful. However, the ruling makes it clear that employers can make it necessary for part-time workers to take steps to exercise their option to join the pension scheme, even though entry may be automatic for full-time workers without their being required to take any action. Trade union representatives need to be aware of this ruling and ensure that part-time workers are told what their rights are and how to exercise them.

The ECJ, in the case of *Steinicke v Bundesanstalt für Arbeit [2003] IRLR 892*, held that European law does not prevent pension rights for part-time workers being **calculated pro rata**, as long as the way that the calculation is done does not mean that the part-time worker gets proportionately less. However, in the case of *Trustees of Uppingham School Retirement Benefits Scheme for Non-Teaching Staff v Shillcock [2002] IRLR 702*, the High Court ruled that the exclusion of workers earning **less than the National Insurance threshold** was justified, even though the outcome was to exclude proportionately more part-time workers.

Part-time workers attending **union training** should get paid for all the hours on the course (see chapter 5 – Rights to time off).

In relation to **overtime pay**, it is not contrary to equal treatment laws to pay enhanced rates only when the part timer has completed the full-time hours *(Stadt v Helmig [1995] IRLR 216).* Nor are part-time workers entitled to have account taken of previous years they had worked full time when their redundancy pay is calculated *(Barry v Midland Bank [1999] IRLR 581).* However, if overtime is only paid once workers have already worked additional unpaid overtime, this may amount to discrimination, if it means that part-time workers have to work proportionately more hours, as the Elsner-Lakeberg case below demonstrates.

A part-time worker who claims to have received less favourable treatment has the right to ask the employer for a **written statement** of the reasons for the difference in treatment, and may take a claim of less favourable treatment to an employment tribunal.

Part-time workers can also take claims based on **sex discrimination**. To do this they have to comparing their terms with those of a full-time worker of the opposite sex. In the case below Edeltraud Elsner-Lakeberg claimed sex discrimination, based on her treatment as a part-time worker.

Edeltraud Elsner-Lakeberg worked as a part-time teacher. All teachers' contracts said that they did not get paid for the first three hours of overtime in a month. As a result Elsner-Lakeberg had to do proportionately more work before being entitled to overtime pay. The ECJ held that this amounted to unlawful discrimination (*Elsner-Lakeberg v land Nordrhein-Westfalen [2005] IRLR 209*).

A claim for the right to work part-time could be taken under sex discrimination law or under the *Flexible Working Regulations* (see Chapter 8: Flexible working). A woman refused the right to work part-time can in some circumstances show that this amounts to indirect discrimination (see Chapter 6: Indirect discrimination). However, each case will depend on its facts. In the case of *MOD v MacMillan EATS/0003/04*, the EAT in Scotland held that refusing an MOD employee the right to work part-time did not amount to detrimental treatment that had a disproportionate effect on women.

Temporary employees

Under the *Fixed-term Employees (Prevention of Less Favourable Treatment) Regulations 2002*, fixed-term employees (also known as temporary employees) have the same statutory rights as permanent employees, for example to maternity leave or not to be unfairly dismissed. Fixed-term employees are those working for a **specified period of time** or those employed to undertake and complete a **specified task**. The UK regulations apply only to employees. A contract is still for a fixed-term even if it contains a clause that would give either party the option to end it earlier.

Mr Allen, a fixed-term employee, was dismissed without his employer following the procedures that would have applied to a permanent employee. His contract had a clause that said the contract could be terminated by notice. The employer argued that the regulations could not apply to this contract since its termination clause meant it was not really for a fixed-term. However, the EAT disagreed (*Allen v National Australia Group Europe [2004] IRLR* 847).

Fixed-term employees have the right to **paid holidays**, pro rata to the length of their contract. In cases where they **work on more than one fixed-term contract**, their service is added together to assess rights to holiday pay in lieu if their contract ends without renewal.

The regulations cover **all contractual terms** including pay and pensions. This means that fixed-term employees have the right to a written statement of their main contractual terms, guarantee pay and medical suspension pay (see chapter 4) in the same way as permanent staff. The right to no less favourable treatment extends to qualifying periods for employment benefits and opportunities for training and permanent employment.

Fixed-term employees can compare their treatment with that of permanent staff employed by the same employer, so long as they are doing the **same or similar work** and are working at the same "establishment" (location). If there is no comparable employee at that establishment, a comparison can be made with the pay and benefits package of comparable employees at other locations.

If there are differences, the employer has to show that the **overall employment package** is **no less favourable**.

Employers can legally **justify less favourable treatment** if they have a good reason. For example, they may be able to justify excluding a fixed-term employee from the occupational pension scheme on the grounds that the contribution would be too low to be viable.

Fixed-term employees who believe they have been less favourably treated have the right to ask for a **written statement** explaining the difference in treatment. This can be used as evidence in a tribunal.

If a temporary employee has been working continuously under two or more contracts for **four or more years,** an employer will have to justify the offer of further temporary employment or otherwise **offer permanent work**.

Temporary employees who are employed for a **short period** can lose out on employment rights that are dependent on length of service, such as unfair dismissal rights that only apply if the employee has worked for at least a year. But those who work on a series of temporary contracts with short gaps between each may be able to establish continuity (see chapter 10 – Qualifying for unfair dismissal rights). The dismissal of fixed-term employees on the grounds of having **asserted their rights under the regulations is automatically unfair**. This means that the dismissed employee can take a dismissal claim even if they have not worked for at least a year or indeed are over the normal retirement age and would thus be excluded from normal unfair dismissal claims. However, the fact that a fixed-term contract ends does not, of itself, amount to less favourable treatment. In the case of *Webley v Department for Work and Pensions [2005] EWCA 1745* the Court of Appeal held that a decision not to renew a fixed-term contract was not unlawful under the fixed term regulations.

Temporary employees may also be able to use **discrimination** law (see chapter 6) to challenge their employers' policies where, in practice, these have a discriminatory impact.

Karen Whiffen, a schoolteacher employed on a series of temporary contracts, did not have her contract renewed. The school wanted to make redundancies and decided to get rid of the temporary staff first. It was only after that stage that they applied the redundancy selection criteria. The Court of Appeal held that the policy of dismissing fixed-term contract holders had a greater impact on women teachers in the school than on men and was therefore indirectly discriminatory *(Whiffen v Milham Ford Girls' School [2001] IRLR 468).*

Temporary employees also have the same protection against discrimination on the grounds of **pregnancy and maternity** as permanent staff. A temporary employee cannot be dismissed, refused renewal of her contract or refused employment for these reasons, according to the ECJ in the cases of *Tele Danmark v Handels [2001]*

IRLR 853 and *Jimenez Melgar v Ayuntamiento de Los Barrios [2001] IRLR 848.*

Employers can no longer require employees to sign a waiver of dismissal or redundancy rights when beginning or renewing a temporary contract. A temporary employee whose contract comes to an end through redundancy, and who has worked for the employer for two or more years, can get redundancy pay. The only exception would be where that person was employed prior to 1 October 2002 and had previously agreed to waive rights to redundancy.

Agency workers

The *Employment Agencies Act 1973* does not allow agencies to charge employees a fee for placing them in work. The Act also regulates the workings of agencies. Workers seeking employment through an agency have the right not to be discriminated against in the offer of employment, including on trade union grounds. The *Conduct of Employment Agencies and Employment Businesses Regulations 2003* place limits on the right of employment agencies to charge fees where a temp employed through the agency is offered a permanent job with an employer where they have been working temporarily.

The **employment status** of temporary workers employed through employment agencies depends on their contract. To qualify for basic employment rights their contracts should, as a minimum, cover the **mutual obligations** to provide work and to undertake it. But, in addition, the employer must exercise an element of control over the employee's work. This makes it unlikely that agency workers can claim they are employed by the agency.

Ms Dacas worked as a cleaner, having obtained the work through an agency. When dismissed, she brought a claim against both the local authority she worked for and the agency. A tribunal ruled that neither employed her. The EAT then held that she was an agency employee. The agency appealed to the Court of Appeal. It held that the EAT was wrong. The majority of the judges in the court held that it might have been possible for Dacas to successfully argue that there was an implied contract of employment between her and the local authority and that it was her employer, but since that issue had not been raised at the appeal they could make no ruling on it *(Brook Street Bureau v Dacas [2004] IRLR 358).*

If there is no contractual relationship, individuals cannot be considered as employees.

In the case of *Hewlett Packard v O'Murphy [2002] IRLR 4*, Mr O'Murphy had set up a company that hired him out through an agency to Hewlett Packard (HP). Working in this way had tax advantages for him. However, after six years HP terminated the arrangement. O'Murphy claimed he had been unfairly dismissed, but the fact that he was found not to be an employee denied him the right to pursue the claim.

There may be circumstances where this rule does not apply. In the case of *Recruit Employment Services v Dillon EAT/0049/02*, the EAT held that there was nothing to prevent a tribunal finding that on a **particular assignment** the individual was an employee of the agency, even though on other assignments she would properly be considered self-employed. In the case of *Montgomery v Johnson Underwood [2001] IRLR 269*, the Court of Appeal ruled that, to decide who (if anyone) is the employer, the tribunals must use the test set down in the case of *Ready Mixed Concrete (SE) v Minister of Pensions and National Insurance [1968]*. It must show that:

- the employee **agrees to work** for the employer;
- in performing the work the employee agrees to be **subject to the employer's control** "in a sufficient degree"; and
- the other provisions of the contract are **consistent with it being a contract of employment**.

The European Commission presented a **draft directive** to the European Parliament to give agency workers the right to be no less favourably treated. The draft says that this right would apply once the agency worker had been in post for six weeks. The UK government had originally opposed the draft directive but at the end of 2004 it pledged that it would work towards an agreement with other EU member states to try to get talks going again on the content of the draft directive. However, it wants a six-month, rather than six week, qualification period before the rights apply, while employers are lobbying for twelve months. Research carried out by the TUC shows that 53% of agency workers would lose out if there was a six-month qualification and a massive 74% would be excluded if the employers' lobby was successful.

Homeworkers

Many workers now work all or part of their time in their own homes.

Their employment status is often unclear and as a result it is difficult to establish what their employment rights are. Although the tribunals have sometimes ruled that **homeworkers can be employees**, there are cases where they have held that there are no mutual obligations between employer and homeworker and that therefore the essential element for a contract of employment is missing. In the case of *Bridges and others v Industrial Rubber EAT/0150/04*, the EAT held that a statement in a homeworker's contract that there were no mutual obligations deprived her of the right to claim that she was an employee.

Public sector workers

Public sector workers, in some circumstances, have alternative avenues for pursuing legal claims. For example, if prison officers and the police (including British Transport Police) are dismissed, the remedy lies not through the tribunals but by way of a **special complaints** body. They are entitled to be treated no less favourably than they would have been by the employment tribunals, or to be given the reasons why they were not *(R v Civil Service Appeal Board ex parte Cunningham [1991] IRLR 297)*. The *Criminal Justice and Public Order Act 1994* places prison officers in the same category as the police, and thus removes their right to strike.

Working outside the UK

With closer ties between European states, more workers will find themselves working outside the UK at some point. One issue for them is deciding in which country they might launch any legal action against their employer. In the case of *Mulox IBC v Geels [1994] IRLR 422*, it was held to be the state where the employee principally works. Similarly, in the case of *Weber v Universal Ogden Services [2002] IRLR 365*, the EAT held that it is the state where the employee has worked the longest. The only circumstance where this rule might not apply is where the employee had worked in a number of states but had recently settled in one. He or she would have to launch any legal challenge in that state, invoking its laws.

Workers who are posted to work abroad are covered by the *Equal Opportunities (Employment Legislation) (Termination Limits) Regulations 1999*. All workers **temporarily working** in an EU country have the right to the **same minimum terms and conditions** as workers permanently in that state. So UK workers transferred to work in another EU state will be entitled to whatever is set as a minimum standard in that state. In turn, workers temporarily working in the UK, no matter what country they were originally employed in, also get the right to at least the minimum laid down in UK law.

In one of the first cases to be taken using this law, three women employed by US company United Airlines won their right to benefit from UK sex discrimination law. The company said that, since they had been hired in the USA and did not habitually work in the UK, UK laws did not cover them, including those guaranteeing job protection to pregnant women. The employment tribunal applied the laws on posted workers and ruled that they were covered.

In the case of *Jackson v Ghost [2003] IRLR 824*, the EAT held that the 1999 legislation does not grant unlimited extra-territorial jurisdiction. It only covers employees who are temporarily posted abroad. In the case of *Serco v Lawson A1/2003/0649/A*, the Court of Appeal held that workers posted long-term to work outside the Great Britain could not lodge claims in the UK tribunals. In this case leave to appeal to the House of Lords has been won and the decision of the UK's highest court will be given later in the year. In the case of *Saggar v MOD A2/2004/1396*, the Court of Appeal held that the whole of a person's employment has to be taken into account in deciding whether they "wholly or mainly" worked outside Great Britain. In this case the employee had, for most of his employment relationship, worked in Great Britain. The fact that he was not working in Great Britain when the alleged discrimination took place did not exclude him from the right to claim under Great Britain discrimination law.

More information: LRD booklets *Disciplinary and grievance procedures (£4.20)*; *Temporary workers (£3.70)* and *Part-time workers (£3.40)*; LRD's *Workplace Report* has quarterly updates on contracts.

3. Starting work and the employment contract

References and employer checks

Most employers require a reference before they will employ someone. Young workers starting work for the first time are likely to come with references from school or college, plus examination results. But from then on job offers will generally rely on employer references.

An employer has a **duty of care** to ensure that a reference does not contain false statements and is not malicious *(Spring v Guardian Assurance [1994] IRLR 460)*. It would also not be reasonable and fair to give information about complaints against an employee where these had never been brought to that employee's attention *(TSB Bank v Harris [2000] IRLR 157)*.

An employer's core duty is to ensure that the reference is **accurate and not misleading.** The fact that it is not sufficiently comprehensive (in the view of the employee) is not challengeable *(Kidd v Axa Equity [2000] IRLR 301)*. There is no legal obligation on the employer to provide a good reference. If a **poor reference** means that an individual does not obtain employment, there is no breach of the duty of care, provided the employer has ensured that the reference is accurate, not misleading and not malicious *(Kirk v Legal and General [2002] IRLR 124)*.

Employers are **not obliged to give a reference**. However, there are some circumstances in which it would be unlawful discrimination for the employer to refuse.

If an employer refuses a reference because the employee has earlier taken a discrimination claim, generally this would be **unlawful victimisation**. In the case of *Jones v 3M Healthcare [2003] IRLR 33*, the House of Lords held that three disabled workers who were denied or given poor references by their ex-employers because they had previously brought discrimination claims, had been unlawfully discriminated against. This protection also covers former employees (see Chapter 6 — Victimisation).

However, there is an **exception** to this rule.

In the case of *Chief Constable of West Yorkshire Police v Khan [2001] IRLR 830,* the House of Lords confirmed that a refusal to supply an employee with a reference amounts to less favourable treatment. However, it went on to hold that it does not necessarily follow that, in every case, a victimisation claim would be upheld. Where the reason for not giving a reference is because the employer and employee are currently litigating a discrimination claim, the existence of that adversarial relationship may reasonably cause the employer to behave in a way that treats the employee less favourably. The test is whether the employer would have continued to deny the employee the reference once the case had ended, regardless of the outcome. If the answer is no, this does not amount to victimisation.

If an employer has made a **job offer subject to a reference** being obtained, the contract will not take effect unless or until this happens. The prospective employer can decide whether the reference is satisfactory. The **test is a subjective one** *(Wishart v NACAB [1990] IRLR 393).* Furthermore, employers are free to **seek references from people other than** those the employee has **nominated**, unless the contract expressly excludes this. There is no implied term that would prevent this *(Purvis v Luminar Leisures EAT/1332/99).* Although it is usually for the employer to decide whether or not the reference is satisfactory, if the employer uses this as an excuse to dismiss an employee when the real reason is discriminatory, it will not be valid. In the case of *Halai v Integrated Asian Advice Service EAT/0855/03*, Ms Halai was dismissed because her references were said not to be satisfactory. The EAT found that the real reason was because she had complained that she was being paid less than a male colleague. The dismissal was discriminatory and furthermore Halai was awarded compensation to reflect the fact that she had not been paid equally during the short period when she had worked.

Under the *Immigration and Asylum Act 1996*, employers are required to ask for documents confirming a **right to work** from all new employees. This can either be a passport or at least two other documents which can be evidence of a National Insurance number, birth certificate or Home Office document showing a right to work. Employers face a fine if they employ anyone without having satisfied themselves of the claimant's right to seek employment. A Code of Practice says that all employees should be treated the same and that existing employees should not be asked for proof of entitlement to work. However, the checks should not be carried out in such a way as to discriminate. For example, employers who only check on black claimants could be challenged using discrimination law. This does not mean that employers can never ask just some groups for sight of a passport. In the case of *Olatokun v Ikon Office Solutions EAT/0074/04*, the EAT held that an employer practice of asking only non-EU citizens for a passport did not amount to unlawful discrimination.

Previous criminal convictions

The *Rehabilitation of Offenders Act 1974* allows individuals whose convictions are regarded as **"spent"** after a period of rehabilitation the right not to have to declare their convictions when applying for a job. *Section 4(3)(b)* of the Act also makes it unfair to dismiss someone because of a spent conviction or to prejudice employment in any way.

The period of rehabilitation varies according to the sentence and age when convicted, although sentences in prison, youth custody or a young offenders' institution of 30 months or more are never spent. As a guide, a conviction of less than six months' imprisonment would be spent after seven years. In some jobs, for example nursing or teaching, convictions always have to be disclosed, whether spent or not.

In the case of *Wood v Coverage Care [1996] IRLR 264*, the job of an employee who had a past conviction was declared redundant. The EAT held that her employer was justified in refusing to consider her for alternative employment in a residential home for the elderly, an area of employment where convictions were never spent. The fact that Wood's duties were administrative only was not relevant.

Although it is unfair to dismiss someone because of a spent conviction, an employee will still need to meet the **normal qualifying conditions** for unfair dismissal (see chapter 10). If a conviction is not spent, but the employer has not asked for details of convictions, there is no obligation on the employee to disclose them. Under the *Police Act 1997*, employers were given the right to ask job applicants for a copy of their criminal certificate. There are two types of certificate — an "enhanced" certificate, where checks are needed on job applicants working with children, the elderly or vulnerable, and a "standard" certificate for other types of work. Under the *Police Act 1997 (Criminal Records) (Amendment) Regulations 2004*, the Criminal Records Bureau, which issues the certificates, can charge a fee of £29 for a standard disclosure and £34 for an enhanced disclosure.

Written contracts

The employment contract is key to any employment relationship. Its provisions determine most of the conditions under which work is undertaken. Employees should know what their contracts provide for and how to enforce their rights. They also need to know what to do if their employer does not honour the contract. The advisory service Acas has updated its guide on *Employment Contracts*. A copy of the guide can be obtained from the Acas website: www.acas.gov.uk.

Once an employer has offered a job and the offer has been accepted there is a **legal contract** between employer and employee, even if there is **nothing in writing**. If an offer has been made and accepted and the **employer withdraws** it, it may be possible to claim damages for breach of contract *(Sarker v South Tees Acute Hospitals [1997] IRLR 328)*. In most cases, damages would be limited to the length of notice required to terminate the contract legally. However, in *Gill and others v Cape Contracts [1985] IRLR 499*, the High Court declared that damages would be based on the wages that would have been due for the whole of the period of their contract, in the case of workers who had been offered a fixed-term contract.

To enforce the contract you need to know **who the employer is**. This should be given in your written statement (see below). Employees of charities and voluntary organisations are likely to be employed by the management committee, even though the individuals on it change *(Affleck v Newcastle Mind [1999] IRLR 405)*. Local authorities employ teachers, even though there may be local management of schools *(Askew v Governing Body of Clifton Middle School [1999] IRLR 708)*. However, school governing bodies do in some cases exercise powers under delegated legislation and can therefore be treated as the employer in constructive dismissal cases. Local authorities are liable for the actions of their elected councillors, where these affect the ability of employees to carry out their duties *(Moores v Bude-Stratton [2000] IRLR 676)*.

Under *sections 1* and *2* of the *Employment Rights Act 1996 (ERA 96)* employees have the right to written particulars of the contract. No later than **two months** after the beginning of employment, every employee must be given a **written statement** that must include:

- the names of the employer and employee;
- the date employment began and the period of continuous employment;
- the scale and rate of remuneration, pay intervals and its method of calculation;
- terms and conditions relating to hours of work and holiday entitlement (including public holidays);
- the job title or description; and
- the employee's place of work.

These must all be detailed in a single document known as the **"principle statement"**. However, provided that they are given within the two-month deadline, other employment particulars can be documented by instalments. These are:

- whether employment is permanent or for a fixed term;
- details of sickness, pensions and notice;
- details of the employer's disciplinary and grievance procedures (see chapter 10 – Disciplinary procedures);
- details of collective agreements affecting employment; and
- details of any requirements regarding work outside the UK.

The statement can **refer the employee to another document** (provided there are opportunities for reading it at work) for employment particulars relating to sickness terms, pay and pension schemes. The *section 1* requirements make no specific mention of **overtime**. In the case of *Lange v Georg Schunemann GmbH [2001] IRLR 244*, the European Court of Justice (ECJ) ruled that if overtime is an essential element of the contractual relationship, so that employees should normally do it if requested, a reference to it must be included in the written statement.

According to the ECJ in the case *of Kampelmann v Landschaftsverband [1998] IRLR 333,* just laying out the **job title** without any further description is not sufficient.

As far as **notice requirements** are concerned, it is sufficient for the statement to refer the employee to the law on the matter (see chapter 10 – Termination with/without notice) or to a collective agreement, providing there are opportunities to see it at work.

If there are **no terms** relating to any of the above items, this has to be stated.

Existing employees must also be given a statement of their written particulars if they request one. There is an **absolute right** to the terms of your contract as notified to you, whether orally or in writing.

If an employer does not comply with these requirements, an employee can go to a tribunal any time while working or **within three months** of leaving or "as soon as is reasonably practicable". The tribunal has the power to order the employer to prepare a statement. But it has no powers to order the employer to remake the original contract on different terms *(Eagland v BT [1992] IRLR 323)*. It will only require that the employer provides information in relation to contract terms as they applied at the date of the tribunal application.

What makes a contract

A contract of employment can also consist of items other than those listed in the written statement. Contract terms can be express, implied, based on works rules or custom and practice and can come from clauses in the collective agreement.

Express terms

Express terms are the most important. They are specifically agreed with the employer. Normally, where a contract has a clearly stated express term, the courts will apply it, even where it is not favourable to the employee. But a term that seeks to deprive an employee of a right that otherwise would have existed has to be very clear indeed. If a contract term is **ambiguous** the courts look at what has happened in practice to interpret it. In one case the employer tried to argue that a bank holiday payment system that had operated for more than 30 years was not contractual because the clause in the contract was open to a different interpretation. The Court of Appeal held that the fact that it was ambiguous meant that it could take account of what happened in practice to decide what employees were entitled to under the contract *(Dunlop Tyres v Blows [2001] IRLR 629)*.

However, if it is **too uncertain** the courts may have difficulty in enforcing it. In one case a contract term that obliged the employer to pay pension contributions, without stating the amount, was held to be too unclear to enforce. There was no way of assessing what might be a reasonable amount, since different employers paid different levels of contribution. Furthermore, the EAT noted that the employee had never suggested to the employer what he thought might be a reasonable contribution *(Fontana v Fabio EAT/140/01).*

Private health insurance, where available, is almost always an express term *(Marlow v East Thames Housing [2002] IRLR 798).*

Courts are likely to uphold challenges to express terms where they seek to stop (restrain) employees from **working for competitors**, particularly after their employment has ended (see below — Restraining clauses).

It may also be possible to use the *Unfair Contract Terms Act 1977* to challenge a term in a contract that is unreasonable. In the case of *Brigden v American Express [2000] IRLR 94* (which did not succeed on the particular facts), the High Court ruled that unfair employment terms could be challenged under the 1977 Act.

The Act can also be used to challenge **pay deductions**. In one case an employee successfully challenged a bus company's practice of making deductions if there were shortfalls in cash takings. The employee argued that, since the company had sometimes used its discretion not to deduct pay when shortages were as a result of a third party theft, its failure to do so on this occasion enabled a challenge under the Act.

An **equal opportunities policy** can, in certain circumstances, amount to an express term. However, where an employer imposes a retirement age, an employee cannot use the existence of the equal opportunities policy to defeat this, even if the policy specifically refers to age. In the case of *Taylor v Secretary of State for Scotland [2000] IRLR 502,* the House of Lords held that an age equality policy is contractual and therefore enforceable only up to the time when the employee reaches retirement age.

Some company policies may only amount to statements of principle, rather than of contract. In the case *of Wandsworth LB v D'Silva [1998] IRLR 193,* the Court of Appeal ruled that the authority's sickness absence procedure was not contractual and could therefore be changed unilaterally without amounting to a breach of contract.

Implied terms

The terms of a contract can be "implied" — i.e. where they are not specifically stated, but without them there would be no contract. They must be terms that both parties would have agreed to, had they thought about it.

Well established implied terms include the duties of **mutual trust and confidence**, which bind both employer and employee. Neither party should operate the contract in a way that would destroy the trust or confidence of the other, including, for example, an obligation to deal properly with an employee's grievance. Offering an employee money to leave can amount to a breach of contract, as the case of *Bates Wells & Braithwaite v MacFarlane EAT/0616/02* demonstrates.

Wendy MacFarlane's baby had cerebral palsy, causing her to want to change her working arrangements. Her employers instead offered her £5,000 to leave. She claimed constructive dismissal. The EAT held that the offer of money to leave amounted to a breach of mutual trust and confidence.

The Court of Appeal has held that **threatening to dismiss** an employee to intimidate them or issuing **threats using intemperate language** will amount to a breach of mutual trust and confidence, giving the employee the right to sue for wrongful dismissal (*Horkulak v Cantor Fitzgerald International [2004] IRLR 942*). Mutual trust and confidence is a **valuable employment right,** as the case below demonstrates.

Marjorie Morrow worked for the supermarket chain Safeway. She was publicly reprimanded by her manager in full view of customers and staff, in a manner which was "humiliating", according to the EAT. This amounted to a breach of the implied term, giving Morrow the right to resign and claim constructive dismissal *(Morrow v Safeway Stores [2002] IRLR 9).*

Treating an employee in an **arbitrary or capricious manner** by not offering the same benefits as are available to other workers can also amount to a breach of the term *(BG v O'Brien [2001] IRLR 496).*

In the case of *Malik v BCCI [1997] IRLR 462,* the House of Lords ruled that the BCCI company (which had gone bust) was responsible for their former employees' inability to secure new employment because of their employer's poor reputation, based on dishonesty or corruption. The employees were entitled to "**stigma damages**", based on a breach of the implied term of mutual trust and confidence. However, the stigma must have a "real or substantial effect" on the employee's ability to get a new job and must have caused actual financial loss, according to the Court of Appeal in a later case *(BCCI v Ali (No 3) [2002] IRLR 460).*

Employers will also be in breach of an implied term if they **negligently misrepresent** a situation and as a result employees take or accept a course of action which they would otherwise have rejected. In the case of *Hagen v ICI Chemicals [2002] IRLR 31*, employees agreed to transfer under TUPE (see chapter 12). They did so because they had been told their pension rights would be more or less the same. This was not the case and some employees lost out substantially. The High Court held that this was a breach of contract and that the employees could sue their old employer for damages.

Employers also have the implied duty to take **reasonable care not to injure** employees' health *(Johnstone v Bloomsbury Health Authority [1991] IRLR 118)* and not to put the employee at risk of **psychological stress** *(Walker v Northumberland CC [1995] IRLR 35)*. The latter is qualified by the requirement that the harm to the employee was **foreseeable**, according to the Court of Appeal in the landmark case *Sutherland v Hatton [2002] IRLR 263*. The House of Lords reviewed the *Sutherland* case in March 2004. The judgement in the case (now known as *Barber v Somerset CC [2004] IRLR 475*) upheld the Court of Appeal interpretation of the implied duty of care in relation to stress. However, it also held that in this case the employer could have foreseen that there would have been damage to the employee's psychiatric health and should have investigated the steps it might take to alleviate the risk and introduced them. This failure to do so meant that the employer was liable in a claim for damages. The majority of the House of Lords judges ruled that, once the judge in the original High Court claim had held that there were steps the employers could and should have taken, the higher courts were bound to accept that assessment.

It is not enough just to show that the employer knew the employee was stressed, unless the demands of the job are unusually stressful or it was known that the employee was vulnerable to psychiatric illness *(Prateley v Surrey CC [2003] IRLR 794)*.

The **duty of care** does not mean that the employer has an obligation to take reasonable steps to agree an **employee's request for a reduced workload**, even if on the grounds of stress. The issue for employers is whether the employee's ill health was foreseeable and whether it was a breach of the duty of care that caused the injury. Equally, employers accused of **bullying** are only likely to have breached the implied duty of care where they had notice or information alerting them to the risk to the employee's health. If they are **aware of the risk** and refuse to negotiate over changes, they could be in breach of the duty of care.

Mr Owen anticipated that on his return from a long overseas driving job he would not be required to do another long job immediately. When instructed to do so he refused and was dismissed. The EAT agreed that he could imply into his contract a term that the employer would not risk his health *(NWT Freight Forwarding v Owen EAT/0643/01).*

Employers are also liable if their employees act in a way that would breach a contract and as a result cause harm to a third party to whom the employer owes a duty of care.

The case of *Scally v Southern Health Board [1991] IRLR 5221*, concerned the right to derive an employment benefit (in that case the right to purchase additional pension entitlement). The House of Lords ruled that, where an employee can only benefit from the right if informed of it by the employer, there is an implied contractual term to **provide the information**. The extent of any implied **duty to inform** was considered in the case of *Ibekwe v London General Transport Services [2003] IRLR 697.*

Daniel Ibekwe was off sick during a period when he would have had to exercise an option regarding his pension scheme. His employer had informed employees of the available options through notices in their pay slips and placed on workplace notice boards. Ibekwe had called into work each week to pick up his payslip but claimed that he had not seen the notices. He claimed that his employers had a duty to inform him of the options and that they had failed to do this. The Court of Appeal ruled that while there was a duty to inform employees of the steps the employers had taken, there was no obligation to check whether individual employees had received the notice.

The duty to inform does not, however, mean that the employer has a legal obligation to advise on the best choice or option *(University of Nottingham v Eyett [1999] IRLR 87)* or indeed to take reasonable care to protect the economic well-being of employees *(Crossley v Faithful & Gould Holdings [2004] IRLR 377).*

An implied term **cannot normally overrule an express term**. For example, in the case of *Reda v Flag [2002] IRLR 747*, the court ruled that a term giving the employer the right to choose to terminate a contract, either at the end of its term or with pay in lieu, left the choice up to the employer. There was no implied term that the choice would be exercised in a way that would be most beneficial to the employee.

Terms can be implied through **custom and practice**. However, if a term is **discretionary**, it will not amount to a custom or practice and thus can never be implied. In the case of *Campbell v Union Carbide EAT/0342/01,* the EAT held that an employee could not benefit from an ill-health severance payment because it was discretionary. The employer could choose whether or not to make the payment. In the case of *Diagonal Computer Services v Plews EAT/0338/02,* the EAT held that an employer's failure to honour a discretionary entitlement could only be challenged if it was clear that they were acting perversely. In the case of *Horkulak v Cantor Fitzgerald International [2004] IRLR 942,* the Court of Appeal held that where there is a discretion it will be regarded as subject to an implied term that it will be exercised genuinely and rationally.

If you **continue working** despite the employer having breached an implied contract term, this may mean you have "waived" (abandoned) your right to pursue a breach of contract claim. You cannot argue that you have had to accept changes under **duress** if you continue to work for your employer without taking any steps to challenge them or to bring the contract to an end. The tribunal is likely to find that this amounts to an acceptance of the change. However, if you are not initially aware that there has been a change, but protest as soon as you become aware of it the courts are unlikely to find that you have waived your right to pursue the breach of contract claim.

An employee's implied terms includes **fidelity and good faith**, for example not giving away trade secrets *(Ticehurst & Thompson v BT [1992] IRLR 219).*

Some terms would **not automatically be implied**. For example, there is no **implied term that on promotion** an employee should be better off.

Mr Fisher accepted promotion to a managerial post. Custom and practice said that on promotion he would receive an increase on his basic pay of at least 5%. This did happen, however, his new grade did not pay unsocial hours' payments and Fisher found that he was actually out of pocket. He went to a tribunal arguing that there must have been an implied term that his actual earnings would increase by at least 5%. The EAT held that there was no such implied term (*London Underground v Fisher EAT/0104/04*).

Works rules and collective agreements

Works rules, guidelines or rules about how work should be carried out can be part of the contract, even if the employee has no option but to accept the rule.

Although most **collective agreements** are not legally binding on the parties who have concluded them — the employer and the union — those items within the agreement that can be **incorporated** into the individual's contract become binding conditions of that contract.

Wood Hall Personnel & Transport reached an agreement with the T&G general union. This gave workers the right to 20 days' holiday plus bank and public holidays. The company then published a staff handbook which said that bank and public holidays were part of the 20 days. The EAT held that the effect of the collective agreement with the union was to amend existing contracts and the employer could not go on to change these in the way that had been tried (*Wood Hall Personnel & Transport v Harris and Gonsalvez EAT/156/02*).

However, the tribunals have to look at the "contractual intention" of the parties when deciding whether the terms of a collective agreement are incorporated. In the case of *Kaur v MG Rover [2005] IRLR 40*, the Court of Appeal held that the terms of a collective agreement which stated that there would be no redundancies were "aspirational" and did not amend the employment contracts. If, through custom and practice, changes agreed in negotiations are incorporated into employees' contracts, employees are bound to accept them. The fact that they **might not like what has been negotiated** is not the main issue, particularly where they then allow time to pass before voicing their objections *(Henry v London General Transport Services [2002] IRLR 472)*.

For example, a collectively agreed policy that the employer can introduce a practice of random **stop and search** to deal with a problem of theft, would be incorporated into the contracts of every employee even if they have not all individually agreed to the policy.

Mr Trotter objected to a new company policy on random searches and as a consequence resigned claiming constructive dismissal. The EAT held that while the policy change did amount to a fundamental breach of contract, the constructive dismissal was fair. The policy had been consulted on with the unions. It was not imposed arbitrarily and it would not be reasonable for the employer to have to differentiate between those employees who had agreed the change and those who had not (*Trotter v Grattan EAT/0179/03*).

If a workplace representative has apparent authority to negotiate, the employer can reach a deal at that level even if the procedures say that the full-time official should be informed of any deals concluded *(Harris v Richard Lawson Autologistics [2002] IRLR 476).*

If the change has **not been agreed by all the recognised unions** it may well be the case that it is not universally incorporated.

South Tyneside MBC wanted to change holiday terms. It had a recognition agreement with two unions but only reached agreement with one of them. Nevertheless, it introduced the change. The EAT noted that collective bargaining "rests upon a foundation of consensus and process" and that the processes for voting agreed between the unions had not been followed. This meant that there was no local agreement to the change and it had not therefore been incorporated into employees' contracts (*South Tyneside MBC v Graham EAT/0107/03*)

Once a change has become incorporated into an employee's contract it becomes a binding contractual term. The employee cannot revert back to the previous contractual arrangement without a further agreement.

Illegal clauses

If the employer proposes something illegal in the contract, for example a method for non-payment of tax by paying "cash in hand", employees need to be wary as it may mean they cannot enforce any part of the contract, including statutory rights under it.

For an employee to be barred from enforcing their employment rights on the grounds of illegality, the following must be found:

- the facts that made performance illegal must be identified;
- the employee must know that it was illegal; and
- the employee must have actively participated in the illegality (*Kaid v Gruppo UKEAT/056/03*).

In the case of *Salvesen v Simons [1994] IRLR 52,* the employee lost his right to pursue an unfair dismissal claim because he had accepted that part of his pay should not be taxed. The fact that he did not realise this was illegal made no difference. Agreeing to such a proposal, even if only for a short period of time, could result in the contract itself being declared illegal, with a resulting loss of all employment rights *(Hyland v J H Barker [1985] IRLR 403).* In another case, the fact that the employee was not fluent in English was held not to be a valid reason for her not to have challenged the fact that she was being paid gross. In that case (*Wheeler v Qualitydeep EAT/0998/03*) the fact that the arrangement had gone on for some time and that the employee too had financially benefited pointed to the contract being illegal. Agreeing to an illegal contract means that **all its terms are unenforceable**. The court will not accept that, where the employer gains more from the illegality than the employee (for example, by avoiding unfair dismissal law), this gives the employee rights which have been lost through illegality *(Soteriou v Ultrachem [2004] IRLR 870).*

The rule may not be strictly applied where:

- employees had sought an arrangement to pay tax and National Insurance but had not successfully persuaded their employer to make the arrangement (*Warp Technologies Holdings v Nunoo and Vermani EAT/0527/04*);
- employees took part in, but **did not gain from**, their employer's fraud *(Hewcastle Catering v Ahmed [1991] IRLR 473);*
- an employee was **paid occasional sums** cash in hand *(Annandale Engineering v Samson [1994] IRLR 59)*; or
- in **discrimination or TUPE** claims.

Employers usually cannot point to the fact that a contract is illegal to avoid claims based on sex, race or disability discrimination *(Leighton v Michael [1996] IRLR 67).* However, in cases where the illegality is entirely due to the employee's actions it may remove the right to take a discrimination claim. In the case of *Vakante v Addey & Stanhope School A1/2003/2753*, the Court of Appeal held that Mihovil Vankante's decision to work without documents was criminal and meant that he could not bring a discrimination claim even though it could have been the case that his employer had discriminated.

Where there is a **TUPE transfer** (see chapter 12) the new employer cannot avoid legal obligations in relation to TUPE by pointing to the fact that some employees may be working unlawfully (*Rosan Heims v Duke EAT/1248/01*).

Restraining clauses

Many contracts contain terms that **"restrain" or limit employees** in some way, for example, by requiring them not to work for competitors. Where such clauses exist, the courts can examine them to declare whether they are enforceable or not. In general, the narrower the range of activity restrained and the shorter the period, the more likely it is that a court will uphold the clause.

The Court of Appeal has ruled that a clause preventing an employee from working for any competitor for a period of 12 months went beyond the protection of trade secrets that an employer can legitimately use. The restriction has to be on something that goes beyond just the skill, experience and know-how acquired by an employee over time *(Wincanton v Cranny [2000] IRLR 716).*

In deciding whether a clause is valid the courts will also look at what other employers in the sector do. **Six-month clauses** are common and more likely to be upheld by the courts *(Dentmaster v Kent [1997] IRLR 636).*

The mere fact that the employer has unilaterally dismissed an employee does not void a restraint term *(Rock Refrigeration v Jones [1996] IRLR 675).* The Court of Appeal has, however, ruled that a clause that denied an employee the right to future contractual commission if he went to work for a competitor was unenforceable *(Marshall v NM Financial Management [1997] IRLR 449).*

While some clauses will be upheld as valid, provided they do no more than **protect a legitimate employer interest**, the employer normally has to show the harm that might be caused. In the case of *Jack Allen (Sales & Services) v Smith [1999] IRLR 19,* the EAT said that the harm has to be "real and not fanciful".

The fact that an employee has accepted more money in return for agreeing to be bound by a restrictive clause does not, of itself, prevent the tribunals from examining the clause. They can still decide whether or not the employer can enforce it, according to the Court of Appeal in the case of *Turner v Commonwealth [2000] IRLR 114.*

Contract changes

Employers should never introduce contract changes without, as a minimum, having **consulted** with the union, or employee representatives if there is no recognised union. If an employer imposes changes without agreement this will be a unilateral variation of contract and will be a breach of contract. Whether or not it is a fundamental breach will depend on the extent of the changes. Sometimes unilateral changes involve the termination of one contract and the offer of a new contract *(GMB v Man Truck & Bus UK [2000] IRLR 636).*

Once the employee has accepted the employment contract the employer should not make changes without agreement.

Ms Aparau's employer changed after a takeover. She was given a new contract, did not sign it but continued to work. A year later her employer tried to enforce one of the new terms. She succeeded in her claim that simply continuing to work did not imply she had accepted the change. The EAT said that where a changed contract term could have an effect only at some indeterminate time in the future, it cannot be unilaterally imposed *(Aparau v Iceland Frozen Foods [1996] IRLR 119).*

There may also be scope for using the rights under the whistleblowing legislation if employers act in breach of contract (see chapter 10 – Automatically unfair dismissals).

Contracts may be changed lawfully:

- if developments, through **custom and practice**, are made over time;
- if the **parties agree** to the change;
- where terms are changed as the result of **collective bargaining**;
- where the contract itself **allows for a change** — for example where there is a mobility clause (but see chapter 6 – Indirect discrimination); and
- where a contract term is offered "**subject to the needs of the service**".

All other forms of contract changes unilaterally imposed will amount to a **breach of contract**.

If employees agree to changes, a **new statement** (see above – Written contracts) incorporating the changes must be issued within a month *(section 4 ERA 96)*. The statement must set out the **changes in full**. There is no provision for statements by instalment, as is the case with the initial statement. Where there is a change of employer's name, this must be stated along with a restatement of the date of the employee's continuity of service.

Employers may simply give **notice to change** the contract but this does not prevent it being a breach of contract if you have not agreed to the change. If the changes are so significant that they effectively terminate the existing contract and replace it with another, an employee in this situation who meets the "qualifying conditions" for claiming unfair dismissal (see chapter 10) may be able to pursue a tribunal claim.

In workplaces where the union is recognised, contract changes usually occur through **collective bargaining**. It is normally taken to be the case that the employee has accepted changes made in this way where, in the past, that is how contracts have been changed (see above – Works rules and collective agreements).

Fundamental breach of contract

Alternatively, where the employer changes the contract without agreement (in legal terms this is called a **breach**), the employee can go to the civil courts to claim that the change has fundamentally altered the contract. Not every change is a **fundamental breach**, but asking an employee to move a considerable distance or accept significant changes in hours or pay (unless specifically allowed by the contract) is likely to constitute one. A **cumulative series of incidents,** each not sufficiently serious to amount to a fundamental breach, can, taken together, amount to a breach of the implied term of trust and confidence (see above – Implied terms).

If the court finds the employer has no right under the contract to change its terms, or where the change proposed was unreasonably implemented, it has the power to order the employer to restore the contract to its original provisions.

A House of Lords ruling *(Rigby v Ferodo [1987] IRLR 516)* looked at the legal implications of an employer's decision to reduce pay.

Engineering workers employed by Ferodo succeeded in a claim for damages for reduced wages after their employer decided unilaterally to cut their pay. The Law Lords said that the fact that the employers, by their action, had clearly intended the contracts to continue (although on different terms) could not allow them to argue that they had offered new contracts. Furthermore, this continuing contractual relationship gave the employees the right to enforce the debt due, that is the difference between what their contracts said they should be paid and what they in fact received. And the fact that they had continued to work could not be taken as an implicit agreement to the change.

Other cases in which the courts have ruled that fundamental changes to contracts have been made include:

- issuing a final written warning without a proper investigation *(Thackeray v Acequip EAT/0396/03)*;
- **reducing pay** and assigning **additional duties**, even if, due to a resulting stress-related illness, the employee does not immediately act on the breach *(Governing Body of St Edmund of Canterbury Catholic High School v Hines EAT/1138/02)*;
- **reducing working hours**, even if in the past there has been agreement to change hours in similar situations *(International Packaging Corporation v Balfour [2003] IRLR 11)*;
- giving an employee a **final written warning** for an offence which any employer acting reasonably would have regarded as minor *(Stanley Cole v Sheridan [2003] IRLR 885)*;
- transferring an employee to a **higher graded post** but where the result is to deprive the employee of previous pay protection *(LB Camden v Collins & Clements EAT/1436/01)*;
- unilateral change of a fixed **London allowance** provided in the contract *(Security and Facilities Division v Hayes [2001] IRLR 81)*;
- **changing retirement age** without agreement. The EAT ruled that while employers could increase the retirement age they could not reduce it without agreement, since the effect was to deprive the employee of the right to claim unfair dismissal *(Bratko v Beloit Walmsley [1995] IRLR 629)*;
- an instruction to an employee to **change her hours** in conflict with her domestic responsibilities *(Greenaway Harrison v Wiles [1994] IRLR 380)*. In that case the employers argued that the employee had "jumped the gun" because the change had not yet been implemented, but the EAT ruled there was a breach of contract;
- an employer's decision to pay the **national rate only**, ignoring the previous collectively agreed local rate which had already become incorporated within the individual's contract *(Gibbons v Associated British Ports [1985] IRLR 376)*;
- a **transfer of employees** to new work where there was nothing in their contract allowing for this *(Hughes v Southwark [1988] IRLR 55)*; and
- the **replacement of full-time work** by part-time and temporary work *(Hogg v Dover College [1990] ICR 39)*.

The ruling in the *Hogg* case was applied by the EAT in the case *of Alcan Extrusions v Yates [1996] IRLR 327* which said that, where radically **different terms are unilaterally imposed**, the employee does not have to choose between staying with the employer and accepting the change or resigning and claiming constructive dismissal. The employee reserved the right to take an unfair dismissal case at a later stage.

Employees who are dismissed can normally only claim compensation under unfair dismissal law (see chapter 10). However, according to the House of Lords in the conjoined cases of *Eastwood v Magnox Electric and McCabe v Cornwall CC [2004] IRLR 733*, employees who are unfairly dismissed may also be able to claim compensation where their employer's conduct prior to the dismissal caused mental illness resulting in financial loss. The court held that employers' duty of care extends to a requirement to protect their employees' mental health and that a failure to do so amounts to a breach of contract. The court thus ruled that financial loss is recoverable if the breach occurs prior to dismissal.

As an alternative to claiming breach of contract, an employee may be able to get an **injunction** to stop their employer from changing the contract (see chapter 10 – Injunctions).

In the case of *Peace v City of Edinburgh Council [1999] IRLR 417,* the Court of Session in Scotland granted an interdict (injunction) preventing the council from adopting a new disciplinary procedure. The employee successfully argued that the established procedure was a term in his contract and that an interdict was the appropriate legal action to deal with a breach of contract that had not yet happened but was **anticipated.**

If an employer breaches a contract this may absolve an employee from contractual obligations. In one case the employer's breach removed the employee's legal obligation to repay relocation expenses which otherwise would have been repayable on termination. However, if the contract stipulates that repayment will be required, no matter what the circumstances leading to the termination, the employee is contractually obliged to repay the money. In the case of *CRS Computers v McKenzie EAT/1259/01,* this meant having to pay back a car loan.

Where the contract change results in a **loss of pay**, employees can also consider using *Part II* of the *ERA 96* (see chapter 4 – Deductions and underpayments) to obtain their wages due under the agreed contract.

There are some advantages in using this Act since the claim is heard at a tribunal — a cheaper, speedier and less formal setting than the County or High Court.

An employer's breach may open up the right to pursue other statutory claims, as in the case of *Mennell v Newell and Wright [1997] IRLR 519.*

Mr Mennell was told his contract would be changed without agreement. He complained that the resulting reduction in pay would be unlawful. The employer then dismissed him. He could not claim under the unfair dismissal rules because he had not worked for the two years required at that time (now one year). Instead he successfully argued that he was dismissed because he was attempting to **enforce his statutory right** not to have an unlawful deduction (see chapter 10). The Court of Appeal accepted his submission and held that the dismissal was unfair.

Employees may also be able to prove unfair dismissal as well as breach of contract, where the contract changes are major. In the *Hogg v Dover College* case (see above) Mr Hogg won an unfair dismissal claim despite having continued in work (though under protest). The EAT recognised that he needed the work but accepted that the change from full to part-time work was a breach of contract by his employer which he had not accepted.

Even where there is a **mobility clause** in a contract, this does not necessarily give the employer unlimited rights to transfer workers *(United Bank v Akhtar [1989] IRLR 507)* and the issue of whether the effect of the clause is discriminatory should also be considered (see chapter 6). However, where the contract is clear on the existence of a mobility clause, the employee has no additional rights, for example to be paid any relocation allowance, unless the contract provides for it.

An employer's refusal to compensate an employee required to move under a mobility clause does not amount to a breach of contract. Furthermore, a request **temporarily to move to a new location**, even where the employee is not bound by a mobility clause, may not amount to a breach of contract. The employer may be able to dismiss fairly for reasons of conduct if the employee **refuses to move** (see chapter 10).

There may be circumstances where a **relocation** can amount to **constructive dismissal**.

Mr McAndrew was told, at short notice, to move to a new location 15 miles away. He resigned claiming constructive dismissal. The Court of Session held that a term that reasonable notice should be given of any relocation could properly be incorporated into the contract *(Prestwick Circuits v McAndrew [1990] IRLR 191).*

What amounts to **reasonable notice** is something for the tribunals to decide. A week could be sufficient. However, the following EAT decision should be noted.

Mr White's contract included a mobility clause. As a result of its operation he suffered a reduction in earnings which were not guaranteed in his contract. The tribunal ruled he had no right to maintain them and that there was no contractual obligation on the employer to introduce the change reasonably. This was so, provided that the move was not "capricious" and that the contractual power was not exercised in such a way as to undermine the implied term of trust and confidence *(White v Reflecting Roadstuds [1991] IRLR 331).*

Tribunals can also take into account the employer's **need for change**, balanced against the injury done to the employee. In the case of *Catamaran Cruisers v Williams [1994] IRLR 386*, the EAT ruled that the contract change could be necessary if not imposed in an arbitrary way. The fact that the union had recommended the change was taken into account.

Where contract changes are less significant, employees have fewer legal rights. For example, a change from manual work to computerised work, which workers argued was in effect a different type of work, was held by the courts not to be a significant change.

In rare cases **employees too can be sued** for breach of contract. In *Attorney General v Blake [2001] IRLR 36*, the House of Lords held that employers can take account of any profits made by an employee as a result of their breach and can claim damages based on these. Normally it would be difficult for an employer to establish the nature of the financial damage caused by an employee's breach. Indeed, in the case of *Giraud v Smith [2000] IRLR 763*, the EAT held that a contract clause saying that employees who left without giving proper notice had to pay the equivalent of their notice to their employer, was unenforceable. Employers could only recoup a pre-estimated loss.

More information: LRD booklet, *Contracts of Employment – a legal guide* (£4.70); LRD's *Workplace Report* provides regular quarterly updates on contract law.

4. Rights to pay and conditions

National minimum wage

Under the *National Minimum Wage Act 1998*, UK workers have the right to a **minimum wage**, currently set at £4.85 an hour for those aged 22 or over. This rises to £5.05 from 1 October 2005. Young people aged 18 to 21 get a lower rate of £4.10, rising to £4.25 from 1 October 2005. Sixteen and 17 year olds have a lower rate of £3.00 an hour. The rate can be paid **net of tax and national insurance deductions.**

Workers, including agency and homeworkers, are covered, as is anyone who works for another person. In one case a tribunal ruled that individuals who were employed through an agency to "house sit" while the occupants of the house were away had the right to be paid the minimum wage. In the case of *Scottbridge Construction v Wright [2003] IRLR 21*, the Court of Session in Scotland held that a night watchman had the right to be paid the national minimum wage for the whole of his nightshift, even though, when not on patrol, he could read, watch television or sleep.

Similarly, in the case of *British Nursing Association v Inland Revenue [2001] IRLR 659*, the Employment Appeal Tribunal (EAT) ruled that **workers working in their own homes** during the night, answering telephone enquiries, had the right to be paid the national minimum wage. It did not matter that they could do other things (including sleep) when not answering the phone. Workers providing a "**round the clock**" service are likely to be treated differently. In the case of *Walton v Independent Living [2003] IRLR 469*, the Court of Appeal held that a carer providing 24-hour cover did not have to be paid for all those hours. Although she had to be available, in practice she was only required to assist her client for around six-and-a-half hours a day. The court held that payment should be based on those hours.

Workers working at home and paid according to what they produce (**pieceworkers**) have the right to a minimum fair piece rate, set of at **least 120% of the national minimum wage**.

Those **excluded from the right to the national minimum wage** are: fishing vessel workers paid by share of catch; people working as volunteers in voluntary organisations; prisoners; apprentices under the age of 19 or who are under 26 but in the first 12 months of their apprenticeship; trainees on government-funded training; students on sandwich courses; trainee teachers; members of the armed forces; and schoolchildren. The EAT has ruled that a **child doing a newspaper round** was not covered by the national minimum wage *(Addison v Ashby [2003] IRLR 211)*.

The **Inland Revenue** has the power to issue **compliance orders** against employers not paying the minimum wage. But if there is a dispute about how much is owed it will be for the tribunal not the Inland Revenue to calculate the amount. Enforcement officers can issue orders covering ex-employees as well as current employees and can amend or withdraw enforcement and penalty notices where these are found to be incorrect (*National Minimum Wage (Enforcement) Act 2003*).

If an employer **fails to pay** the national minimum wage a claim can be made to an employment tribunal and it is up to the employer to prove that the minimum has been paid. You can also claim if your employer **reduces your hours** to keep your wages at what they were before the new minimum came into force. If an employer **increases the productivity target** to fund an increase in the national minimum wage and, as a result, an employee unable or unwilling to meet the new target is dismissed, the dismissal is automatically unfair (see chapter 10 – Automatically unfair dismissals) *(Bopari v Grasshopper EAT/284/01)*. If an employer **reduces an existing bonus** or attendance payment to fund an increase in the national minimum wage, this can amount to an unlawful deduction (see below – Deductions and underpayments).

Pay slips and pay intervals

Every employee must be given, by their first pay date, an itemised pay statement that lists **gross wages, deductions** and **net wages** *(Employment Rights Act 1996 (ERA 96) section 8)*. If an employer fails to give a statement an employee can go to a tribunal to get it.

If employees are currently **paid in cash** this should remain as part of their contractual rights and the usual rules for contract changes apply (see chapter 3 – Contract changes). Employers can be challenged if they move existing employees onto cashless pay without agreement, but only if the resulting breach was fundamental. An employer dismissing an employee who refuses to agree to a change to cashless pay may attempt to argue that this is a dismissal "for some other reason" (see chapter 10). But each case would depend on the individual facts and circumstances.

Employers must each year give every employee a **certificate (P60)** that shows annual gross pay, take-home pay and total deductions.

Deductions and underpayments

Fixed deductions from pay do not need to be itemised separately on the pay statement. However, there are certain legal rules covering deductions. *Section 13 ERA 96* says that employers cannot make deductions from wages unless the **deduction is by statutory power** or there is **a term agreed in writing** in the worker's contract which precedes the deduction. Deductions by statutory power would include income tax and national insurance contributions. Workers who have signed an authorisation form for **union subscriptions** to be deducted (check-off) will have the deduction shown on their pay slip. All other deductions are likely to be unlawful if not agreed in advance.

Wages include fees, bonuses, commission, holiday pay, guarantee pay, sick pay and maternity pay. But *ERA 96* cannot be used to claim notice pay, or pay in lieu, which can be recovered through a claim of wrongful dismissal.

Ms Delaney was dismissed without notice and given a cheque for pay in lieu of notice, which subsequently was stopped. She was also entitled to holiday pay and commission, neither of which was paid. She claimed payment on all three counts, arguing that the non-payment was a deduction under the Act. The House of Lords upheld her claim for holiday pay and commission, as these were wages, but not for pay in lieu of notice classified as appropriate for a claim for damages for wrongful dismissal *(Delaney v Staples [1992] IRLR 191).*

The law can be used to claim **shortfalls**, for example non-payment of a shift allowance or a bonus or commission *(Kent Services v Butterfield [1992] IRLR 349)*. However, where payments are genuinely discretionary it can be difficult to establish a contractual entitlement to them. But in the case of *Chequepoint UK v Radwan Court of Appeal, 15 September 2002*, the Court of Appeal held that once an employer confirms that a discretionary bonus is due, it becomes contractual.

This interpretation was confirmed in the case of *Farrell Matthews & Weir v Hansen [2005] IRLR 160.* The courts have also confirmed that employers cannot exercise discretion in an irrational or perverse way *(Clark v Nomura International [2000] IRLR 766).* The Act cannot be used to claim **car allowances**. Claims over failure to pay these are based on a breach of contract and are pursued in the County or High Court.

Under the *Attachment of Earnings Act 1971*, employers must make deductions from earnings where employees have had an **attachment of earnings** order made against them by the courts.

Even where the employee has breached the contract (for example, by leaving without giving the appropriate notice) there is no automatic right to deduct pay. Any deductions made without authority from a final pay packet would be unlawful.

Ms Chambers and others walked out without notice following a dispute. Their final pay packets had shortfalls said by the employer to offset claims for damages for breach of contract. The EAT stated that these amounted to deductions and were unlawful *(Chiltern House v Chambers [1990] IRLR 88).*

Deducting money from an employee's final pay packet because that employee has taken more **statutory holidays** than have been accrued amounts to an unlawful deduction. The law says that a worker has the right to be paid wages **properly due** and any shortfall is effectively a deduction, unless it is an error of calculation. But, as an EAT case *(Yemm v British Steel [1994] IRLR 117)* makes clear, where employers make a conscious decision not to make a payment, because they believe there is no contractual entitlement, they are not making an "error of computation".

If an employee has the right to a **fixed allowance** (for example, overnight expenses) the employer cannot unilaterally reduce the rate by arguing that the new allowance still covered the actual expenses incurred by the employee *(Security and Facilities Division v Hayes [2001] IRLR 81).*

Part II of *ERA 96* can be used to **challenge contract changes**. For example in the case of *Kerr v Sweater Shop [1996] IRLR 424*, the EAT held that a change in the calculation of **holiday pay**, communicated to workers by way of a general notice only, did not comply with the law, making the resulting pay reduction unlawful. In the case of *International Packaging v Balfour [2003] IRLR 11* the court held that a decision to put employees on **short time** amounted to an unlawful deduction. In the case of *Jowitt v Pioneer Technology [2003] IRLR 356,* the Court of Appeal reversed an earlier EAT ruling and held that an employer's failure to pay the employee his **contractual permanent health insurance** because the insurers had decided the employee could do some work, although not his own job, did not amount to a deduction. The insurance scheme only required a payment to be made when the employee was unable to do either their own job or any other paid work that they might realistically be expected to do. In the case of *Bruce v Wiggins Teape [1994] IRLR 536,* the law was used to reinstate an **overtime rate** that the employer had scrapped unilaterally. And in the case of *Saavedra v Aceground [1995] IRLR 198,* the Act was used to reclaim a **share of tips** that the employer had unilaterally reduced. However, in the case of *Nerva v UK [2002] IRLR 815,* the ECJ confirmed that **tips added to a credit card** payment were not the property of the employees and that the employer's decision not to pay them to staff did not amount to an unlawful deduction.

Where the employer had a **contractual right** to impose the change the resulting deduction will be lawful.

In the case of *Hussman Manufacturing v Weir [1998] IRLR 288* the employee's **shift was changed** and as a result his pay was reduced. He claimed that this amounted to an unlawful deduction, but lost the case when the employer showed that there was a contract term giving them the right to make changes to shifts.

Any other deductions, for example for dishonesty, poor work or misconduct, can be made provided the worker has **agreed in advance in writing** to the deduction. But the agreement must be specific and clear and made before any incident which would give rise to a deduction. Where the employee had signed a form agreeing to repay **training costs** if he left employment, one tribunal said this did not constitute authority to deduct *(Potter v Hunt Contracts [1992] IRLR 108).*

An employer who persuaded his employee to sign a form agreeing to **future deductions** in respect of previous stock shortfalls did not make a lawful deduction *(Discount Tobacco v Williamson [1993] IRLR 327).* Employees may also be able to use the *Unfair Contract Terms Act*

1977 to challenge pay deductions (see chapter 3 – Express terms).

Retail workers have additional protection limiting deductions for cash shortages or stock deficiencies to a maximum of 10% of any one pay packet, except for the final one.

If an employer's deductions contravene the Act a worker can **complain to a tribunal** *(section 23 ERA 96)*. The complaint has to be made within **three months**, calculated from the date when the last disputed payment should have been made *(Group 4 Nightspeed v Gilbert [1997] IRLR 398)*. If the complaint is upheld the tribunal can order the employer to make good the unlawful deduction. The position of workers taking **action short of a strike** is explained in chapter 9. Claims regarding such deductions cannot usually be pursued through the employment tribunals. However, what the tribunal can consider is whether industrial action has taken place. It cannot just rely on the employer having alleged that there has been industrial action (*Gill v Ford Motor Co [2004] IRLR 840*).

An employee can also take a claim for breach of contract in the civil courts if an employer makes a deduction without prior agreement.

Overpayments

If an employer incorrectly calculates the amount of pay due, resulting in an overpayment, there are specific rules on how and when the money is to be paid back. The employer will be expected to **act reasonably**, staging deductions for repayment over a period of time agreed with the individual. Whatever the circumstances of the overpayment, the employer should never make a deduction to rectify it without first **consulting the employee**. An employer may not recover an overpayment if the employee was led to believe there was an **entitlement to the payment** and a **right to receive it**, and as a result had **adjusted their spending**. If employees genuinely believe that the money is due to them and spend it, the employer will not be able to recoup it *(Kleinwort Benson v Lincoln City [1998] 3 Weekly Law Reports 1095)*. However, in the case of *Commerzbank v Price-Jones A2/2003/ 0070*, the Court of Appeal held that an overpayment which was clearly a mistake on the employer's part could be reclaimed unless the employee could show that it would be inequitable for them to be required to repay it.

Section 14 ERA 96 states that the general restrictions on deductions (see above) do not apply when the employer's purpose in making the deduction is to reclaim an overpayment of wages. The case of *SIP v Swinn [1994] IRLR 323*, confirmed that the Act cannot be used to challenge such deductions and that employees must pursue those claims in the County or High Courts.

Guarantee pay

Employees **laid off** or on short time should still receive their **normal pay** *(Miller v Hamworthy Engineering [1986] IRLR 461)*, unless there is a clear contractual term or custom to the contrary. This is particularly the case for salaried employees whose pay is expressed as an annual sum.

In one case the collective agreement said that short-time working could be introduced, but only where "approved as an alternative to redundancy" by the union. Introducing it without that consent gave employees the right to use *Part II* of the *ERA 96* to claim their full wages since their employer had made an unlawful deduction under the Act *(Davies v Hotpoint [1994] IRLR 538)*.

If the employment contract specifically gives the employer the right to lay off employees without pay, they can claim **statutory guarantee pay** as long as they have been working for the employer for **at least a month**. The provisions for this are found in *section 28 ERA 96*. Although calculated on normal hourly earnings, guarantee pay is offset against contractual pay and limited to a maximum of five days' pay in any three-month period. The maximum paid for a day is £18.40 (2005/06) *(section 31 ERA 96)*. Employees laid off because of industrial action taken by others employed by their employer cannot qualify for guarantee pay.

If employees are offered **suitable alternative work** for the days laid off, which they refuse, no guarantee pay is payable. If employees are denied guarantee pay in circumstances where they believe they have an entitlement, they can make a claim to a tribunal **within three months** of the day payment is claimed for *(section 34 ERA 96)*. Employees laid off for a period of **at least four weeks** may be able to claim redundancy (see chapter 11 – Qualifying for redundancy pay).

Medical suspension pay

Employees suspended by their employer on medical grounds because of a statutory requirement are entitled to medical suspension pay *(section 64 ERA 96)*. This applies where there is a **potential danger to a worker's health**, for example from lead, rubber, chemicals or radioactive substances.

The same requirements, exclusions and obligations to accept suitable alternative work apply as for guarantee pay (see above). However, payment is based on the week's pay calculation (see chapter 10 – Compensation) and is currently set at a maximum of £280 (2005/06). Contractual earnings are offset against this and the maximum period of entitlement is 26 weeks. Employees who have been refused medical suspension pay must lodge their claim with the tribunal **within three months** *(section 70 ERA 96)*.

Equal pay

It is unlawful for an employer to discriminate on the grounds of sex, which includes paying one sex less than the other. The *Equal Pay Act 1970* lays down the circumstances in which workers can claim equal pay. It says that an equality clause is presumed to operate in every employment contract, giving women the right to equal treatment with men. You can claim equal pay with someone of the opposite sex whose job is comparable to yours, but you have to show that there is an appreciable difference in pay between the two jobs and that one is carried out almost exclusively by one sex and the other by the opposite sex. In the case of *MOD v Armstrong [2004] 672*, the EAT made it clear that the "fundamental question is whether there is a causative link between the applicant's sex and the fact that she is paid less than the true value of her job as reflected in the pay of her named comparator". Your employer should not attempt to put pressure on you to withdraw a claim, as the following case demonstrates.

Ms Derbyshire, along with 38 colleagues, took an equal pay claim against her employers. Their response was to write to all staff pointing out that the cost of settling the claim would result in redundancies and to write to Derbyshire and her colleagues urging them to settle. The EAT held that the letters amounted to victimisation (*St Helens MBC v Derbyshire and others [2004] IRLR 851*).

A "credible suggestion" that there might be a pay difference is not enough *(Nelson v Carillion Services [2003] IRLR 428)*. Furthermore you have to establish that there is a case of **pay discrimination based on a sex difference**. Just pointing to the fact that someone earns more than you is not enough *(Parliamentary Commissioner for Administration v Ferandez [2004] IRLR 22)*. In the case of *Home Office v Bailey*, the Court of Appeal held that female prison officer staff might be able to compare their pay with that of male colleagues even though the comparator group was all male, while the women's grade was mixed in gender.

Employees who believe they may have grounds for an equal pay claim can use a **questionnaire procedure** to get information from their employer about pay and grading in the workplace. But you need to make sure that you do not ask for information that would go beyond finding out about your comparators. In one case the employee asked for information about the pay of everyone on her pay band. The EAT held that just because employees are all on the same pay band or grade does not imply that they are doing like work or work of equal value (*Villalba v Merrill Lynch EAT/9461/04*). If employers refuse to respond to the questionnaire, tribunals can **infer that there is unequal pay**.

An Equal Opportunities Commission (EOC) *Code of practice on equal pay* provides **practical guidance** and suggests good practice. In particular the code recommends that employers carry out equal pay reviews. The code is admissible in evidence in sex discrimination proceedings. Employers who ignore the code's recommendations can have this fact used against them at a tribunal. Trade unions, concerned that the gap between men's and women's pay persists, would like the government to go further than just recommending equal pay reviews, to impose a legal obligation on employers to **audit their pay systems**. Workplace representatives should consider negotiating with their employers to get agreement to audit the pay system.

The *Equal Pay Act (EPA)* covers not only basic pay, but also other **terms and conditions** such as sick pay, holiday pay, special retirement privileges (for example travel concessions, pensions, redundancy pay) and any "fringe" benefits that can be defined as pay, including discretionary bonuses. In the case of *Redcar and Cleveland v Degnan [2005] IRLR 179*, the EAT held that bonuses and allowances paid for attendance were part of the normal working hours and should be included in the hourly rate. This meant that women comparing their pay with that of male workers who did get attendance bonuses could base their claim on what the men earned with the bonus. Each term stands separately, so an employer cannot justify one unequal term by saying that the employee benefited under another, different term *(Jamstalldhetsombudsmannen v Orebro [2000] IRLR 421)*. Employers may offer different terms if they have an **equality objective**.

Mr Lommers was denied a place for his child at a work-subsidised nursery. Places were mainly offered to female employees as a way to encourage their participation in the labour market. Noting that male single parents might also be offered places, the ECJ held that the practice was not contrary to the equal treatment directive (*Lommers v Minister Van Landbouw [2002] IRLR 430)*.

In another case, the European Court of Justice held that a scheme, which paid an additional allowance to women made redundant to take account of evidence that they were more likely to remain out of work following redundancy, was lawful (*Hlozek v Roche Austria Case C-19/02*) The Act applies equally to **part-time workers**. The European Court case of *Bilka Kaufhaus v Weber von Hartz [1986] IRLR 317*, established that refusing to allow part-time workers access to a company pension scheme infringed the law on equal pay. **Pieceworkers** can also use the Act. According to the ECJ in the case of *Specialarbejderforbundet i Danmark v Dansk Industri [1995] IRLR 648*, where there is an appreciable difference in pay the employer has to prove there is no sex-based discrimination. The fact that there may be a **few men employed** doing the same work as women does not itself bar an equal value claim where women are comparing their jobs with those of other male workers *(Pickstone v Freemans [1988] IRLR 357)*.

A woman does not have to have worked for a particular length of time before claiming equal pay. She can claim **any time while in the job**, or **within six months of leaving it**. This applies even if she is still working for the same employer but in a different job. Under the *Equal Pay (Amendment) Regulations 2003*, the six months is assessed from the end of employment or the end of a **stable employment relationship**.

Comparing jobs

Section 1 of the *EPA* says that women have the right to equal treatment in pay where they carry out:

- **"like work"** to that of a man;

- "**work rated as equivalent**" to a man's; or
- "**work of equal value**", in terms of, for example, effort, skill and decision making, compared to a man's.

Like work is defined as when a woman is doing "the same or broadly similar" work to a man where differences, if any, are not of practical importance. Tribunals will look at how work is carried out in practice to determine this. Where there are differences in the work, they will look to see the frequency with which these occur.

Work rated as equivalent refers to work rated under a **job evaluation scheme**. The existence of a job evaluation scheme may act as a **bar to workers** taking equal value claims to a tribunal (see below), unless it was not specifically applied to the group of workers. For example, a job evaluation of health workers in Britain did not bar a claim by Northern Irish workers *(McAuley v Eastern Health & Social Services [1991] IRLR 467).* Women can claim equal pay where a job evaluation scheme exists if they can show that the **scheme itself is discriminatory**, for example, if factors generally seen as favourable to women were excluded or wrongly weighted, or if it is outdated. Where a job evaluation exercise has resulted in a different score for women and their male comparators, but because a grading system based on bands would in effect place both scores in the same band, there is an entitlement to equal pay *(Springboard Sunderland v Robson [1992] IRLR 261).* The job evaluation scheme also has to be thorough in analysis and must be capable of impartial application (*Diageo v Thomson EAT/ 0064/03*).

Once jobs have been rated as equal, employers cannot **reduce the pay** for the jobs of one sex while leaving those of the opposite sex untouched. In the case of *Ratcliffe v N. Yorkshire CC [1995] IRLR 439*, the House of Lords said that reducing the pay of school meals workers to win an in-house contract was contrary to equal pay laws. The women's work had been evaluated as equal to that of male workers who did not face a wage cut.

To claim **equal value** a woman must show that her job is of equal value to that of a more highly-paid male employee (the male **comparator** – see below), as measured by criteria like skill and decision making. Tribunals cannot "strike out" (reject) a claim on the basis that there are "no reasonable grounds" for it or because there is an existing job evaluation scheme. Instead, under the *Equal Pay (Amendment) Regulations 2003*, the tribunal can **assess the job evaluation scheme** and reject it where it has a "reasonable suspicion" that it discriminates.

Claims will not succeed in some circumstances. For example, it may be lawful to pay workers different rates to reflect their **different qualifications**, even though in practice they appear to perform similar work. They can also be paid differently on account of their **job performance**, provided it is an assessment of their actual work, not their work potential (*Brunnhofer v Bank der Österreichischen Postsparkasse [2001] IRLR 571*). Different or additional tasks can also provide a justification for different rates of pay. In the case of *Christie and others v John E Haith [2003] IRLR 670*, the EAT held that a requirement that male employees had to **lift heavy loads** was lawful grounds for the pay difference.

A difference in pay resulting from pay protection after a **TUPE transfer** (see chapter 12), is also justifiable under equal pay law. Different pay rates based on length of service may also be justifiable, although this issue is being considered in the case of *Cadman v HSE v [2004] IRLR 921*, where the Court of Appeal said that it was impossible to say that length of service as a criterion for determining pay rates need never be justified. The court referred the issue to the ECJ whose ruling was awaited as this booklet was being produced.

An employer cannot pay someone of the opposite sex doing the same work more because it is believed that they will perform better, according to rulings from the European Court of Justice and the UK courts. But the courts will look for some evidence of sex-based differences.

In the case of *Glasgow City Council v Marshall [2000] IRLR 272*, the House of Lords held that school instructors doing almost identical work to schoolteachers, could not claim equal pay. The pay differences were for historical reasons but there was no evidence to show that these were in any way linked to differences based on sex.

The EAT has also held that women **transferred to alternative work** for health reasons **during pregnancy** have no right to pursue an equal pay claim in respect of the alternative work. Equally, men do not have the right to claim equality in respect of any additional lump sum or loyalty bonuses paid to women on maternity leave *(Abdoulaye v Renault [1999] IRLR 811).*

Comparable worker

To win an equal pay claim you have to be able to show that there is a **comparable worker of the opposite sex** who is being paid more. Normally, the worker will be in the same establishment (workplace). It is very important to choose a **comparator who is most similar** in terms of length of service, age and so on. This is because any material differences may explain the difference in pay and defeat the claim.

A woman can compare her job to that of a man in **other workplaces** owned by the same employer, if they work under the same terms and conditions *(British Coal v Smith [1994] IRLR 342).* Some workers, for example those in NHS trusts and local authorities, may be able to compare their pay with that of workers in other trusts or local authorities.

In the case of *Scullard v Southern Region Council for Education [1996] IRLR 344,* the employee was able to claim equal pay with those employed by other regional councils. All were funded by the Department for Education and Employment and the fact that the employers were different did not bar the claim.

In another case the Scottish Court of Session upheld the right of teachers to claim equal pay with colleagues employed by a different local education authority on the ground that their pay scales were all under the control of the secretary of state *(South Ayrshire v Morton [2002] IRLR 256).*

The extent to which comparisons with other employers can be made is, however, limited. The EAT in England and Wales has suggested that the *Morton* case was wrongly decided and should not necessarily be followed. In the case of *Robertson v Department for Environment, Food and Rural Affairs* A1/2003/2774, the Court of Appeal has ruled that civil servants working for different civil service departments could not compare their jobs under equal pay law as there was no single source for their rate of pay, with each individual department setting its own terms and conditions. In the case of *Lawrence v Regent Office Care [2002] IRLR 822,* a claim under equal pay law that **contracted-out workers** be paid the same as those who had remained in-house was ruled against by the ECJ. It held that it was not the fact that the comparison was with workers employed by a different employer that caused the claim to fail. To win the workers would have needed to show that there was a "**single source**" responsible for the inequality of treatment.

In the case of *Allonby v Accrington & Rossendale College [2004] IRLR 224,* the ECJ ruled that agency worker Debra Allonby could not compare her rate of pay with that of a directly-employed male worker, even though they both worked at the "same establishment". They had different employers and there was no common controlling entity regulating their pay. However, while rejecting the claim for equal pay the court held that Allonby's exclusion from the **right to join the college pension scheme** could be challenged under sex discrimination law, if the provision detrimentally affected a greater proportion of women. Allonby's claim now goes back to the UK courts for them to rule on her claim for equal access to the pension scheme (see chapter 6 — Discrimination).

Taking an equal pay claim

The basic procedures for taking equal pay claims are the same as for all other tribunal claims (see chapter 1). But there are special procedures for taking **equal value claims** to tribunals. There is provision for the appointment of an **independent expert**, instructed by the tribunal to evaluate the jobs being compared. The expert examines the jobs and presents the resulting report as evidence. A tribunal can, however, decide on a claim without using an expert, but has to first give the parties the opportunity to appoint their own experts, before giving its ruling on the claim *(William Ball v Wood EAT/89/01).*

With effect from 1 October 2004 the law has been amended to introduce procedural changes to how the tribunals operate. The new procedures are intended to be less complex and aim to inform the parties better about the time a case will take and its chance of success. The government says that the changes will result in reduced costs for both sides, as well as savings to the taxpayer.

The employer has two defences against equal pay claims:

- where there is a **"material difference"** justifying the pay gap (in like work cases); or
- where there is a **"material factor"** justifying the pay gap (in equal value cases).

A **material difference** can include aspects like merit pay, red circling (protecting previous earnings), longer hours and so on. But the employer has to show that the difference is genuine and accounts for the whole of the pay disparity. However, if a measure has been introduced for budgetary savings, the fact that it has not achieved the gains anticipated will not, in itself, cancel out the employer's defence. An ECJ ruling, however, suggests that budgeting constraints can never be used to justify sex discrimination, unless there is a legitimate social policy behind it *(Jorgensen v Foreningen [2000] IRLR 726).*

Material factors include matters like skill shortages or an employee's special role in giving advice and training. Once the employer has shown genuine reasons, unconnected with sex, for the pay difference, there is no further obligation to justify the difference *(Strathclyde RC v Wallace [1998] IRLR 146).* The existence of a collective agreement, however, laying down different pay rates cannot be a material factor, even if untainted by sex discrimination.

In the case of *Barber v NCR [1993] IRLR 95*, a reduction in hours of work for male workers gave them a higher hourly rate than that of equally evaluated women. The women won the right to the higher hourly rate.

The ECJ has held *(Enderby v Frenchay HA [1993] IRLR 591)* that the fact that rates of pay are set by **two different collective processes** which, considered separately, had no discriminatory effect, does not provide an "objective justification" for defence to an equal pay claim. Although it accepted that market forces could be an objective justification, if this only accounted for part of the pay difference, the women were entitled to that proportion of the difference that could not be objectively justified. In this case speech therapists successfully compared themselves with clinical psychologists and negotiated a compensation deal averaging around £50,000 for each employee.

Back pay of up to six years from the date of the original claim *(Levez v TH Jennings [1999] IRLR 36)*, can be claimed. Back pay can be claimed for more than six years in two particular circumstances. One is where the employer "deliberately concealed" relevant facts from the claimant. Provided a claim is brought within six years of the discovery of this fact, the claimant can claim. Other circumstances are where the claimant is a minor or "of unsound mind" (suffering from a disability).

Working hours and breaks

The *Working Time Regulations 1998* limit the length of the working day and the working week. The regulations cover "**workers**" not just "employees" and state that, in general, a worker should work no more than **48 hours in a week**, averaged over what is called a "reference period". This is normally 17 weeks, but can be extended to 26 weeks in some cases. It can also be extended to 52 weeks by agreement only. Employers cannot make workers do more than these hours *(Barber v RJB Mining [1999] IRLR 308).*

The regulations do not apply to **senior managers** and others whose **working time is not pre-determined** and where they can exercise control over their own hours of work. Since August 2003, transport sector workers have been included within the protection. **Junior doctors**, who are currently excluded, will be covered by the regulations with effect from 1 August 2004.

The regulations allow individuals to **opt out of the 48-hour** limit, but they can opt back in at any time by giving notice of not less than seven days and not more than three months, depending on what their contract says. Following a review of the opt-out provision by the European Commission (EC) there are proposals to amend the working time directive. These would include provisions that limit the maximum number of hours in the week that an opted out worker can do to 65. They would also extend the reference period from 17 weeks to a year and make it clear that time spent on call but not worked would not count as working time. However, in the case of *Pheiffer v Deutsches Rotes Kreuz [2005] IRLR 137*, the ECJ held, not only that emergency workers are covered by the directive. It also held that the provisions on opt-out have to be defined strictly and that any worker who opts out has to have done so freely and with full knowledge of all the facts.

If a worker does **more hours than are permitted** under the regulations that, of itself, does not give a right to be paid for the additional hours, in the absence of a contractual term specifying payment *(Forbouys v Rich EAT/144/01).* Working hours can include **time on call**, provided that the employee has to remain on the employer's premises, even if not obliged to work *(Sindicato de Medicos v Consumo de la Generalidad*

Valenciana [2000] IRLR 845). This ECJ ruling was followed in the case of *Landeshauptstadt Kiel v Jaeger [2003] IRLR 804.*

The ECJ held that Norbert Jaeger, a doctor who when on call could sleep in a hospital room and rarely spent more than half of the time on call actually working, nevertheless should **include all of that time** within the definition of working time. This meant that Jaeger had the right to compensatory periods of time off immediately following the period he had been on call.

However, where someone is on call but **not required on the premises**, the hours on call are not counted

There are additional rules covering **night workers**. In general, these state that a worker should not do more than eight hours a night, when averaged over four months. Employers have to provide free health assessments for night workers.

Employers are also bound by an implied contractual duty not to require that employees work such long hours as to **damage their health** (see *Johnstone* case, chapter 3 – What makes a contract).

The regulations also give workers the right to a **break of at least 20 minutes** if the working day is more than six hours. This break does not have to be paid. The regulations state that breaks can be deferred and compensated later where "the worker's activities involve the need for continuity of service". The Court of Appeal, in the case of *Alpha Catering Services v Gallagher [2005] IRLR 102,* held that the focus is on the worker's activities, not the employers. Employers cannot, for example, understaff to avoid giving workers the right to breaks. In the case of seafarers, where there are separate regulations, short breaks are included within the definition of working hours (*P&O Ferries (Bermuda) v Spencer EAT/0433/04*). Workers are also entitled to a daily rest break of at least 11 hours and a weekly rest of not less than 24 hours, which can be averaged over two weeks. Young workers have additional protection (see chapter 2 – Young workers).

Under the *Sunday Trading Act 1994 (STA)* shopworkers who were in employment prior to 24 August 1994 and were not Sunday workers, or who have given their employers a written opted-out notice saying they do not wish to work on Sundays, are **"protected shopworkers"** and do not have to work on Sundays. There may also be situations where a requirement to work at particular times offends against the law on religion or belief (see chapter 6 — Discrimination).

Holidays

Under the *Working Time Regulations 1998*, all workers have the right to at least **four weeks' paid holiday** a year, regardless of whether they are employed on permanent or **temporary contracts** of whatever length. In the case of *Byrne Bros v Baird [2002] IRLR 96*, the EAT held that building workers whose contracts clearly required them to "personally perform services" were workers and therefore had the right to four weeks' paid holiday.

Under the statutory scheme **holidays must be taken in the year in which they accrue**, they cannot be paid for in lieu, unless the worker is leaving work and has not been able to take that year's holidays. However, in an important case decided in 2002, the EAT held that where the employer had refused to give his workers any holiday entitlement during the whole of their employment, they had the right to be compensated for all the holidays they would have accrued for the whole of their period of employment and not just those for the current year *(List Design v Douglas EAT/0966/00)*.

Pay during holidays is calculated on **normal weekly earnings**. However, a worker who is also entitled to commission will not automatically have this included in the calculation of normal earnings for holiday pay purposes *(Evans v Malley Organisation [2003] IRLR 156)*. The way that the law has been interpreted in the UK excludes **overtime pay** from the calculation of normal earnings. In the case of *Bamsey v Albion Engineering [2004] IRLR 457*, the Court of Appeal upheld this interpretation.

Holiday rights are accrued on a monthly basis. In the first year, a worker gets entitlement to a twelfth of the statutory annual leave for every month worked. The amount of time that can be taken at any one time within the **first year of work** can be rounded up by up to half a day. Someone working five days a week who has worked for two months would be entitled to take three and a third days and so could take three and a half days' leave. Workers wanting to take leave need to give notice of at least twice the length of the holiday requested. Employers have the right to ask for the leave to be **deferred**, provided they tell the employee in advance, giving notice which is at least as long as the leave requested. The right applies to **"workers"** not just "employees (see chapter 2 – Employee or self-employed).

The law does not allow employers to claim that an existing hourly rate includes an element of holiday pay without the agreement of the employee. In the case of *Gridquest v Blackburn [2002] IRLR 604*, the Court of Appeal held that an employer could not unilaterally decide that a week's pay included a holiday element, unless it was something clearly agreed between employer and worker.

Some employers will try to assert that holiday pay is already **included in a worker's basic pay** (known as rolled up holiday pay) and that there is no obligation to pay again when holidays are actually taken. This kind of argument is most frequently used in respect of temporary or casual staff. The EAT in Scotland held that payments included in the basic hourly rate are unlikely to satisfy the requirement of the working time regulations for entitlement to paid holidays *(MPB Structure v Munro [2002] IRLR 601)*. However, in the case of *Caulfield v Marshalls Clay Products [2004] IRLR 564*, the Court of Appeal ruled that rolled up holiday pay is compatible with the working time regulations provided that the contract allocates a proportion of the hourly rate to holidays.

The *Marshalls* case, together with the case of *Robinson-Steele v RD Services Case 1800174/04)*, has been referred to the European Court of Justice for a ruling on whether rolled up pay is lawful under EU law. The court's decision is awaited. And in the case of *JJ Cafferkey v Byrne [2005] IRLR 72*, the EAT refused to accept that a daily rate said to include an element of holiday pay actually does, unless an amount can be identified as a true addition to the daily rate.

If an employer **refuses to pay statutory holidays** a tribunal claim can be made for pay to cover the holidays lost. The claim must be brought under the Working time regulations. This was decided by the Court of Appeal, in the case of *Commissioners of Inland Revenue v Ainsworth & others A2/2004/0349&0350*, overruling *List Design v Douglas [2003] IRLR 14*.

A ruling by the EAT in the case of *Kigass Aero Components v Brown [2002] IRLR 312*, had suggested that workers on long-term sickness absence might still remain entitled to paid holidays during their period of sickness absence. However, the Court of Appeal, in the case of

Commissioners of Inland Revenue v Ainsworth and others A2/2004/0349&0350, has held that the *Kigass* case was incorrectly decided. The court held that a worker absent on long term sickness could not be said, at some arbitrary period during that absence, to be on leave. Additionally, leave in these circumstances could not be said to serve a health and safety purpose, as envisaged under the EU law. The ruling means that workers, who are absent from work long-term, will not accrue holiday entitlement during that absence.

Bank holidays can be included in the four weeks' holiday. Where they are not, payment for bank holidays depends entirely on what the contract says. In the case of *Campbell & Smith Construction v Greenwood [2001] IRLR 588*, the EAT confirmed that, unless it is in the contract, there is no right to **bank holidays**, other than for bank workers themselves.

Employees who are told not to work during their notice period (commonly called "**garden leave**") continue to accrue holiday entitlement.

The only circumstance in which a worker can be **paid in lieu of statutory holidays** is when the **contract ends** without the worker having taken all of the days due. The law clearly states that the employer "shall make" a payment in lieu. The right to pay in lieu is absolute and any clause in a contract that seeks to deny it is void *(Witley & District Men's Club v Mackay [2001] IRLR 595)*. If statutory holidays are outstanding when an **employee leaves**, the rate of pay for each day's leave is calculated by taking annual pay and dividing it by the number of days worked in the year (*Leisure Leagues v Maconnachie [2002] IRLR 600)*. If they have taken more statutory holidays than would have accrued by the time they leave, workers have no statutory obligation to repay any money for the additional days. If any money were deducted without consent, this would amount to an unlawful deduction *(Hill v Chapell [2003] IRLR 19)* (see above – Deductions and underpayments).

If **contractual holidays** have not been taken when employment ends and are paid in lieu, the employer can calculate the pay at 1/365th for every day not taken. However, in making this calculation, account has to be taken of non-working days. For example, if a worker leaves work with 10 days' holiday owing (two weeks for a five-day worker) holiday pay is calculated at 14/365ths to take account of the non-working weekends.

Pay in lieu of contractual holidays is only payable if the contract provides for it. There may even be circumstances where there is no express contractual term, but the court can imply a term *(Janes Solicitors v Lamb Simpson EAT/323/94)*.

Time off for public duties

Employees who hold certain **public offices** have the right to a "reasonable" amount of time off to perform their duties. This covers such things as justice of the peace, local councillor or member of a tribunal, an NHS trust, a school governing body, a police authority, environmental agency or board of prison visitors. In deciding what is reasonable, the employer can take account of the effect of the time off on the business and can also assess how much time off is required and how much has already been given overall.

However, in the case of *Riley-Williams v Argos EAT/811/02*, the EAT held that the right to time off for public duties has to be assessed on what a **reasonable amount of time off** would be to meet the requirements of the office. In this case the employee had been appointed as a magistrate. Her letter of appointment said that she would have to serve a minimum of 26 half-day sessions a year. The EAT said a reasonable employer should allow that amount.

The *Employment Relations Act 2004* gives a new protection to employees who are **called for jury service**. With effect from 6 April 2005 they have the right not to be dismissed or suffer any other detriment because they are summoned or absent from work on jury service.

There is **no statutory right to be paid** for the time off, unless the employee's contract provides for this.

An employee who has been refused the right to time off in respect of any of the above functions can take a complaint to a tribunal. This has to be done within **three months** of the action complained of.

Other statutory rights to time off are explained in the following chapters: trade union duties and activities — chapter 5; ante-natal care, family emergencies, parental and maternity leave — chapter 8;

alternative work in a redundancy situation — chapter 11; and employee representatives and pension fund trustees — chapter 5.

There is no law giving a right to leave to take part in other activities, for example, sport, voluntary work, travel or activities in the Territorial Army. It should be noted that members of the **volunteer reserve force** are legally obliged to tell their employers of their reserve status under regulations effective from April 2004. Many workplaces will, however, have agreements that include entitlement to time off. Employers are likely to take account of the degree of disruption an employee's absence would cause. They may also consider whether the organisation benefits, either in terms of prestige or in employee morale, by conceding the time off.

More information: LRD booklets, *Winning equal pay (£3.70)*; *Working time (£4.25)*; LRD's *Workplace Report* contains regular updates on pay and working time cases, as well as equal pay developments.

5. Union and collective organisation

The right to recognition

To gain access to many of the rights covered in this chapter the union must be **recognised by the employer**. The *Employment Relations Act 1999 (ERA 99),* provides a mechanism through which unions can gain statutory recognition, even where the employer is implacably opposed to it. However, the law does not apply to small employers — that is those with **20 or fewer workers**. The legislation extends to workers and not just employees. However, those who work freelance may be excluded from the calculation of the number of workers *(R v CAC [2003] IRLR 460).*

To apply for recognition under the statutory procedure a union has to submit a **request in writing** to the employer. If it is unable to negotiate a recognition agreement, it makes a formal application in writing to the Central Arbitration Committee (CAC).

When making a formal application the union has to **identify the "bargaining unit"** for which it is seeking recognition. This is the group of workers it wants to represent. It is important to **choose the bargaining unit carefully**, as the outcome of any eventual ballot can hang on who is, or is not, included in the unit. The law says that the CAC must examine whether a bargaining unit is **"compatible with effective management"**. The courts have interpreted this to mean that the union's bargaining unit will usually only be successfully challenged where the employer can show that it is not compatible with management. It does not have to be the most effective unit of organisation, as long as it is not an ineffective one. If the employer successfully challenges the union's preferred bargaining unit, the CAC can impose a different one. At this stage the union may choose to **withdraw the application**.

The *Employment Relations Act 2004,* obliges employers to provide the union and the CAC with an **up-to-date list of workers** in the bargaining unit. It also imposes a legal obligation on a union to provide the CAC with information about its membership. The Act also creates the concept of "unfair labour practices" which would mean that employers, who intimidate employees in the run up to a recognition ballot, could face a recognition award being imposed on them. These changes were due to come into force in April 2005 but have now been delayed until 1 October 2005.

The procedure

The CAC has to first **accept the application as valid**. It will do this only if the union demonstrates that it already has **at least 10% of the bargaining unit in membership** and that a majority of the workers in the unit would be likely to favour recognition. The union has to produce **evidence in support** of these two requirements. This will usually consist of its own membership records and any letters, petitions and other evidence from the workforce showing that there is likely to be majority support for recognition. This information remains confidential — the employer is not given copies of any documents relating to workers' intentions regarding recognition or whether individuals are union members.

Normally, only one union can apply for recognition for the bargaining unit at a time. Where **more than one union** wishes to gain recognition for the same group, they must apply together and show that they are capable of co-operation. If they cannot do this, both applications are invalid. A union cannot apply for statutory recognition where there is already a recognised union, even if the recognised union does not have the support of the majority of the workforce in the bargaining unit. An employer can even decide to recognise another union anytime until the CAC accepts the application as valid, which would block the first union from making a statutory claim. However, the body with which the employer comes to a deal must be an independent union. Entertainment union BECTU challenged cinema group City Screen when it signed an agreement with a body whose membership consisted solely of four managers and which had no source of funds other than that provided by the company. The CAC held that this was not a union and therefore did not bar the BECTU claim for recognition (*BECTU v City Screen TURI/309/2003*).

The aim of these restrictions is to avoid competition between unions for the same group of workers. It is not necessary that the agreement on recognition include a requirement to negotiate on pay, hours and holidays even though these are referred to in the legislation. In the case of *T&G v Asda [2004] IRLR 836*, the CAC held that a "partnership agreement" which did not include pay bargaining was nevertheless a recognition agreement and thus barred another union from making a statutory claim for recognition. However, it means that there will be situations where a union has the majority of members but cannot gain recognition because the employer has reached a voluntary recognition agreement with another union, which could include non-TUC unions. This occurred in the case *NUJ v CAC [2005] IRLR 28*, where the court held that even though the union that the employer signed an agreement with had very few members and had not engaged in collective bargaining, the National Union of Journalists which did have a large membership was barred from seeking recognition under the legislation.

If the union has recruited **more than half the workers** in the bargaining unit, the CAC may be able to award recognition without the need for a ballot. Only a minority of unions have achieved statutory recognition this way. Generally the claim goes through a series of procedures and is most likely to be concluded by means of a **secret ballot** of workers.

The **ballot** can either be held by post sent to the individual's nominated address, or at the workplace, or a combination of the two. It is up to the CAC to decide. Regardless of the employer's attitude to the union, they have a legal duty to **co-operate generally** with the union and with the person appointed to conduct the ballot and to provide the CAC with a list of workers' names and addresses. In the case of *R (on the application of Ultraframe v CAC)*, the CAC ordered that a ballot should be re-run where the union had lost the ballot by just a few votes but had complained to the CAC that some members had not received ballot papers.

Unions must be given reasonable **access to the workforce**. A Department of Trade and Industry **code of practice** on access to workers during recognition and derecognition ballots gives advice to employers and unions on what arrangements should be made so that the union gets the opportunity to put its case to workers in the bargaining unit. This can be through mass meetings and/or surgeries. The code suggests a mass meeting lasting at least 30 minutes every 10 days of the access period with at least a day set aside for surgeries. The government issued a consultation document in late 2004 seeking views on its plans to give unions improved rights of access in the workplace. These are contained in a revised consultative *Code of practice on access and unfair practices during ballots for trade union recognition or derecognition*. The consultative code defines "unfair practices" that the parties must not engage in during the balloting period. They include employer inducements or threats to workers over how they will vote, including any disciplinary action taken by an employer against workers, for the purpose of influencing their vote.

A **CAC ruling** in a recognition claim by the T&G general union against King Asia Foods recommended that workers should have the right to attend at least two 15 minute private surgeries and up to four mass meetings, each lasting at least 30 minutes. It also said that the union should be given a noticeboard to display its material without restriction as to its content.

The *Employment Relations Act 2004* gives unions the **right to make contact** with workers in the bargaining unit once the CAC has accepted their recognition application. The union can make a request to the CAC to appoint a "suitable independent person" (SIP). This new right to access will not give the union the right to face-to-face contact, but does give it the right to pass on information about the recognition claim to workers through the SIP. The Act defines "unfair labour practices" giving workers protection from employers who try to bribe or intimidate them out of having their union recognised. Equally, if individuals allege bribery or intimidation by the union in its campaign for recognition, they will have a claim against the union. However, these changes do not come into force until 1 October 2005. The Act gives the CAC the power to speed up the procedures in recognition claims, for example, by making an early determination on the bargaining unit. It will also give postal voting rights to workers who are absent from work on the date of the recognition ballot.

Whatever the methods agreed, they should ensure that the union has the **same access** to the workforce as the employer. If the employer puts out a circular with arguments against recognition, the union should be allowed to circulate its arguments in favour.

To win a recognition ballot it is not enough simply to get a majority of the votes cast (50% plus one). **At least 40%** of the entire bargaining unit must also vote in favour of recognition. In effect, abstentions count as votes against the union.

If the ballot goes in the union's favour, or if the CAC declares that there should be recognition without a ballot because the union already has more than 50% of the workforce in membership, the employer and union have to try to **negotiate a collective bargaining procedure**. With a statutory recognition award the union is limited to an agreement to negotiate over pay, hours and holidays. **"Pay"** had been **defined widely** by the CAC to include pension rights but the *Employment Relations Act 2004* reverses this position, making it clear that pensions are excluded from the definition of pay. While the Act also gives the secretary of state the power to extend the bargaining coverage of statutory recognition, it contains no timetable for when this change might be introduced.

If employers and unions cannot reach an agreement on procedures, the CAC will impose one. This will normally involve the setting up of a joint negotiating body and a six-stage bargaining procedure, with each stage having a specified timetable.

Although the law on recognition appears extremely complicated, unions have had **significant successes** during its first five years of operation. It has led both to statutory awards for recognition and to a significant increase in voluntary recognition, as employers realise that they could secure a more acceptable agreement through co-operation.

The legislation also sets out the circumstances where the employer or workers can apply to the CAC to have a union with statutory recognition **derecognised**. In general, these provisions are not operative unless statutory recognition was granted more than three years earlier. However, in one of the first cases on the issue, the CAC issued a derecognition award at the employer's request because evidence was offered to show that the bargaining unit was no longer in existence.

Membership rights

Most of the law affecting trade unions is contained in the *Trade Union and Labour Relations (Consolidation) Act 1992 (TULR(C)A 92)*, which lays down the status of a union and its duties in respect of keeping accounts, submitting returns and the conduct of elections.

While unions can now gain statutory recognition using the law (see above), there are legal limits on the right to enforce **100% union organisation** (the "closed shop"). *Section 222 TULR(C)A 92* states that all industrial action to enforce 100% union membership agreements or to cause an employer to discriminate against a non-member is unlawful, leaving the union at risk of legal penalties. In addition, any dismissal of a non-union member to enforce 100% membership is automatically unfair.

Under *section 137 TULR(C)A 92,* there is a statutory right not to be **refused work on the grounds of membership or non-membership** of a union or because of refusal to leave or to join a union. The EAT has held that a refusal to hire a known trade union activist, because he was believed to be "uncooperative and anti-management", came within the definition of discriminatory action on the grounds of union membership *(Harrison v Kent CC [1995] ICR 434).*

It will always be difficult to prove an allegation of **refusal to hire** because of an individual's trade union membership. If a prospective employer is known to systematically exclude trade union members; refuses to process an application or makes the claimant withdraw; refuses employment or makes a spurious offer of employment; and the grounds are believed to be because the individual is (or is not) a trade union member, that person can complain to a tribunal. Complaints can also be made over advertisements or against employment agencies that seek similarly to exclude claimants *(section 138 TULR(C)A 92).* A successful claimant in a claim may be awarded compensation. The **maximum amount** that can be awarded is £56,800 (2005/06), which may include a sum for injury to feelings.

Under *section 3* of the *Employment Relations Act 1999 (ERA 99),* the secretary of state has the power to make regulations prohibiting the **compilation of lists** of individuals who have been **union activists**, if these are used to discriminate in recruitment or employment. Draft regulations, published in February 2003, state that if employers or employment agencies are found to be using such lists they can be required to pay compensation. Although there was consultation on the regulations, the government stated that the regulations would not come into force unless and until there was fresh evidence of employers using lists to exclude union activists.

The *Human Rights Act 1998* (see Introduction – Civil Liberties and employment law) guarantees the **rights to peaceful assembly and freedom of association**. Unions should consider whether they have a claim under the Act where there have been attempts by an employer to restrict their freedom to associate.

Victimisation

Individual members of unions have protection against victimisation by their employer. They have the right not to have **action short of dismissal** (for example, suspension) taken against them, together with the right not to be **dismissed** because of membership of a trade union (see chapter 10 – Automatically unfair dismissals) and the right not to be **selected for redundancy** for that reason (see chapter 11 – Selection for redundancy). The *Employment Relations Act 2004* extends the protection to workers and came into force on 6 April 2005. It also reverses the burden of proof and removes the exclusion of employees over their normal retirement age.

Mr Williams was selected for redundancy on the grounds of the **manner in which he carried out his union duties.** The EAT held that provided that the behaviour to which the employer objected was carried out as a trade union activity and not just a reflection of Williams' own personality, his redundancy selection amounted to unlawful discrimination on trade union grounds *(Krupp Camford Pressings v Williams EAT/397/01).*

In an important ruling in 1991, the Court of Appeal said that dismissal because an employee had been an **active union member in a previous job** was unfair and fell within the protection afforded by *section 152 TULR(C)A 92 (Fitzpatrick v British Railways Board [1991] IRLR 376).*

The key issue is **why the employer dismissed** the employee.

Ms Lindsay was dismissed shortly after joining a union. Her employer denied the dismissal was anything to do with her union membership, claiming it was because of her timekeeping. Lindsay successfully argued that it was only after she had joined the union that her employer started complaining about her timekeeping. The EAT agreed that this amounted to a dismissal for trade union reasons *(Lindsay v General Contracting EAT/1126/00).*

Section 146 TULR(C)A 92 protects trade unionists from action short of dismissal by employers where this involves either preventing or deterring them from joining or taking part in union activities. If an employer decides to **no longer recognise a shop steward** who has been duly accredited by the union, this amounts to action short of dismissal for the purpose of deterring the individual from taking part in union activities *(Farnsworth v McCoid [1998] IRLR 362)*. An employee carrying out his trade union duties at an appropriate time, who is **disciplined on account of those activities**, is unlawfully victimised *(LB Islington v Hutchings EAT/34/01)*. The protection covers employees who have ceased to be union activists but who have action taken against them on the grounds of their past involvement in union activities.

However, according to the Court of Appeal in the case of *Gallacher v Department of Transport [1994] IRLR 231*, an employer's **refusal to promote** someone on the grounds that their trade union duties had prevented the individual from acquiring relevant experience does not fall within the protection.

The Court of Appeal held that **withholding a pay rise** from an employee until such time as she agreed to give up her union duties amounted to unlawful victimisation. The employers argued that they had not taken action against her, but that they had merely "omitted" to take action in her favour, but the court rejected this explanation *(LB Southwark v Whillier [2001] ICR 1016)*.

In this case the employers were relying on a 1995 House of Lords ruling in the case of *Associated Newspapers v Wilson [1995] IRLR 258*, and an accompanying amendment to the law. Dave Wilson, a journalist, had been refused pay increases because he would not give up his collectively agreed terms and conditions. The judges said that what the employers had done was lawful. At the same time the then Conservative government amended the law in line with the legal ruling to make it clear that employers could **refuse pay increases** to individuals who did not agree to opt out of a collective agreement. *Section 17* of the *ERA 99* attempted to reverse the law by giving the secretary of state the power to make new regulations to protect employees against any detriment short of dismissal resulting from "any act or any deliberate failure to act". This meant that employers could not treat trade union members less favourably by not extending to them a benefit available to non-members. However, this still allowed employers to pay higher wages or bonuses to workers who opted out of collective bargaining, as long as the employment contract did not bar union membership and the payment is for services provided by the worker.

In 2002, the *Wilson* case went on appeal to the **European Court of Human Rights**. The court held that UK law including *section 17*, was still in breach of *Article 11* of the *European Convention on Human Rights*. In the UK there is no protection to employees unwilling to renounce an essential freedom, that of trade union membership and collective bargaining.

The *Employment Relations Act 2004* gives workers the right to seek compensation at a tribunal where employers offer inducements to give up union membership. Even with the new law, it is still the case that employers could offer personal contracts that exclude collective bargaining, but the law makes it clear that any inducement to individuals to relinquish union representation is unlawful.

Victimisation claims must go to the tribunal within **three months** of the date when the action complained of occurred, and if the claim is upheld the tribunal will order the employer to pay compensation that is "just and equitable". There is no length of service requirement to pursue the claim. If the victimisation results in a dismissal, a minimum of £3,800 (2005/06) basic compensation will be awarded. In addition the tribunal can make a compensatory award of up to £56,800 (2005/06), which could include damages for injury to feelings. The EAT, in the case of *LB Hackney v Adams [2003] IRLR 402*, held that damages for **injury to feelings** are as relevant in trade union cases as in any other field of discrimination law.

Disciplinary **action against union representatives** should not be dealt with under the organisation's normal disciplinary procedure but should be covered by a special procedure. The ACAS code of practice on disciplinary and grievance procedures says: "Disciplinary action against a trade union official can lead to a serious dispute if it is seen as an attack on the union's functions". For this reason, while normal disciplinary standards should apply, no action beyond an oral warning should be taken until the case is discussed with a senior trade union representative or full-time official.

Rights to time off

Union lay officials, including shop stewards, staff reps and branch secretaries of recognised unions, have the right to **time off with pay** (based on average hourly earnings) to carry out trade union duties *(section 168 TULR(C)A 92).* If an employer refuses a right to time off in circumstances where it would have been reasonable to provide the right, the union representative can take a claim to an employment tribunal. The tribunal can award financial compensation, even in cases where the representative has not incurred any financial loss *(Skiggs v SW Trains EAT/0763/03).*

Trade union duties are those concerned with negotiation with the employer over what are termed "*section 178(2)*" matters (terms and conditions, recruitment, suspension, dismissal, work allocation, discipline, union membership, time off facilities and procedures). Alternatively, with the employer's agreement, they can be for functions related to these matters but which are not within the scope of negotiations. To benefit from the time-off rights, the union must be recognised by the employer for the *section 178(2)* matter for which the time off is required.

Trade union officers have the right to **time off for training**, again if related to *section 178 (2)* matters. This right is qualified by the words "reasonable in all the circumstances". The ACAS *Code of practice on time off for trade union duties and activities* gives, as examples of "reasonableness", the employer's need for safety and security at all times, the size of the organisation, the production process and the need to maintain a service to the public. There is **no service qualification** for this right. Employee representatives appointed or elected for consultation on redundancy and business transfers (see chapters 11 and 12) similarly have the right to time off for training in their duties. An employer who persistently refuses time off, arguing that there are **staff shortages**, is likely to be in breach of the law where no efforts are made to overcome the shortages.

The EAT has held that time off is not rigidly limited to the *section 178(2)* matters since an employer acting reasonably has to take account of factors like the history, timing and agenda of the meeting in question *(London Ambulance Service v Charlton [1992] IRLR 510).*

Trade union representatives on the management committees of their **company pension schemes** have the right to paid time off for training on pensions, even where the pension scheme itself is not negotiable, according to the EAT.

Part-time workers should be paid for the same number of hours as a full-time employee when attending union training.

A ruling of the European Court in the case of *Arbeiterwohlfahrt der Stadt Berlin v Botel [1992] IRLR 423,* held that an employee whose working day is shorter than that of other employees, but who takes part in a course with hours in excess of the employee's contractual hours, should be paid for the hours on the course at the same level as the full-time workers. This interpretation was re-adopted by the ECJ in the case of *Kuratorium v Lewark [1996] IRLR 637.*

All members of recognised unions, not just representatives, have the right to reasonable time off without pay to take part in **trade union activities**, except for industrial action *(section 170 TULR(C)A 92).* These would include shiftworkers attending trades council and union branch meetings. Circumstances where the time off rights have been held to apply to workplace union representatives include attendance at trade union meetings and at a conference dealing with new laws on working conditions. However, the EAT ruled, in the case of *Luce v LB Bexley [1990] IRLR 422*, that there is no right to time off to attend a **lobby of parliament** in protest over legislation not significantly specific to the workers concerned.

An employee can take a claim relating to time off to a tribunal, but only where the time off has been requested and denied *(Ryford v Drinkwater [1996] IRLR 16).* The claim must be presented to a tribunal **within three months** (*section 171 TULR(C)A 92).* If the claim is successful, the tribunal will make a declaration of the employee's rights and may award "just and equitable" compensation.

Employee representatives in workplaces with no recognised union who are elected for consultation on redundancy and business transfers (see chapters 11 and 12) have rights to time off with pay for their duties.

Union learning representatives also have the right to a reasonable amount of paid time off to carry out their duties. These would include addressing learning or training needs, providing information and advice and promoting the value of learning. They also have the right to time off for training in understanding the different methods for identifying learning needs, drawing up learning plans and working with employers to promote the value of learning.

Rights to information

Section 181 TULR(C)A 92 says that, **for the purpose of collective bargaining**, employers have a duty to disclose, to representatives of independent recognised unions, information:

- without which representatives would be impeded in carrying out collective bargaining; or
- which, in accordance with good industrial relations practice, should be disclosed.

This can include an order to an employer to give the union information on the **distribution of percentage pay awards** across certain staff groups and information about the amount and distribution of overtime.

The Acas *Code of practice on information disclosure* states that items that should be disclosed include:

- **pay and benefits** — structure of the payment system, earnings analysed by work group, details of fringe benefits;
- **employee numbers** — numbers employed by age and sex, turnover, absenteeism;
- **performance** — savings from increased productivity; and
- **financial** — assets, liabilities, loans, transfer prices.

This right to disclosure is, however, **limited** by *section 182 TULR(C)A 92*. This states that an employer can decline to give the information on the grounds of: national security; that the information has been obtained in confidence; that it relates specifically to an individual; or that it would cause "substantial injury" to the employer's undertaking. The ACAS code of practice gives examples of what would amount to "substantial injury".

Complaints over an employer's failure to disclose must be presented in writing to the Central Arbitration Committee (CAC), which will attempt first to mediate to resolve the matter. Failing this it may, if it finds the claim justified, make a ruling *(section 183 TULR(C)A 92)*. Claims under *section 183* are presented by the union, not by individuals.

Trade unionists may also have the right to information about potential redundancies (see chapter 11 – Consultation).

Employee reps and European works councils

In companies with operations in two or more European Union states employing more than 1,000 employees in total, a European works council (EWC) must, if requested, be established to provide a forum for informing and consulting employees. EWC members need not be trade union representatives, although in practice in most large workplaces where there are recognised unions they will nominate candidates for election. The rules for setting up an EWC are laid down in the *Transitional Information and Consultation of Employees Regulations 1999.*

Companies have to supply information about their structures and organisation where requested. The ECJ, in the case of *Betreibsrat v Bofrost [2001] IRLR 403*, held that this is a **legal requirement** even if it has not, at that stage, been possible to establish whether the company itself is the controlling undertaking. The court held that information on company structure is essential to the opening of negotiations on the establishment of an EWC. Where the company headquarters is located outside the EU, the largest employer based in an EU state in the group has to assume responsibility for the provision of information to assist the establishment of the EWC *(Gesamtbetriebsrat der Kuhne & Nagel v Kuhne & Nagel [2004] IRLR 332).* Where the central management is based in an EU state, a company must supply other undertakings in the same group with information needed for the establishment of an EWC (*Betriebsrat der Firma ADS Anker Gmbj v ADS Anker GmbH C-349/01*).

In May 2004, the European Commission launched a formal process that could lead to a revision of the EU directive upon which the 1999 regulations are based. The review covered the process of initiating the establishment of an EWC, the effectiveness of information and consultation, facilities for EWC members and trade union involvement in EWCs.

An EU directive obliges employers to **consult with employee representatives at national level.** The *Employment Relations Act 2004* transposes these requirements into UK law. Under the

Information and Consultation of Employees Regulations 2004 effective from 6 April 2005, UK employers have to establish information and consultation bodies (I&C) if 10% of the workforce request it. Once in place the terms of reference of the I&C can only be changed if 40% of the workforce vote in favour. The I&C would be the body through which the employer would consult with reps on the situation, structure and probable development of employment and on future job plans. However, initially the law only applies in firms where there are **150 or more employees**. In March 2007, workplaces with 100 to 150 workers will be included and this will be extended in March 2008 to workplaces with 50 to 100 workers. Part-time workers are counted, although those working fewer than 75 hours per month can each be counted as half an employee if the employer so wishes. The legislation additionally excludes casual and agency staff from the calculation of the number of employees.

Internal union matters

A number of internal union procedures are also regulated by legislation. These are dealt with only briefly in this booklet. The main areas covered by the law are bars on membership, internal union elections, ballots on political funds and discipline of members.

Union members also have rights as defined by the **union's rulebook**. These can lay down the circumstances under which a member can expect support or representation from the union. The rulebook defines the **contractual relationship** between the member and the union.

Under *section 17 TULR(C)A 92*, a union may not refuse to accept into membership or expel anyone except on the grounds of the individual's conduct. Section 33 of the *Employment Relations Act 2004* gives unions a specific right to expel members on the grounds of their activities as a party member if these are contrary to the rules or objectives of the union. This means that unions can lawfully expel racist activists from their membership.

Sections 24-61 of *TULR(C)A 92* lay down the procedures to be adopted by unions in relation to:

- maintaining a **register of members' names and addresses;**
- submitting **annual returns**; and

◆ conducting **union elections**.

When conducting **elections** unions must ensure that:

◆ all members of a union's national executive body, including its president and general secretary, are **elected at least every five years** *(section 46)*;
◆ elections must be by **secret postal ballot** *(section 1)*;
◆ elections must be supervised by **independent scrutineers** who are responsible for inspecting the membership register and producing a report on the election *(section 49)*;
◆ an **"independent person"** must undertake the administration of the vote (this person may also serve as scrutineer); and
◆ **members must be told** who the scrutineers are to be and their names must be included on the ballot paper *(section 51)*.

Section 65 says that a union may not **"unjustifiably discipline"** a member and defines this as where the member:

◆ fails to **participate in or support industrial action**;
◆ seeks to take **legal action against the union**;
◆ **fails to agree to check-off** arrangements; or
◆ **works with non-union members** or non-union employers.

Political fund ballots must be conducted **every 10 years** and are subject to the same general rules. There is a right of complaint to the **Certification Officer** or the courts if any member believes the ballot has not been conducted according to the rules.

The government-appointed Certification Officer has **prime responsibility** for checking the finances and independence of unions and for assisting individuals with complaints against their unions.

A complaint has to be submitted to the tribunal within **three months** of the action complained of.

More information: LRD booklets *Time off for trade union duties and activities (£4.25); Learning and training (£4.20); Worker representation in Europe (£10.95), Information and consultation (£5.15)*

6. Discrimination

The law prohibits discrimination in employment on the following specific grounds: **sex, race and nationality**, **disability, sexual orientation, religion or belief** and **transsexuality**.

Discrimination in pay is covered by the equal pay legislation (see chapter 4 – Equal pay).

There are significant similarities in the way that the law deals with the different forms of discrimination, and rulings in one type of discrimination claim usually apply to other types. This chapter first provides an overview of the different grounds for unlawful discrimination and then explains how direct and indirect discrimination, harassment and victimisation operate in relation to these protected groups. There are important differences, however, in how the law relating to disability discrimination operates, so this is dealt with under a separate heading.

Types of unlawful discrimination

Sex and race

Under the *Sex Discrimination Act 1975*, discrimination on the **grounds of sex** occurs when an employer **treats one sex differently** from another or people of one sex are disadvantaged. For example, excluding women from certain jobs, even if on the assumption that the jobs are hazardous, would amount to sex discrimination. The only circumstances when it is lawful to do this is in cases of pregnancy or maternity. The Act protects men as well as women.

Under the *Race Relations Act 1976* discrimination on **racial grounds** includes treating someone less favourably on the grounds of colour, race, nationality or ethnic or national origins.

Sexual orientation

The *Employment Equality (Sexual Orientation) Regulations* 2003, which came into force on 1 December 2003, outlaw discrimination on the grounds of sexual orientation, defined as an orientation towards:

- persons of the same sex;
- persons of the opposite sex; or
- persons of the same sex and the opposite sex.

The regulations cover discrimination based on a person's perceived sexual orientation. So if an employer discriminates against a worker because he is thought to be gay, he has the right to pursue a claim even if in fact he is not gay.

The regulations were challenged by a consortium of trade unions in March 2004 since they allow religious organisations to discriminate on the grounds of sexual orientation "so as to comply with the doctrines of a religion" or "to avoid conflicting with the strongly held religious convictions of a significant number of the religion's followers". Although the High Court rejected the claim, the ruling indicated that teachers in faith schools are likely to have protection under the regulations and that the religious exemption would only apply narrowly to ministers of religion.

Gender reassignment

Transsexual people have the right to be protected from direct discrimination under the *Sex Discrimination (Gender Reassignment) Regulations 1999*. Gender reassignment is defined as "a process, which is undertaken under medical supervision, for the purposes of reassigning a person's sex by changing physiological or other characteristics of sex, and includes any part of such a process". The comparison in treatment is made with a person (actual or hypothetical) whose relevant circumstances, other than in relation to gender reassignment, are the same.

In a landmark ruling in 2002, the European Court of Human Rights held that post-operative transsexual people must have all of the rights available to their new sex, including the right to marry a person of the opposite sex. The ruling also means that post-operative transsexual people have the right to state benefits appropriate to their new sex *(Goodwin v UK [2002] IRLR 664).*

In a key ruling in 2003, the ECJ held that pension fund rules must be interpreted so as to ensure that the **survivor of a partnership** where one is a post-operative transsexual has the **right to a pension** if it would have been available had they been married (*KB v The NHS Pensions Agency [2004] IRLR 240*). In another case heard by the Court of Appeal the facts were as follows:

A post-operative transsexual police constable was refused a job where she would be required to undertake searches of female prisoners. The court ruled that she should be regarded as female and that she should have been given the opportunity to work, even if it meant that her gender status could not be kept confidential *(A v Chief Constable of the West Yorkshire Police [2004] IRLR 573).*

The *Gender Recognition Act 2004* gives legal recognition to those who can demonstrate that they have taken decisive steps towards living permanently and fully in their acquired gender. The Act provides that applications for legal recognition in the acquired gender should be considered by a Gender Recognition Panel. If the panel issues a Gender Recognition Certificate, a new birth certificate is issued.

Where an individual is going through the process of gender reassignment they have to undergo a "**real life test**". This involves having to live as a member of their adoptive sex. Employers need to consider whether any adjustments should be made during that period and the question of appropriate toilet facilities may arise. In the case of *Croft v Royal Mail [2003] IRLR 592*, the Court of Appeal held that it was appropriate for the employer to suggest the use of the disabled facilities for an interim period only, prior to gender re-assignment having been concluded.

Religion or belief

The *Employment Equality (Religion or Belief) Regulations 2003* cover not just cases where a person is discriminated against on the grounds of their religion or belief, but on the grounds of the perceived religion or belief of an individual. For example, if someone is discriminated against because he or she is thought to be a Muslim, they can use the law even if in fact they are not of that (or indeed any) faith. The regulations define religion or belief as "any religion, religious belief, or similar philosophical belief".

The *Fair Employment and Treatment (Northern Ireland) Order 1998* also covers religious (and political) discrimination and obliges employers to **register** with the Equality Commission for Northern Ireland and file **annual monitoring returns**. Employers are also required to regularly review their employment practices and to assess whether affirmative (positive) action policies are necessary.

The Northern Ireland Court of Appeal held that an employer who accepted the resignation of a Catholic barworker who feared for his safety when working in a public house in a Protestant area, was guilty of discrimination. It was no excuse to allege that he would have responded similarly had he employed a Protestant in a public house in a Catholic area *(Smyth v Croft Inns [1996] IRLR 84).*

Under the Northern Irish legislation, political discrimination is not limited to sectarian political opinions, but covers all discrimination on **political grounds**, according to the Court of Appeal case of *McKay v NIPSA [1995] IRLR 146.*

Age

The government is also required, under the EU Employment Framework directive, to outlaw **age discrimination**, but has until 2006 to do so. In December 2004, it published its plans for the new law which sets 65 as a default retirement age but gives employees the right to work beyond that age. In the meantime there is only a **voluntary code of practice**, *Age diversity in employment.* This calls on employers to review their practices to prevent age discrimination. In the case of *Secretary of state for trade and industry v Rutherford and Bentley [2004] IRLR 892*, the Court of Appeal held that the statistics did not reveal that men were more disadvantaged than women over the different retirement ages. In February 2005, leave for Rutherford and Bentley to appeal to the House of Lords was granted. The appeal had still to be heard as this booklet went to press.

Direct and indirect discrimination

Both **direct** and **indirect** discrimination are unlawful under the *Sex Discrimination Act 1975 (SDA),* the *Race Relations Act 1976 (RRA),* the *Employment Equality (Sexual Orientation) Regulations 2003 (SO 03),* and the *Employment Equality (Religion or Belief) Regulations 2003 (RB 03).* Normally, a claim is pursued for either direct or indirect discrimination, but there are cases where claimants can claim both *(Jaffrey v Department of Environment, Transport and the Regions [2002] IRLR 688).* However, an individual who claims both direct and indirect discrimination must declare this in the claim form to the tribunal (*Ali v Office of National Statistics [2005] IRLR 201*).

Both **employees and workers** (see chapter 2 for definition) are protected by discrimination law, so long as there is an employment relationship between the parties. In the case of *Mingeley v Pennock and Ivory t/a Amber Cars [2004] IRLR 373*, the Court of Appeal rejected a discrimination claim taken by a private hire taxi driver against the company that allocated work to him because his contract did not meet the definition of an employment relationship.

Direct discrimination

Direct discrimination in employment occurs when someone is **treated less favourably**, including in recruitment, training and promotion. The right to no less favourable treatment is laid down in *section 1* of the *SDA* and the *RRA* and under *regulation 3* of the *SO 03* and *RB 03*. Discrimination on the grounds of **marital status** is also unlawful. This covers not only discrimination against someone because they are married, but also because of whom they are married to *(Chief Constable of the Bedfordshire Constabulary v Graham [2002] IRLR 239)*. Subjecting someone to **detriment** amounts to less favourable treatment.

In the landmark case of *Shamoon v Chief Constable of the RUC [2003] UKHL 11*, the House of Lords held that even if the action taken against an employee (in this case removing some responsibilities from her post) **did not result in a loss of pay or grading** it could nevertheless amount to a detriment. But doing something that puts the individual at a **disadvantage** is not a detriment, if the same action would have been taken against comparable employees.

Dismissing or refusing to hire a woman because she is **pregnant** comes within the definition of direct discrimination. It is automatically unfair to dismiss a woman while pregnant or on maternity leave for any reason connected with her pregnancy (see chapter 8 – Appointment and dismissal).

Having a workplace **retirement** policy where women retire earlier than men would also be sex discrimination, and can lead to a claim of unfair dismissal (see chapter 10).

It is unlawful to discriminate against someone because they are black and also if they have a distinct ethnic origin, for example if they are

Jewish, Sikh or gypsy. Discrimination on grounds of **nationality** is unlawful, and is not the same as citizenship. This means that it is unlawful to discriminate against a Scottish person in favour of an English person, or vice versa, even though they are both British citizens.

A tribunal will **compare the treatment** of the claimant with that of a person in a similar position, but who is of a different sex, race, sexual orientation, or religion or belief or is transsexual. The fact that the alleged perpetrator of a discriminatory act may be of the same sex, sexuality, religion, national or ethnic origin as the individual making the complaint is irrelevant.

The first thing to **establish is who the comparable person is**. Only where there is no comparable person can the tribunal try to assess how the employer would have treated a **hypothetical** comparator.

The claimant must show that there was **"less favourable treatment"**. This can include: setting different questions at interview; only asking women about their domestic commitments; asking intrusive questions only of workers who are believed to be gay; making assumptions of how individuals will respond based on their perceived religion or belief; instructing employees to discriminate; paying different redundancy pay to women or black workers; presuming that some work is unsuited to women or black workers; using racist name calling or allowing it to continue unchecked; language tests; culturally biased aptitude tests; word of mouth recruitment; and maintaining quotas.

Below are some case law examples of direct discrimination claims.

In the case of *LB Tower Hamlets v Ogunlokun EAT/762/01,* the EAT held that failing to follow the equal opportunities policy, marking the claimant differently from his comparator and giving unhelpful and evasive answers, all amounted to less favourable treatment. This allowed the tribunal to infer that there had been discrimination.

Marlene Morgan succeeded in her claim of race discrimination because she had failed to progress in the organisation in the same way as her white colleagues. The employer circulated a memo to her colleagues warning them that she was taking the case and the EAT held that this amounted to victimisation *(Commissioners of Inland Revenue v Morgan EAT/851/99).*

There may be circumstances where a **dress code** imposed only on one sex could amount to discrimination. In a test case brought by PCS on behalf of around 8,000 members who worked for JobCentre Plus, the EAT held that a requirement for men to wear ties does not necessarily amount to discrimination but it could do. JobCentre Plus had a "smartness code" that stipulated that men (but not women) must wear ties. The question that the tribunal should have asked was whether or not the men could only achieve the required level of smartness by wearing ties. As a result of the decision PCS settled the claim and the JobCentre Plus collar and tie rule was abolished. *(Department for Work and Pensions v Thompson EAT/0254/03).* The employee in this case, Matthew Thompson, was seeking to appeal to the Court of Appeal as this booklet went to press.

Refusing to appoint someone on discriminatory grounds is unlawful. However, if someone applies for a job knowing that there is no chance of success, simply to raise the issue of equal opportunities, the failure to offer the job will not amount to detrimental action. Furthermore, the case of *Cardiff Women's Aid v Hartup [1994] IRLR 390,* confirmed that no complaint can be pursued unless the individual has actually applied for the job. Only the Commissions (see below) have the status required to bring claims about discriminatory adverts.

Indirect discrimination

In cases of sex discrimination and those based on discrimination against transsexual people, indirect discrimination occurs where the employer imposes a **"provision, criterion or practice"** which:

- would be to the **detriment of a considerably larger proportion** of women;
- which is **not justified**; and
- which is **to the detriment** of the woman making the complaint.

The employer must have at least some knowledge that the provision, criterion or practice is, or may be, discriminatory. In sex discrimination cases therefore it is necessary to establish whether **statistically more of one sex are affected** by the practice. The *Employment Equality (Sex Discrimination) Regulations 2005,* which will amend the definition of indirect discrimination in sex discrimination cases to be consistent with the definitions for all other forms of discrimination (see below), were published for consultation in March 2005. The regulations will come into force on 1 October 2005

In **race, sexual orientation** and **religion or belief** cases the definition of indirect discrimination does not require statistical comparisons. It is where the employer imposes a **"provision, criterion or practice"** which:

- puts persons of that group at a **disadvantage** compared to members of a different group;
- puts that **individual at a disadvantage**; and
- which the employer cannot show to be a **proportionate** means of achieving a legitimate end.

There is a further complication. In race cases, the definition of indirect discrimination is dependent on what the claim is based on. Where it is taken on the basis of a person's colour or nationality, then the test is whether the employer has imposed **"a requirement or condition"** (rather than a provision, criterion or practice) which applies equally to persons not of that colour or nationality, but where the proportion of the colour or nationality that can comply is "considerably smaller" than the proportion of the other group, which is not justifiable and which is to the individual's detriment.

The provision, criterion or practice can be an express or implied term. In the case of *BMA v Chaudhary EAT/1351/01*, the EAT held that the association's refusal to support a member in taking a case was itself discriminatory. The member had alleged that his exclusion from the medical register was for discriminatory reasons. His association refused to support his challenge because it had a policy not to question decisions taken by the medical register. Whatever the nature of the indirect discrimination, claimants also have to show that they have suffered a **detriment**. In other words, they have lost out in some way as a result of the imposition of provisions or requirements. In one case, an investigation into a fraud, which lasted longer than it would have done if the employee under investigation had been white, was held to amount to a detriment, even though the employee did not lose out financially *(Garry v LB Ealing [2001] IRLR 681)*.

Justification

The law says that an employer can justify indirect discrimination where it is a **proportionate means of achieving a legitimate aim**. In the case of *Schonheit v Stadt Frankfurt am Main [2004] IRLR 983*, the

ECJ held that the justification that the employer has at the time of the legal challenge does not have to be the same one used when the original act of discrimination occurred.

There are also exemptions where there is a **genuine occupational qualification** (GOQ) that employees be from a specified group. Advertising a job as suitable for an "Afro Caribbean worker" to maintain a racial balance in a daycare centre comes within the GOQ requirements *(Tottenham Green Under Fives v Marshall [1991] IRLR 162)*.

Similar provisions apply in the regulations on sexual orientation and religion, although the former allow an additional exemption for religious organisations (see above – Sexual orientation).

Harassment

Harassment, which previously could only be challenged under general definitions of discrimination, is now specifically unlawful. However, the harassment has to be on account of one of the strands of discrimination protected by law (*Brumfitt v MOD [2005] IRLR 4*). Employers are legally obliged to take steps to protect employees against harassment. If employers foresee acts that could cause physical or psychiatric injury to employees and do nothing about it, they are liable in negligence claims *(Waters v Commissioner of Police of the Metropolis [2000] IRLR 720)*. If an employer fails to investigate a claim of sexual harassment, and this is due to the sex of the employee making the complaint, this will amount to unlawful sex discrimination *(Home Office v Coyne [2000] IRLR 838)*. Employers will also be liable for undue delay in investigating complaints.

In cases of **race, disability, sexual orientation and religion or belief**, harassment is now defined as:

- violating another's dignity; or
- creating an intimidating, hostile, degrading, humiliating or offensive environment for the other.

It also says that harassment occurs where its effect (rather than just its purpose) is to violate dignity. The definition of harassment based on sex or transsexuality is currently dependent on case law ruling. The *Employment Equality (Sex Discrimination) Regulations 2005* amend the definition of harassment in sex discrimination cases to be consistent with the definitions for all other forms of discrimination (see above). The regulations were published for consultation in March 2005 and are due to come into force on 1 October 2005. In the meantime, however, case law rulings confirm that sexual or transsexual harassment does amount to unlawful discrimination.

It is the person on the receiving end who defines harassment. Once they have made it clear that behaviour is **unacceptable and unwelcome**, it will amount to harassment, even where other workers would not see the same behaviour as offensive *(Reed & Bull v Stedman [1999] IRLR 299)*. For example, the fact that a male supervisor is also vulgar and lewd in dealing with male employees does not mean that there cannot be a claim from women *(Driskel v Peninsula Business Services [2000] IRLR 151)*.

Harassment can include remarks that cause distress if they are "unwanted" and "uninvited" *(Insitu v Heads [1995] IRLR 4)*. In the case of *Moonsar v Fiveways Express Transport [2005] IRLR 9*, the EAT held that Rea Moonsar had been discriminated against when colleagues with whom she shared an office downloaded pornographic material. Moonsar had not complained at the time but did later, following her selection for redundancy. The EAT agreed that her colleagues' behaviour could be regarded as degrading and offensive and was obviously less favourable treatment. In the case of *Jones v Tower Boot [1997] IRLR 168*, the employer was held responsible for racist insults and attacks committed by employees where the employer had not responded to the insults and attacks.

A case can be successful even if there has only been a single act of harassment, as the following case shows.

Two male employees subjected Ms Darby to a serious sexual assault. Despite her complaints the matter was not properly investigated. She resigned claiming unfair dismissal. The EAT upheld the claim saying that the employer's failure to act was a breach of contract *(Bracebridge Engineering v Darby [1990] IRLR 3)*.

The tribunals will differentiate between harassment and verbal abuse, that is not directed at an individual. In the case of *Thomas v Robinson [2003] IRLR 7*, the EAT held that for a remark to amount to harassment, the individual making the complaint must show that they suffered distress as a result. If an individual produces no evidence to show the impact of the remark when it was made, it is unlikely to amount to harassment.

Employers are under a **duty of care** to take reasonable steps to protect employees from sexual harassment once it has been brought to their attention. The tribunal will look to see whether the employer took any steps to prevent the discrimination. It will then consider whether there was anything else that the employer could have done *(Canniffe v E Riding of Yorkshire Council [2000] IRLR 555).*

The **employer is responsible** for any harassment carried out by employees. It is not enough to show that the employee concerned was initially disciplined if the harassment continued without any further action from the employer. Employers are not, however, responsible for acts of harassment by **third parties**. In the joined cases of *Rhys Harper, D'Souza and others v Relaxion Group [2003] IRLR 484*, the House of Lords held that employers are not liable for the actions of third parties with whom they had neither a contractual link nor control over the other party.

Although in most cases the appropriate response from the employer would be to suspend the alleged harasser pending an investigation, there may be rare cases where this could amount to a breach of the implied term of mutual trust and confidence (see chapter 3 – Implied terms). In the case of *Gogay v Hertfordshire CC [2000] IRLR 703*, the immediate suspension of a female employee over what turned out to be a completely unsubstantiated allegation of sexual abuse, which led to the employee suffering clinical depression, amounted to a breach of contract.

Under *section 11* of the *Industrial Tribunals Act 1996 (ITA 96)*, tribunals have discretionary powers to **protect the identity** of the parties or witnesses in sexual misconduct cases, although, except for serious cases of indecent assault, this protection applies only until the tribunal decision is given. This does not prohibit the attendance of the media at the hearing, but prohibits reporting while the order is in force. It does not, however, give an automatic right of protection to the employer.

In the majority of claims the employee will still be in employment, but where the harassment has resulted in the employee being forced to leave work, there may also be a separate claim for **constructive dismissal** (see chapter 10).

The rules on **time limits** in cases of continuing harassment are the same as those for continuing discrimination (see below – Taking a discrimination claim).

Harassment at work can also be dealt with under the *Protection from Harassment Act 1997*. The Act covers both criminal and civil harassment and, although it has rarely been used in employment situations, there are circumstances where it might be appropriate. In one case, two male employees who had indecently assaulted a colleague were given prison sentences of 12 and 21 months.

Victimisation

The victimisation of workers by **treating them differently because they are pursuing a discrimination claim** or have made a complaint of discrimination, is unlawful. Workers who give evidence in support of someone else's claim are also protected. In a European Court of Justice landmark case, an employer's refusal to supply a reference to an ex-employee, who had earlier taken a sex discrimination claim, was held to amount to victimisation *(Coote v Granada Hospitality [1999] IRLR 452)* (see chapter 3 – References and employer checks).

That interpretation initially appeared to apply only to victimisation by former employers in sex discrimination cases. However, in the case of *Rhys Harper v Relaxion Group [2003] IRLR 484*, the House of Lords held that it protected employees in all types of discrimination cases.

The *Relaxion* case was one of three successful appeals heard together, where the House of Lords decided that victimisation protection applied to former employees. Another linked case was that of *Jones v 3M Healthcare [2003] IRLR 484*.

Gerald Jones was dismissed and refused access to his workplace to allow him to recover some of his personal property from his desk. Jones was able to show that his employer would not have refused him access except that he had earlier made a disability discrimination claim against the employer.

In victimisation cases too, the employee has to identify the comparable employee to demonstrate how their treatment was, or would be, different. Where there is no actual comparator the tribunal can consider how a **hypothetical comparator**, who had not taken a discrimination claim, would have been treated.

The other essential factor is that those who are alleged to have perpetrated the victimisation need to have known that the employee had earlier taken a discrimination claim. If they did not know, there is no victimisation.

Selecting a woman for **redundancy** because she had earlier complained about discrimination amounts to victimisation, as does singling out workers for different treatment because they have claimed discrimination. An example of this is where an employer halted an enquiry into racial discrimination because the employee making the complaint had brought proceedings before an employment tribunal.

An employer who refused an employee **time off** to see an adviser about a race discrimination claim, and who would have given employees time off for domestic reasons, victimised the employee, according to the Court of Appeal in the case of *TNT Express v Brown [2000] ICR 182*.

Victimisation can be unconsciously motivated. In the case of *Nagararajan v LRT [1999] IRLR 572*, the House of Lords held that where an individual had been refused a job, the fact that his previous discrimination complaints may have subconsciously influenced the interviewing panel was enough to uphold a claim.

Proving and inferring discrimination

Proving that discrimination has taken place can be difficult, but it is important to bear in mind that the tribunal should **look at the employee's entire employment history** to see whether there are facts that would infer discrimination. Additionally, the changes to the definition of indirect discrimination (see above) make it a little easier for employees to prove discrimination. The law says that where the worker proves facts from which the tribunal could conclude, "in the absence of an adequate explanation", that there has been less favourable treatment, the complaint will be upheld, unless the employer proves there was no discrimination.

The burden of proving the case shifts from the worker, who initially has to make the case, to the employer. In the case of *Barton v Investec*

Henderson Crosthwaite Securities [2003] IRLR 332, the EAT set out two tests on proving discrimination. These are that the: claimant has to prove, on the balance of probabilities, that the discrimination has taken place and the tribunal may draw inferences so that firm proof is not necessary; and that the burden then shifts to the employer to prove that the treatment is not on discriminatory grounds and again the tribunal may draw inferences since the employer too may not be able to provide firm proof. The shift in burden of proof is now contained in the relevant discrimination legislation.

The *Barton* test was refined in the case of *Igen v Wong [2005] IRLR 258,* a Court of Appeal ruling given in February 2005. The court held that the first stage is that the claimant has to prove facts from which it could be concluded that there was discrimination. If this is not proved the claim will fail but the tribunal can rely on inferences of discrimination.

Where **more than one form of discrimination** is alleged, for example sex and race discrimination, each must be separately proven. In the case of *Bahl v The Law Society [2004] IRLR 799*, the Court of Appeal held that the unreasonable treatment of an employee cannot in itself lead to an inference of discrimination. In the case of *Igen v Wong EAT/0944/03*, Ms Wong showed that she had been treated to disciplinary action which was confrontational in tone and unreasonable. Her employers were unable to give an adequate explanation for its behaviour and the EAT held that this meant that the tribunal could conclude that Wong had been discriminated against on the grounds of her race.

There is a special **questionnaire procedure** for all types of unlawful discrimination. Claimants can send a questionnaire to their employer asking for information about the alleged discrimination. This can be used in evidence in a tribunal claim. Employers are not obliged to respond, but if they do not do so within eight weeks or if the tribunal views the reply as inadequate, the tribunals can infer that there has been discrimination.

Tribunals may also **infer** from the facts that **discrimination** has occurred. The most important case is that of *Anya v University of Oxford [2002] IRLR 337*. In that case, the Court of Appeal pointed out that, particularly in race discrimination claims where often the discrimination is covert, the tribunals have to infer what has happened by looking at the entire situation, not just the events leading to the specific complaint. If it finds evidence of different treatment, this could signal the existence of unlawful discrimination.

In one case **paying an employee's bonus late**, failing to invite her to an important function and a delay in holding an appeal on her grievance all raised an inference of disability discrimination. The matters complained of had all occurred shortly after the employer became aware of the fact that the employee had a disabling illness. In another case the tribunal inferred race discrimination.

Ms King, who is Chinese, applied for a post for which she believed she was suitable but was not shortlisted. The tribunal noted that the employer (The Great Britain-China Centre) employed no Chinese people. No records of race were kept but the tribunal inferred that there had been discrimination. The Court of Appeal upheld the tribunal's right to make such an inference, despite the fact that the burden of proof initially lies with the claimant *(King v The Great Britain-China Centre [1991] IRLR 513).*

If an employer **dismisses employees of one nationality** and replaces them with employees of another, there will be an inference of discrimination.

Positive action

While employers have a legal obligation not to discriminate **against** an individual, they also have an equal obligation not to discriminate **in favour** of anyone. In some circumstances what is permitted is "positive action". This is where a measure, often of a temporary nature, is adopted to re-establish equality of opportunity by removing the effects of discrimination. It may be lawful to give a **preference to women candidates** even though there is an equally qualified male candidate, but only if this forms part of an equality policy to address existing imbalances between the sexes *(Badeck and others [2000] IRLR 432).* However, an appointments' system that automatically favours a female candidate, even where there are more highly qualified male candidates, is contrary to equal treatment law *(Abrahamsson v Fogelqvist [2000] IRLR 732).* Giving absolute and unconditional priority to one sex would breach discrimination law. In the case of *EFTA Surveillance Authority v Kingdom of Norway [2003] IRLR 318*, the court held that by not even allowing male candidates to be assessed as suitable, the employer had breached EU law.

There are other situations when positive action is allowed. *Sections 47-48 SDA* allow employers and training bodies to introduce **training schemes** specifically for women where the proportion of women doing the work is comparatively small. *Section 49* allows trade unions to maintain **reserved or additional seats** on their elective bodies.

The legislation on **sexual orientation** and **religion or belief** has a similar provision for training. The main difference is that the test is whether, in the employer's view, the training **"prevents or compensates for disadvantages"** linked to the specific form of discrimination.

The *RRA* also contains a provision regarding **training** (*sections 37 and 38*). Additionally, under *section 35*, employers may provide persons of a particular **racial group** with special access to facilities or services to meet the needs of that group "with regard to education, training or welfare or any ancillary benefits".

The *RRA* (amended by the *Race Relations (Amendment) Act 2000*) places a **duty on public authorities**, such as local authorities and the prison service, not to discriminate on the grounds of race. Specifically, the authorities have a legal obligation to **promote race equality** and must consider how each of their policies affect race equality. They have to publish **Race Equality Schemes** to explain how they will meet their legal duties. Where they employ more than 150 staff they must also **monitor** grievances, disciplinaries, appraisals, training and dismissals for discrimination. Similar provisions are contained in the *Disability Discrimination Act 2004* and are likely to be in force in June 2006.

Disability discrimination

All employers, regardless of size are obliged to comply with disability discrimination laws. It is unlawful for any employer (other than the armed services) to treat a disabled person less favourably on the grounds of disability, without a justifiable reason. From October 2004, changes to the law under the *Disability Discrimination Act 1995 (Amendment) Regulations 2003* introduced new definitions of direct discrimination, harassment and the employer's duty to make reasonable adjustments. As with other areas of discrimination law, the burden shifts to the employer once the disabled person has established the facts from which inferences of discrimination could be drawn.

The law covers recruitment, selection and promotion and applies to **contract** workers as well as directly employed workers. It also applies to **dismissal**, including constructive dismissal. Selecting an employee for **redundancy** because they were disabled would amount to less favourable treatment. Failing to consult with a disabled employee off sick on account of her disability, over an impending redundancy would also amount to unlawful discrimination. Failing to **exercise a discretion** can amount to detrimental treatment. In the case of *Bancroft v Mitie Property Services (Southern) EAT/0494/04*, the EAT held that the refusal to exercise a discretion to pay a disabled employee full pay while off sick amounted to detrimental treatment.

Defining a disability

To gain the protection of the *DDA 95 (as amended)*, a person must have a disability. This is defined as a **physical or mental impairment**, causing a **substantial and long-term effect** on their ability to carry out **normal day-to-day activities**. **"Long term"** means a year or more, but an individual does not have to be disabled for as long as a year to claim, provided that the disability is likely to last that long or is recurring *(Greenwood v BA [1999] IRLR 600)*. If an employee has **previously suffered** from a recurring impairment, the first instance needs to have had a substantial, long-term adverse effect in order to claim that it is long term. The tribunal also has to find not just that the impairment is likely to recur, but that the substantial adverse affect of it is likely to occur (*Swift v Chief Constable of Wiltshire Constabulary [2004] IRLR 540*). A disability only dates from the time when the diagnosis of the impairment is made. Even if an employee suffers from symptoms, if there is no medical evidence that identifies a specific condition the employee is not disabled under the terms of the Act (*Millar v Commissioners of Inland Revenue EATS/0022/04*).

Impairment

It is the duty of the claimant to make clear the nature of the impairment on which the claim of discrimination is being made. The burden of proof is on the claimant who needs to **obtain the relevant medical evidence**. It is not the duty of the tribunal to present evidence (*McNicol v Balfour Beatty Rail Maintenance [2002] IRLR 711).* The fact that **treatment may alleviate** the symptoms of the impairment is not relevant. A person can be disabled but free of symptoms due to medication. However, they must provide evidence to that effect.

A **mental illness or impairment** must be one that affects memory or the ability to concentrate, to come within the definition of a disability. In the case of *Hewett v Motorola EAT/0526/01*, the EAT held that an **inability to interact socially**, due to the employee suffering from autism, amounts to a mental impairment.

The impairment has to be **well defined**. This usually means that it either has to be listed by the World Health Organisation or well known and referred to in publications. In effect, it needs to be a "diagnosed or diagnosable clinical condition or other mental disorder of a recognised type" *(Morgan v Staffordshire University [2002] IRLR 190)*. A physical impairment, even if it arises from a mental condition that is not a diagnosed clinical condition, can still amount to an impairment. So if an employee has mobility difficulties it does not matter whether or not these are psychological in origin. Even if the nature of an employee's impairment **does not meet the definition of a disability**, there still may be an obligation on the employer to negotiate with the employee over possible alternative work.

Medical conditions that can amount to a disability include cerebral palsy, asthma, migraine, neurotic depression, paranoia and ME. There are some conditions explicitly excluded from the legal definition of a disability, including **alcohol and drug addiction**. However, if these give rise to a condition coming within the definition of a disability, the individual will be classed as disabled. For example, depression arising from addiction could be classified as a disability.

Annette Power was off work through depression and alcoholism and as a result was dismissed. Power claimed protection under the *DDA*. The EAT noted that her depression had a long-term adverse affect on her ability to carry out normal day-to-day activities. The fact that it may have arisen due to her addiction was not relevant to the question of whether or not she was disabled *(Power v Panasonic [2003] IRLR 151).*

Day-to-day activities

To come within the protection of the Act the impairment must have a significant impact on the individual's day-to-day activities. Something is a **"normal" activity** if it is not **abnormal or unusual**, according to the EAT *(Ekpe v Commissioner of Police of the Metropolis [2001] IRLR 605).* It does not have to be something that the majority of the population engages in. If someone's mobility is severely impaired, this will amount to a disability even in the **absence of medical evidence** explaining the cause of the physical impairment, according to the Court of Appeal in the case of *College of Ripon & York St John v Hobbs [2002] IRLR 185.*

Day-to-day activities cover mobility, dexterity, co-ordination, continence, memory, speech and so on. Examples of such activities could include polishing furniture, shaking out quilts and other household tasks. It can also cover using public transport or travelling by air. Someone may be able to perform their work, but not "normal day-to-day activities", and still be disabled *(Vicary v BT [1999] IRLR 680).* **Sporting activities** are specifically **excluded**. This means that if, as a result of an impairment, an individual cannot participate in sporting activities they cannot argue that their normal day-to-day activities have been affected.

The condition has to have a **substantial detrimental impact** on day-to-day activities. So someone who never, or rarely, travels to London would not be able to show that an inability to use the London Underground substantially impacted on their day-to-day activities. If normal day-to-day activities can only be carried out in pain or with difficulty, this may amount to a substantial adverse effect, but it will be up to a tribunal to assess it on the particular facts. An illness, physical or mental, may run its course to conclusion but leave behind an impairment. If this continues to have a substantial effect on day-to-day activities, the *DDA 95* will still apply

A worker may also be classified as disabled as a result of the work that they are doing. For example, if working with fumes triggers asthma attacks, which affect normal day-to-day activities, the worker will be classed as disabled. However, if transferred to work where there are no fumes, the worker is not disabled under the Act *(Cruickshank v VAW Motorcast [2002] IRLR 24).*

Some **conditions are progressive**. This may mean that at the time of the discriminatory treatment the claimant is not suffering from an impairment that has a substantial impact on day-to-day activities. Here the claimant must show, through medical or statistical evidence, that it is more likely than not that at some stage the impairment will have a substantial impact *(Mowat-Brown v University of Surrey [2002] IRLR 235).* In progressive conditions such as cancer, the Court of Appeal, in the case of *Kirton v Tetrosly [2003] IRLR 353*, held that an impairment that arises as a consequence of it could come within the definition of a disability.

The *Disability Discrimination Act 2005* guarantees protection from discrimination to individuals with long-term, non-symptomatic, progressive conditions, like cancer, HIV and multiple sclerosis.

Less favourable treatment

An employer discriminates against disabled employees if they are treated less favourably. In general, assumptions cannot be made about how the law should operate by looking at what happens in sex and race discrimination cases. In the case of *Clark v TGD Novacold [1999] IRLR 318*, for example, the Court of Appeal said that the **less favourable treatment** of a disabled person is discriminatory if unjustified and if the reason for the treatment does not, or would not, apply to others.

An example of less favourable treatment would include failing to renew a temporary contract on the grounds of a worker's disability.

Tribunals can also **infer disability discrimination** from the facts presented to them. In one case, the fact that the employer held a disciplinary hearing in the absence of an employee who was off work because of her disability, raised a presumption of less favourable treatment *(Rowden v Dutton Gregory [2002] ICR 97).*

Duty to make adjustments

Employers have to make **reasonable adjustments** to working conditions or to the workplace to avoid putting disabled workers at a disadvantage. In deciding what adjustments could be made the employer should focus on what the employee can do, and not on what she/he cannot do. Normally a requirement to **extend the payment of sick pay** beyond the contractual entitlement would not be a reasonable adjustment. However, if the tribunal believes that the employer has failed to make reasonable adjustments it can take account of any failure to extend the contractual sick pay arrangements (*Nottinghamshire CC v Meikle [2004] IRLR 703*). Nor is there any requirement to provide training which might assist a worker in overcoming a disability. In one case (*Bruce v Addleshaw A1/2003/2676*), the Court of Appeal held that there was no obligation on an employer to adjust the selection criteria for a job. The disabled person (Mr Bruce) had not been selected for a post because he did not have the relevant experience, however, the fact that he did not was nothing to do with his disability.

Failing to make reasonable adjustments is an act of unlawful discrimination and an employer refusing to employ a disabled worker, without having considered making adjustments, can be liable in a discrimination claim.

GB Electronics intended to announce redundancies. It called all those affected, including Mr Berry, who is profoundly deaf, to a mass meeting and made the announcement. No adjustments were made to take account of Berry's disability, despite his obvious anxiety about events that were taking place and which he did not understand. This amounted to a failure to make reasonable adjustments, which could, for example, have included breaking the news to him separately with a signer present *(Berry v GB Electronics EAT/0992/00)*.

In the case of *Archibald v Fife Council [2004] IRLR 651,* the House of Lords has held that on occasions the duty to make reasonable adjustments can require an employer to treat a disabled worker more favourably than other staff.

Susan Archibald was a road sweeper but following complications arising from surgery she was no longer able to walk. She retrained, applied for more than 100 posts with the council, but was unsuccessful and dismissed for capability reasons. Although she lost her claims in the lower courts, with the assistance of the Disability Rights Commission, she appealed to the House of Lords. It ruled in her favour and held that the council could have transferred Archibald in to one of the 100 jobs she had applied for without requiring her to attend an interview.

The duty to make adjustments only applies if the job can be **reasonably altered** to accommodate an individual's disability. Examples of reasonable adjustments might include relocating the employee or assessing the criteria for selection and making adjustments where otherwise they would produce a discriminatory outcome. The important point is that the employer should have given consideration to whether adjustments could reasonably be made, as the case of *Mid Staffordshire General Hospitals NHS Trust v Cambridge [2003] IRLR 566* shows.

Teresa Cambridge experienced a serious throat condition caused by dust in her workplace. She was unable to return to work full-time and was dismissed. The EAT held that while dismissal could have been justified, the employer should have carried out a proper assessment of what was required to eliminate the disadvantage she faced. The failure to do this made the dismissal unfair.

The tribunal will look at the **nature of the adjustments** proposed and the extent to which they might have overcome the medical condition that prevented the employee's return to work *(Fu v LB Camden [2001] IRLR 186)*. In the case of *BT v Pelling EATS/0093/03*, the EAT held that the adjustment should have included allowing an agoraphobic employee to work from home, as homeworking had been permitted for some employees, this would have been a suitable adjustment.

The employer has an obligation to offer **alternative employment** if the job a disabled person is doing is no longer suitable. According to the case of *Kent County Council v Mingo [2000] IRLR 90*, this extends to giving priority to disabled employees over redundant employees, when looking at possible redeployment. However, this does not mean that there is an obligation to "red circle" a disabled employee's post so as to maintain their previous earnings in their new job. Nor is there a requirement to offer an alternative job that has terms that differ from those the employee had been employed under.

Employers cannot ignore **health and safety** legislation in order to accommodate a disabled employee. For example, if a risk assessment reveals a need to wear protective clothing and it is unsuited to a disabled employee and no reasonable alternatives exist, the employer can lawfully dismiss.

An employer has no obligation to make any adjustments unless an actual or potential job applicant would require this.

Justification

The *DDA* currently gives the employer the right to **justify** direct discrimination, whereas in other areas of discrimination law employers can only use justification in indirect discrimination cases. In one case, the failure of an employee suffering from schizophrenia, who was working in a school, to take **appropriate medication** amounted to a justification for his dismissal. A risk assessment showed him to be at greater risk of having an attack due to the stressful nature of the work *(A v LB Hounslow, CA/1155/98)*. In the case of *Murphy v Slough BC (1) governing Body of Langleywood School A2/2004/1239*, the Court of Appeal held that a school could justify the refusal of paid leave to a disabled employee who was about to receive her surrogate child on the basis of its "precarious financial position".

Where **no reasonable adjustments** can be made this may amount to a justification for the failure to make any. Similarly, where the nature of the employee's disability means that even with adjustments they would be unable to work, the employer would not be unlawfully discriminating just because adjustments had not been made.

However, an employer who cannot justify the failure to make adjustments is likely to be found to have discriminated.

Ms Beart was off sick suffering from depression. A medical report recommended that she be relocated, but instead her employer disciplined and dismissed her because they found out that she had been working while off sick. The Court of Appeal held that the employer had failed to produce evidence to justify the failure to make adjustments and that this was highly significant to a finding of discrimination *(Beart v Prison Service [2003] IRLR 238)*. In a second ruling on this case (*Prison Service v Beart (No 2) [2005] IRLR 171*) the EAT held that the wrongdoer should not benefit from her/his own wrongdoing.

The fact that the employer did not **know about a disability** is not an absolute justification.

Mr Tuck suffered from an illness that neither he nor his employer believed would be substantial or long term. For this reason his employer made no adjustments. The EAT ruled that a late attempt to make adjustments was not sufficient and the employer could not rely on the fact that he did not have sufficient information about the nature of the disability *(Tuck v Fish Brothers EAT/0380/01)*.

However, in some cases an employer may be able to rely on the defence of justification, if at the time of the discriminatory action they had no

knowledge of the disability and were therefore unaware of the duty to make adjustments *(Quinn v Schwarzkopf [2002] IRLR 602)*.

Taking a discrimination claim

If taking a tribunal claim, claimants should always consider whether they should **register the claim under one or more of the four headings — direct, indirect, harassment or victimisation**. This is because it may turn out during the tribunal hearing that what seemed to be a direct discrimination case was in reality one of indirect discrimination and it may be too late to lodge a second claim.

The **time limit** for all discrimination cases is **three months** from the date of the discriminatory act (not the date when any decision leading to discrimination was taken) and, as long as the impact of the **discriminatory act continues**, the right to complain to a tribunal exists. If the employer imposes a requirement that is indirectly discriminatory, then each occasion where this operates to the detriment of the employee amounts to a fresh act of discrimination, according to the Court of Appeal *(Rovenska v GMC [1997] IRLR 367)*. This is usually referred to as "**continuing discrimination**". Where employees can show that for the whole of their career they have been held back on discriminatory grounds, they should consider whether there is the basis for a continuing discrimination claim *(Fearon v Chief Constable of Derbyshire EAT/0445/02)*. If a woman is claiming discriminatory treatment, the fact that she does not suffer this while she is away from work on **maternity leave** does not break the continuity of discrimination *(Spencer v HM Prison Service EAT/0812/02)*.

The concept of "continuing discrimination" also applies in disability cases. In the case of *Hendricks v Commissioner of Police of the Metropolis [2003] IRLR 96*, the Court of Appeal ruled that so long as the employment relationship exists, an employee may be able to argue that there is continuing discrimination. It held this to be the case even if the employee's absence for sickness meant she was out of the environment where the discrimination occurred.

Where an employer has promised to take remedial steps to improve the working environment to prevent a recurrence of discrimination, but then fails to do so, this falls within the definition of continuing discrimination *(Littlewoods v Traynor [1993] IRLR 154)*. So too does a case where an employer has more than once rejected an employee for promotion on discriminatory grounds *(Owusu v London Fire and Civil Defence Authority [1995] IRLR 574)*.

Where the claim is based on an employer's **discriminatory recruitment policies**, the three months run from the date of the last refusal of employment. An individual who is not an employee cannot claim continuing discrimination where certain of the employer's policies remain unchanged. Refusal of a job because of a discriminatory policy occurs only when that job is refused and the individual must bring a claim within three months of that date *(Tyagi v BBC World Service [2001] IRLR 465)*.

In **disability** cases, the tribunal must take account of any medical evidence of the nature of the employee's disability, but can come to its own decision on whether or not the person is disabled.

Although it is always advisable to keep within the time limits, there are situations when it is possible to **submit a late claim**. You should never decide not to pursue a discrimination claim solely because the time limit has expired. In the case of *British Coal v Keeble [1997] IRLR 336*, the EAT ruled that claims based on **new interpretations of the law** by European and domestic courts can be heard even if the **time limit has passed**. In the case of *Southwark LBC v Afolabi [2003] IRLR 220*, the Court of Appeal held that even if a claim is based on events years ago, the tribunal still has the power to consider extending the time limit, if just and equitable to do so.

When making the claim it is enough to **set out the broad outline**. For example, if a race discrimination complaint is based on the allegation that a supervisor dislikes black people and has said so to a third party, it would be enough to name that party. It would not be necessary to set down the exact words used.

Workers have the right to take discrimination claims **regardless of how long they have worked**. Workers **employed outside Great Britain**, posted to work in other EU states, are also covered (see chapter 2 – Working outside the UK).

The Court of Appeal, in the case of *Martins v Marks & Spencer [1998] IRLR 326*, has recommended that in most discrimination cases it would be good practice for tribunals to hold a meeting for preliminary directions. This ensures that the **issues to be tried are identified** in advance of the full tribunal hearing.

Claims of discrimination can be taken against **bodies other than employers**. Partnerships, trade unions, qualifying bodies, vocational training bodies, employment agencies and statutory bodies are all covered under the legislation. Claims can also be taken against work colleagues where they have discriminated or harassed. Separate claims in the civil courts for personal injury (physical or mental) can also be pursued *(Sheriff v Klyne Tugs [1999] IRLR 481)*.

Tribunals have the power to: **make an order** declaring the rights of the parties; **award compensation** to the employee discriminated against; and **recommend action** for the employer to take within a specific period.

Compensation

There is **no upper limit for compensation** in discrimination claims. Compensation can include any actual **financial loss sustained** and damages for **injury to feelings**. Compensation for loss of earnings is assessed by taking the sum the employee would have earned at work, deducting what might have been earned elsewhere and then reducing this by a percentage to reflect the possibility that the employee might have left the employer at some stage anyway *(MoD v Wheeler [1998] IRLR 23)*. The fact that the employer **"unintentionally" discriminated** is not a defence. Tribunals can also award compensation in these cases.

The size of the injury to feelings award will reflect the length of time over which the discrimination occurred as well as the seriousness of the act. It can also take into account the time it took an employer to resolve the employee's grievance *(BT v Reid, [2004] IRLR 327)*. The size of the award can also be affected by the seniority of the person who has discriminated and how persistent the discrimination has been. In cases of serious injury this can amount to around £25,000, according to the Court of Appeal in the case of *Vento v Chief Constable of West Yorkshire Police [2003] IRLR 102*. It held that injury to feelings awards should be a maximum of £25,000 and a minimum of £500.

Awards above or below these limits should only be made in exceptional circumstances. Injury to feelings awards are not grossed up to take account of any tax liability the claimant might have (*Orthet v Vince-Cain [2004] IRLR 857*)

In the case of *Essa v Laing [2004] IRLR 313*, the Court of Appeal held that an employer was still liable to pay compensation for injury to feelings even if it could not have been foreseen that the discrimination would have affected the employee's health so badly. The court held that there was a strict obligation on employers to pay compensation where health was damaged.

The tribunal can also award **aggravated damages** for the manner of the discrimination, in other words, for how the employer went about discriminating against the employee. These are separate from any damages for injury to feelings and will usually only be awarded where the discriminatory conduct was high-handed, malicious, insulting or oppressive. In one case this led to an award of £7,500. There may be circumstances in which the tribunal will award compensation for **psychiatric injury** in addition. In the case of *MoD v Cannock [1994] IRLR 509*, the EAT held that compensation could also be claimed for hurt caused by **loss of a chosen career.**

However, the tribunals **cannot award exemplary damages** — that is damages that are punitive rather than compensatory *(MoD v Meredith [1995] IRLR 539).*

If an individual who has made the **discrimination complaint dies**, the claim for compensation can be continued by relatives or beneficiaries *(Executors of Soutar v James Murray [2002] IRLR 22).*

In determining compensation in **harassment** cases, tribunals will take account of the impact of harassment and how the employer responded to it. The tribunal may also take account of factors like the age of the victim (for example, as a young person was she or he particularly vulnerable), whether the employer's attitudes had encouraged the harassment, or whether complaints had been ignored.

The commissions

The **Equal Opportunities Commission (EOC)** and the **Commission for Racial Equality (CRE)** were established under the *SDA 75* and the

RRA 76 respectively. They have a dual role that involves conducting formal investigations and offering advice and support to persons taking discrimination claims.

The commissions have powers to decide whether to institute proceedings with a view to helping an aggrieved person and to offer representation. But this is normally limited to particularly complex cases or where a question of legal principle is involved.

The **Disability Rights Commission** was established under the *Disability Rights Commission Act 1999*. Its powers are similar to those of the EOC and the CRE.

The government intends to replace the commissions with a new single equality body to be called the **Commission for Equality and Human Rights**. This commission, which will commence its work in 2006, will enforce all areas of discrimination law, including age, religion and belief and sexual orientation and will also promote human rights in the public sector. The Bill to establish the statutory basis for this new single commission was published in March 2005. In February 2005, the government established two reviews, an equalities review and a discrimination law review to support the development of a single equality commission and to work towards the creation of a Single Equality Act.

Northern Ireland has a single **Equality Commission for Northern Ireland** which covers all forms of unlawful discrimination

Codes of practice

The commissions also have the power to issue codes of practice and these contain much useful information on which to assess the strength of a discrimination claim. Every union representative should have a copy of the codes, which can be obtained free of charge from the EOC, the CRE and the DRC (see Further information).

There are also two codes of practice on the scope of the *DDA*. One covers employment and occupation, the other covers the **responsibilities of trade unions** towards their disabled members. There is a CRE code of practice, *Racial equality in employment*, together with an EOC code of practice. The codes give practical guidance and can be taken into account in tribunal hearings. In 2004, the CRE consulted on a new code of practice on racial equality which it is expected will come into force in 2005.

More information: LRD booklets, *Discrimination at work (£4.50); Lesbian and gay workers' rights (£4.00)*; Legal Action Group handbook *Discrimination Law*; LRD's *Workplace Report* has quarterly updates on sex and race discrimination and regular updates on disability discrimination law.

7. Sick pay and sickness absence

Statutory sick pay

Employees who do not have a right to better occupational sick pay from their employer should receive, when off work on account of sickness, statutory sick pay (SSP) of £68.20 a week (2005/06), provided they are earning at least £82 a week. SSP is paid by the employer in the way you would normally be paid.

SSP can only be claimed by those **under pension age** and **in work**. It cannot be claimed if the illness begins while the individual is **on strike** (see below).

Pregnant women can claim, and will only be excluded from SSP if sick for a pregnancy-related reason any time after four weeks before the baby's expected week of birth (see chapter 8 – Maternity pay). But women in receipt of Statutory Maternity Pay (SMP) cannot claim SSP at the same time.

To claim SSP workers have to be ill for at least four days in a row, and their period of absence from work must include **three "qualifying days"**. These are days agreed in advance with the employer and normally include all working days. If these conditions are met, a claim can be made after the fourth day. So a worker who works a normal Monday to Friday week, whose "qualifying days" are also Monday to Friday and who falls sick on a Saturday cannot claim SSP until the following Thursday, providing the illness lasts that long. Where there is a second period of illness within eight weeks, the two can be **linked** together in one claim.

The second set of conditions that must be met cover **notification** of the illness to the employer. This is usually required by the end of the first day off, but a doctor's certificate cannot be demanded before the end of seven days' illness.

Workers who have **frequent periods of sickness absence** may be asked to attend a medical examination by the Department for Work and Pensions (DWP) after a fourth period of absence. Workers refused SSP can **appeal**. The Inland Revenue handles appeals. **Claims for non-payment** of SSP cannot be pursued against the employer as unlawful deductions through the employment tribunals. They have to be pursued through the DWP.

Employers may **opt out of the SSP rules**, if they operate an occupational scheme that pays at least the SSP rate. They will not have to keep SSP records for any payment of contractual remuneration that equals or exceeds the amount of SSP payable. If the employer offers better arrangements under the occupational scheme, these can be linked to a requirement to submit to medical examination. In the case of *Stirling & Mair v Meikle EAT/27/02*, the employee's refusal to be **examined by the company doctor** made it lawful for the employer to stop his occupational sick pay.

Most occupational sick pay schemes will set out a period of entitlement to pay. A typical scheme might pay three or six months' full pay followed by three or six months' half pay and in some cases there may be additional **discretionary entitlements**.

Mr King worked for the fire service. He was off on long-term sick leave, suffering from depression. Unfortunately, his wife was also off sick and as a consequence their family income was reduced. King argued that his employer should have exercised a discretion to extend his period of full pay given that his illness was work related and that his financial situation was poor. The EAT rejected this argument. There was no obligation to exercise the discretion (*West Yorkshire Fire and Civil Defence Authority v King EAT/0961/03*).

Where an occupational sick pay scheme does give the employer some **discretion** over whether or not to pay occupational sick pay at all (as opposed to whether to extend the period of entitlement) the tribunals are likely to impose a narrow discretion on the employer. In one case, the EAT ruled that once it had been established that the employee's sickness was genuine, an entitlement to occupational sick pay was established (*Scottish Courage v Guthrie EAT/0788/03*). If the employee's doctor says that they are fit to return to work, but the employer wants further medical checks, the employee should be paid full wages while waiting for the checks to take place. A person **willing to work** has a common law right to be paid *(Beveridge v KLM UK [2000] IRLR 765)*.

If an employer changes an occupational sick pay policy, this does not necessarily amount to less favourable treatment of **disabled employees**, according to the case of *London Clubs Management v*

Hood [2001] IRLR 719. In this case, the reason for the change was not to do with the fact that an employee was disabled and, in the absence of any evidence that the disabled employee had significantly more periods of absence, the change did not contravene disability discrimination law (see chapter 6 – Disability discrimination).

Women who are **off sick during their pregnancy** but prior to the time when they could be required to begin their maternity leave could lose out on entitlement to occupational sick pay if their employer operates a scheme which gives a fixed maximum amount of sick pay entitlement over the year. In the case of *North Western Health Board v McKenna C-191/03*, the ECJ held that these schemes were discriminatory on the grounds of sex and were therefore unlawful.

SSP is payable to workers **sick while on holiday** but can be offset against any contractual entitlement to holiday pay. Workers can only take holidays in lieu where there is provision to do so in the employment contract.

Dismissal while sick

Dismissal for sickness can come within the range of permitted dismissals for "capability" or "some other substantial reason" (see chapter 10 – Fair dismissal). A dismissal following an unacceptable but genuine level of sickness absence could be a fair dismissal for "some other substantial reason" *(Wilson v Post Office [2000] IRLR 834)*. If a dismissal is triggered by the sickness absence procedure, the tribunal **will not normally take account of the background to the last period of sickness**. For example, if an employee has been through various stages of the sickness absence procedure and then is off sick after an accident, or even after having been a victim of a crime, the dismissal can still be fair. Even if the employee's illness is a result of their work (for example, where they are suffering from work-related stress), this does not mean that the employer cannot dismiss for sickness. However, in the case of *Frewin v Consignia EAT/0981/02*, the EAT held that this is not the same as suggesting that the cause of the illness be completely disregarded.

Tribunals will normally take into account matters like the size of the firm, difficulties in arranging for short-term replacements, the employee's service, the nature of the illness and whether, taking all things into account, the employer's decision to dismiss was one a **"reasonable" employer** would have taken. Employers dismissing for sickness will normally be required to have:

- given **warnings**;
- **consulted a doctor** about the nature of the illness; and
- **consulted the employee** about alternatives to dismissal.

The employer should have taken some steps to **investigate** the sickness and absence. In one case, the EAT accepted that the employer's attempts to contact the employee by phone and by letter without response amounted to a reasonable investigation.

Where there is a **sickness absence code** providing guidance to supervisors on how absences should be dealt with, you will need to establish if it is **contractual** so that both parties are bound by it. To be contractual, it would have to always be applied and the employer would not be able to exercise any discretion in applying it. In many cases it will be. This means that if an employer fails to follow the procedure, any attempts to stop the employee's sick pay entitlement could be unlawful *(Robertson v Rockware Glass EAT/107/01)*. If, however, the sickness code does not form part of the employee's contract, the employer can change it unilaterally *(Wandsworth BC v D'Silva [1998] IRLR 193).*

Many sickness absence procedures set down rules for **keeping in touch during sickness absence**. They may require employees to contact their employer at regular, even pre-set, intervals, but should not be exercised in a manner which would be regarded as totally unreasonable. Some procedures give the employer the right to make contact, which may be intrusive if the employer turns up unexpectedly or telephones too frequently or at inappropriate times of the day. In rare situations, employees in the public sector may be able to use the *Human Rights Act 1998* to argue that the employer's intrusion breaches their right to a private life (see Introduction – Civil liberties and employment law). However, the case would have to be a very serious one to succeed.

Mr Ridge complained that the employer had made a **secret video** of him while he was off sick and had used the video at a disciplinary hearing, resulting in his dismissal. He argued that his human rights had been breached. The EAT held that the employer had the right to video an employee who it suspected was not genuinely sick (*Pendragon Motor Co v Ridge EAT/962/00*).

In the case of *McGowan v Scottish Water [2005] IRLR 167*, the EAT held that the employer (a public corporation) investigating what was effectively criminal activity had the right to protect the assets of the company and surveillance was not disproportionate and therefore did not amount to a breach of Article 8 rights.

Although the employer is obliged to take steps to discover the true medical position before dismissing, the overriding principle is one of **"reasonableness"**, so that a failure to consult with the employee's GP is not an absolute guarantee that the resulting dismissal is unfair. But at the same time, there is **no corresponding obligation** on the employee to inform the employer of the prospects of recovery *(Mitchell v Arkwood Plastics [1993] ICR 471).*

Ms Slaughter was dismissed because she was unable to lift heavy loads due to a back injury. A tribunal tried to reduce her compensation on the grounds that she had an obligation to inform her employer of her medical condition. The EAT rejected this view and said that whilst she had an obligation to co-operate with her employer's medical enquiries, she was under no obligation to instigate them *(Slaughter v Brewer [1990] IRLR 426).*

A dismissal could also be unfair, even if the employer had followed the sickness absence procedure, where an illness was caused or worsened by the employer's malicious or wilful negligence *(Edwards v Governors of Hanson School [2001] IRLR 733).*

Employers will not normally be able to dismiss employees because of a **short sickness absence**, but that is not to say that dismissal can never occur.

In cases of **intermittent absences** due to ill health, the employer may not have the same obligation to obtain medical evidence. The EAT has said that the employer has to have regard to the whole history of the employment and to take account of a range of factors including the nature of the illness and the likelihood of its recurrence, the length of absences compared with the intervals of good health, the employer's need for that particular employee, the impact of absences on the rest of the workforce and the extent to which the employee was made aware of the position *(Lynock v Cereal Packaging [1988] IRLR 510).*

The tribunal will still be able to look at whether the dismissal was reasonable in cases of intermittent but genuine sickness absence.

The case of *Leeson v Makita Manufacturing Europe EAT/0911/00* held the dismissal of an employee who had frequent absences for genuine reasons to be unreasonable. It had more to do with the employer's wish to **make an example of the employee** to deter others, than with dealing with the employee's genuine sickness.

The dismissal of **disabled employees** should be dealt with under the *Disability Discrimination Act 1995* (see chapter 6 – Disability discrimination).

Consultation with the employee is essential, and a failure to do this may make a resulting dismissal unfair.

Mr Daubney's employers commissioned a medical report on his sickness absence, which recommended he be retired. He was then dismissed without consultation. The EAT said this was unfair (*East Lindsey District Council v Daubney [1977] IRLR 181).*

The employer is also under an obligation to consult over the possibility of **alternative work**.

A growing number of employers provide **permanent healthcare insurance (PHI)**, which insures them against the financial costs of long-term illness while providing a financial safety net for employees. The High Court has held, in the case of *Aspden v Webbs Poultry [1996] IRLR 521*, that there is an implied term in a contract that an employee will not be dismissed, except for redundancy, if a PHI scheme requires the individual to remain an employee to receive the benefit.

In the case of *Villella v MFI Furniture [1999] IRLR 468*, the employer paid into a PHI scheme. The insurers investigated the employee's illness and decided they would no longer pay out on the policy. The EAT held that the fact that the insurers were no longer paying did not alter the employer's contractual obligation to pay wages, since the employee's rights under the PHI scheme were not dependent on how the scheme viewed the employee's state of health.

The only circumstances where employees entitled to benefit from a PHI scheme can legitimately be dismissed is where they have fundamentally breached the contract. In the case of *Briscoe v Lubrizol [2002] IRLR 607*, the Court of Appeal held **that refusing to attend a meeting with management** amounted to such a breach, even if it did not amount to gross misconduct.

Where there is a PHI scheme, the fact that an employee may be **doing some work** does not necessarily negate the contractual right to make a PHI claim *(Brompton v AOC [1997] IRLR 639)*. For example, in the case of *Walton v Airtours [2003] IRLR 161*, the Court of Appeal held that where an employee's medical condition allowed him to try an alternative job this did not deny him the right to PHI, since there was no evidence that he could permanently follow the new occupation.

Workers **sick before the beginning of a strike** are not viewed as taking part in it. Workers who are off sick have no obligation to supply their labour and therefore cannot be said to be withdrawing it. This would not apply, however, where the sick employee was somehow actively participating in the strike.

Employers cannot therefore dismiss them by relying on their general right to dismiss strikers (see chapter 9 – Dismissal).

Mr Smith was off sick for the whole period of a strike. Every week he would go to work to hand in his doctor's certificate and would stop to chat to the pickets on the gate. The EAT had to determine whether he was taking part in the strike, and on the facts they held that merely talking to pickets did not amount to taking part in a strike (*Hindle Gears Ltd v McGinty [1984] IRLR 477)*.

However, if the **sickness begins after the strike begins** the worker is usually considered to be taking part in it and could be fairly dismissed.

Employers can use sickness as a method of **selecting for redundancies** (see chapter 11 – Selection for redundancy).

Under unfair dismissal legislation, employees may have their award of **compensation reduced** where, by their action, they have contributed to the dismissal (see chapter 10). However, this rule is rarely appropriate in sickness dismissal cases. Any award of compensation made by a tribunal in an unfair dismissal claim can be reduced to take account of SSP or Incapacity Benefit already paid *(Puglia v C James & Sons [1996] IRLR 70)*.

Frustration

Although employment contracts are normally terminated with notice (except in cases of gross misconduct, see chapter 10 – Fair dismissal), there is one situation when no notice is required. It is when an employee's absence through illness frustrates, or ends, the contract because the nature of the illness or period of absence means either that they can no longer do the job, or that someone else is needed to do it. Once a contract has been frustrated, it no longer exists and all rights to claim under the contract end.

Neill Donaldson worked as a heavy goods vehicle driver but lost his licence due to illness. He was paid sick pay until it ran out, after which there was no contact with his employer for about a year. He was then offered a new job by the employer. Later, when made redundant, his employers calculated his service from the date of the new job. Donaldson argued that his contract had continued during the whole period when he had not worked and that his redundancy pay should be based on all of his years of service. The EAT noted that he had not been able to carry on his old job due to illness. This meant that the old contract had been frustrated and that no account could be taken of it in assessing his service for redundancy *(Donaldson v D&T Campbell EAT/771/01)*.

Even in cases where a worker is **disabled** and has protection under the *Disability Discrimination Act 1995* (see chapter 6 – Disability discrimination) a contract can still be frustrated provided that the employer has complied with the obligations imposed by the legislation to consider any adjustments, and finds that there are no further steps that can reasonably be taken *(Thorold v Martell Press EAT/0343/01)*.

Medical reports

The *Access to Medical Reports Act 1988* gives employees (and prospective employees) the right to see medical reports prepared by their own GP in connection with their employment. The Act says that the employer must obtain the individual's consent before seeking a report from her/his doctor; that the individual has the legal right to have a copy of the report before it is forwarded to the employer; that the individual can query items in it; and that, if the doctor refuses to accept it, the individual's objection may be appended to the report.

The *Access to Health Records Act 1990* gives individuals the right to apply for access to records relating to them that are held by a health professional. Unlike the 1988 Act, the definition of "health professional" in the 1990 Act would cover a company doctor.

More information: LRD booklet *State Benefits & Tax Credits 2005* (£5.45); LRD's *Workplace Report* has monthly updates which highlight any relevant new cases on sickness.

8. Leave for working parents

The rights of working parents to time off and pay to care for their children have improved in recent years. The flat rate of statutory maternity pay has risen significantly and is now £106.00 (2005/06) compared to £75 a week in 2002 and the period of statutory maternity leave is now a minimum of 26 weeks. There are also rights to **adoption** and **paternity leave**.

There are also specific rights for pregnant workers as employers have a general duty to **protect their health and welfare**. This includes carrying out a **risk assessment** of any working arrangements that might have an effect on pregnancy wherever they employ women of childbearing age, regardless of whether or not any employees are pregnant at the time.

In February 2005, the government published a consultation paper outlining its proposals for longer paid statutory maternity pay and leave, together with proposals to extend the right to request flexible working. These include a proposal to extend paid maternity leave to nine months, with a longer term aim of increasing it to a year.

Antenatal care

Pregnant women have the right not to be **unreasonably refused time off** work for antenatal care, including time off for parenthood and relaxation classes.

Under *section 55* of the *Employment Rights Act 1996 (ERA 96),* there is a right to be **paid for time off** at the appropriate hourly rate. If requested by the employer, she must provide a copy of a certificate showing she is pregnant and written **proof of the antenatal appointment**, for all except the first one.

If an employer unreasonably refuses time off an employee can submit a complaint to a tribunal. Normally this should be done **within three months** of the refusal. If the claim is upheld, the tribunal can order the employer to pay her at the appropriate rate. She is entitled to this even if the employer's refusal to allow time off meant she worked, and was paid, during the time when the appointment would have occurred.

Maternity leave

Every woman in work has the right to maternity leave. There are **three types** of leave:

- **ordinary** maternity leave — 26 weeks' leave, which everyone gets;
- **compulsory** maternity leave — two weeks within the period of ordinary leave (four weeks in the case of factory workers) immediately following the birth, which has to be taken; and
- **additional** maternity leave — a further 26 weeks.

To get **ordinary maternity leave** a woman must still be in work by the 14th week before the baby is due. By the 15th week she has to have given her employer **notice of her pregnancy** and of the date when she intends to begin her maternity leave. She can change her mind about this date but has to give her employer at least 28 days' notice of the new start date. If her employer requests it, she also has to provide a **copy of a doctor's or midwife's notice** that she is pregnant. She can begin the leave anytime after the 11th week before the baby is due, up to the week it is born. She must, as a minimum, be off for the whole of the **compulsory leave** period.

While on **ordinary or compulsory** leave she has the right to statutory and/or contractual maternity pay (if qualifying) together will **all non-wage contractual benefits**. She has the right to be given the opportunity for assessment, wherever the pay system is performance based. In the case of *Boyle v EOC [1998] IRLR 717,* the European Court of Justice (ECJ) confirmed that where the pension provision is entirely funded by the employer, all of a woman's statutory maternity leave, including any unpaid leave, is to be taken into account in calculating length of service for pension purposes. As far as statutory holiday rights are concerned, a woman who is on maternity leave must be able to exercise the rights even if that means taking her holidays at a time that does not coincide with when her colleagues take leave.

She also has the **right to be told of any jobs** that become available while she is on maternity leave, for which she might be interested in applying. A failure to give this information amounts to a breach of trust and confidence, according to the EAT in the case of *Visa International Service Association v Paul [2004] IRLR 42.* If she has been serving a probationary period and, due to her maternity leave, has had less time in the job the employer must **extend her period of probation** if the alternative is dismissal for failing her probation *(Haines Lee v Relate Berkshire EAT/1458/01)*.

To get **additional** maternity leave a woman has to meet all of the requirements for ordinary leave and have been **working for the employer for at least 26 weeks** by the 14th week before the baby is due. Additional leave starts at the end of the period of ordinary leave and lasts for another 26 weeks. In total, therefore, a woman with at least 26 weeks' service can have up to a year's maternity leave.

While on additional leave, a woman will only have the right to pay if her contract provides for an extended period of occupational maternity pay. She will accrue statutory annual leave, but whether she accrues any occupational annual leave depends on what the contract provides. An employee on additional maternity leave is **covered by certain non-wage contractual terms** — specifically, she retains the right to notice before termination of the contract, to redundancy pay and to benefit from any disciplinary or grievance procedures (for her entitlement to pay see below). She is also still covered by any express or implied confidentiality or non-competition clauses in the contract.

A woman who is on maternity leave and who decides that she does not want to return to work at the end of it should **resign by giving whatever notice** her contract states she should.

Maternity pay

To get Statutory Maternity Pay (SMP) a woman has to fulfil four requirements:

- she has to have worked for her employer for at **least 26 weeks** by the 15th week before the baby is due;
- in the eight weeks (or two months if monthly paid) prior to the 15th week she has to have had **average earnings of at least £82 a week**;
- she has to have given her employer medical evidence of her pregnancy and at least 28 days' notice of the date when she intends to stop work and start claiming SMP; and
- she must have actually **stopped work**.

She will then get **six weeks' pay at 90%** of average earnings (higher rate SMP) and **20 weeks' at a flat rate** of £106.00 (2005/06). SMP starts in the first week of maternity leave and continues until 26 weeks have passed or the employee returns to work, whichever happens first.

SMP is **paid by the employer through the normal pay packet**. The employer then reclaims most of it back through the national insurance scheme. If a woman is refused SMP and believes she is entitled to it she should apply to the Inland Revenue office for a formal decision.

A woman not qualifying for SMP may be able to claim **Maternity Allowance (MA)** through her local Jobcentre Plus office. MA is a flat rate of £106.00 a week (2005/06) payable for 26 weeks. The condition for this benefit is that she has had at least 26 weeks' employment, that need not be continuous, within the previous 66 weeks. Women who meet the service requirements for SMP, but who earn less than £82 a week but at least £30 a week, even from different jobs, will get 90% of their actual earnings for 26 weeks. Those with fewer than 26 weeks' employment have no entitlement to payment.

Rights to SMP are **not dependent on returning to work**. However, rights to more generous occupational maternity pay can be linked to returning to work for a specified period, and this is not unlawful according to the ECJ in the case of *Handels-og Kontorfunktionaeremes [1999] IRLR 55.*

The ECJ has ruled that it is not contrary to the directive on equal treatment to pay less than full pay during maternity leave. However, the calculation of maternity pay must be based on what a woman is earning immediately before she begins her maternity leave.

In December 1995, Michelle Alabaster received a pay increase. However, on starting her maternity leave a few weeks later, she received maternity pay based on her earnings before the increase, not on her final earnings. The ECJ held that Alabaster could use a 1985 EU directive which protects the health and safety of pregnant women to ensure that she had the right to pay at the rate it would have been paid at if she had not been on maternity leave *(Alabaster v Woolwich [2004] IRLR 486).*

As a consequence of the *Alabaster* ruling the law was changed with effect from April 2005. Pay increases between the beginning of the 15th week before the baby's expected birth and the end of the maternity leave period are taken into account.

Sometimes a pregnant woman will experience sickness leading to absence at work. The ECJ (in the *Handels* case above) held that a woman could not be denied sick pay just because her sickness was pregnancy-related. However, if she **chooses not to work** before the beginning of her maternity leave, for what the ECJ described as "routine pregnancy-related inconveniences", she would not get sick pay.

Returning to work

Employers now have a **legal duty to calculate the employee's date for return to work** and to give her that information in writing. This should normally be done in response to (and within 28 days of) the woman's notification to the employer of her pregnancy. If an employer **fails to provide this information** or provides it less than 28 days before she would have been required to return to work and, as a result, it proves impossible to return on time, the employer may not take action against her.

A woman returning from ordinary or additional maternity leave need do no more than **turn up for work** on the date already notified to her by her employer. She can also choose to return to work before her maternity leave period ends, but has to give the employer at least 28 days' notice of her return. An employer cannot refuse to let her return to work before the end of her maternity leave period, provided she has given notice.

In a case taken to the ECJ, *Busch v Klinikum [2003] IRLR 625*, the court ruled that there was no right to bar an employee's return. The court held that view even though the woman's reason for returning early was that she had exhausted her maternity pay and was pregnant again. Returning to work and then immediately commencing another period of maternity leave gave her a new right to maternity pay.

Provided that a woman returns to work at the end of her ordinary maternity leave, she has the right to **return to her own job.** If, however, she is returning after a period of additional maternity leave, the **right to return is less comprehensive**. A woman would have the right to return to the job she was doing or, if not reasonably practicable, to another suitable or appropriate alternative. She returns on terms and conditions **no less favourable** than had she not taken maternity leave, with her seniority and pension rights as they would have been had she not taken leave. Her employer cannot refuse to take her back just because her replacement is found to be a more effective worker. The

ECJ, in the case of *Land Brandenburg v Sass [2005] IRLR 147*, has held that even if a woman takes more maternity leave than the minimum provided by law she still has the right to have all of the leave period included in calculating her service. The fact that a woman is **sick and unable to return** to work on the agreed date does not give the employer a right to treat her contract as terminated, according the Court of Appeal in the case of *Kwik Save v Greaves [1998] IRLR 245*. Any company sickness absence policy only applies at the point when the woman should have returned to work. At that point comparisons can be made with how male sick employees would be treated. Her period of illness, for the purpose of comparing her sickness record with that of other employees, runs from the end of her maternity leave. Her absence while on maternity leave cannot be taken into account.

These pay, leave and return-to-work provisions are all **minimum statutory requirements**. Many women will have **better arrangements**, negotiated by the union, contained in the contract of employment. Under *section 78 ERA 96* a woman who has the right to maternity leave under a contract, in addition to the statutory rights, may not exercise the two rights separately, but may take advantage of whichever right is the more favourable.

Appointment and dismissal

If an employer **refuses to hire** someone because she is pregnant this amounts to discrimination. A woman has **protection against dismissal** for a pregnancy-related reason during the pregnancy itself and while on maternity leave, regardless of the hours worked or length of service. As long as the employer knows she is pregnant and intends to take maternity leave, she gains the protection. Her employer will escape liability if there is no knowledge of her pregnancy. For this reason it is advisable for an employee to inform her employer of the fact that she is pregnant if symptoms of her pregnancy make it difficult for her to carry out her normal duties (*Ramdoolar v Bycity EAT/0236/04*). Even if another manager knows she is pregnant, if this is not the manager who dismisses then there is no liability as a pregnancy dismissal (*Eildon v Sharkey EATS/0109/03*). It does not matter that there might have been other reasons for the decision to dismiss her. Provided that at least part of the reason for dismissing her was to do with her pregnancy, a woman will be regarded as dismissed for an automatically unfair reason.

The European Court, in the case of *Hertz v Aldi Marked K/S [1994] IRLR 31*, laid down that a woman has the right to be protected from dismissal on pregnancy-related grounds for the whole period from the date of her pregnancy to the end of her maternity leave. In the case of *Webb v EMO Air Cargo [1995] IRLR 645*, the House of Lords held that dismissing an employee because she was pregnant was unlawful, even in circumstances where she had been hired as a replacement for an employee on maternity leave.

Protection against dismissal also extends to **temporary workers**. Where an employer chooses to replace a temporary worker on maternity leave with a permanent employee, this will amount to unlawful discrimination. The fact that, due to the nature of her contract her employer could lawfully have replaced her at any time, is not relevant *(Patefield v Belfast City Council [2000] IRLR 664)*. The rights of pregnant temporary workers have been strengthened by two rulings from the ECJ (see chapter 2 – Temporary employees).

A pregnant woman must be treated **no less favourably** than a male employee.

In the case of *Iske v P&O European Ferries [1997] IRLR 401,* the employer failed to offer a pregnant employee alternative work, although they would have done this for a male employee unable to perform his normal duties. This amounted to discrimination, according to the EAT.

Employers should not go ahead with a **disciplinary hearing** in the absence of an employee where this is due to a pregnancy-related illness *(Abbey National v Formoso [1999] IRLR 222)*.

A woman dismissed during pregnancy for a pregnancy-related reason has the right to take a claim under **sex discrimination law**, in addition to her rights to claim unfair dismissal. In sex discrimination cases there is **no upper limit** on the compensation award (see chapter 6 – Compensation).

Even in cases of **genuine redundancy** the tribunal can still determine whether the dismissal of a particular employee is connected with her pregnancy. Equally, if an employee on maternity leave is made redundant and not offered alternative work, this amounts to unfair dismissal, even if the alternative work arises sometime after the redundancy, but while she is still on maternity leave *(Philip Hodges v Kell [1994] IRLR 568).*

Section 92 ERA 96 states that any woman dismissed while pregnant or on maternity leave must be given a **written statement** giving reasons for her dismissal.

Paternity leave

Qualifying fathers or partners of someone on maternity or adoption leave have the right to **paid paternity leave**. The leave is specifically **to care for the new baby** or to **provide support** for the baby's mother.

To qualify the employee must **be an employee** who has worked for their employer for at least 26 weeks by the 15th week before the baby is due and be earning at least £82 a week. The employee has to give the employer **notice** of his intention to take paternity leave **before the 15th week** before the expected week of the baby's birth.

Statutory Paternity Pay (SPP) amounts to a maximum of **two weeks' paid leave**. Payment is set at £106.00 a week, or 90% of earnings if they are less than this.

The leave must be **taken as one period of either one or two weeks** within **eight weeks** of the baby's birth. It cannot be taken as separate days or in more than one period.

A **same-sex partner** of someone taking maternity or adoption leave can claim paternity leave if qualifying under the conditions listed above.

Adoption leave

Adoptive parents have rights to leave and pay broadly equivalent to those for statutory maternity leave. To qualify the parent must be **newly matched** with a child for adoption by an approved adoption agency. They must also be **employees** and have worked for their employer for at least 26 weeks by the date when they are matched.

Adoption leave must begin either from the date of the child's placement or up to 14 days before that date.

An adoptive parent has the right to 26 weeks' ordinary adoption leave followed by 26 weeks' additional (unpaid) leave. During their ordinary adoption leave they have the right to **Statutory Adoption Pay (SAP)** provided they are earning at least £82 a week. SAP is payable for 26 weeks at a flat rate of £106.00 (or 90% of earnings if these are less than £106.00 a week). The rights to return to work on conditions no less favourable are the same as apply to maternity leave. The partner of a person claiming adoption leave can claim paternity leave.

Parental and dependency leave

Employees are entitled to time off for parental leave under the *Maternity and Parental Leave etc Regulations 1999* and to **time off to deal with family emergencies** under *section ERA 96 57A*.

Working parents have the legal **right to a period of unpaid leave** of up to four weeks in a year and overall no more than **13 weeks** within the first five years of their child's life. For **adopted children** the leave is available in the five years from the time of adoption, provided that the child is still under the age of 18.

If a child is **disabled**, up to **18 weeks'** unpaid leave in total can be taken up to the child's 18th birthday.

Parental leave is available to parents who have worked for their employer for **at least a year**. Leave has to be taken in **blocks of no less than a week**. The right applies to each parent and for each child. Employees taking less than a week off lose a week of their entitlement In one case an employee who requested a day's parental leave to look after his son, was never formally given permission but nevertheless took the leave and was not covered by the parental leave regulations, according to the Court of Appeal. Since the regulations only gave a right to at least a week's leave his request for a day's leave could not have been made under the regulations. (*South Central Trains v Rodway A2/2004/1818*.

An employee who wants to take parental leave has to give at least **21 days' notice**. Where taking the leave at a particular time would cause undue disruption to the business, the employer can make the employee postpone the leave for a period of up to six months, except in the case of leave immediately after the child's birth.

Leave for **urgent family reasons** gives employees the right to reasonable unpaid time off to deal with family emergencies involving parents, children, a spouse or co-habitee, or anyone who looks to the employee for assistance. A family emergency is defined as sickness, accident, criminal injury, death, funerals, absence of the carer for a family member or serious problems at the child's school.

In the case of *Qua v John Ford Morrison [2003] IRLR 184*, the EAT made it clear that the right to time off is either to **deal with a variety of unexpected or sudden events** involving a dependant or to **make arrangements for their care**. The law covers time off following a dependant's death to make funeral arrangements and to attend the funeral. However, according to the EAT in the case of *Foster v Cartwright Black Solicitors [2004] IRLR 781*, it does not extend to the right to compassionate leave as a result of bereavement.

The EAT held that the tribunals need to ask whether time off was taken or requested. They then need to establish how frequently it was taken and if the employee had informed the employer of the likely length of absence, where possible. If both answers are positive the tribunal should then look at whether the request was for time off which falls within the entitlement and whether the amount of time off requested was reasonable.

Flexible working

An employee with responsibility for the upbringing of a child under the age of six (18 in the case of a disabled child) has the right to request, **in writing**, a flexible working pattern to **enable them to care for the child**. The request has to set out their desired working pattern and include an explanation of how the employer could accommodate the request. Employers have a statutory duty to consider the application seriously, rejecting it only if there are **clear business reasons** for doing so. Parents have the right provided that:

- they are **employees** working under a contract of employment;
- they have worked for their employer for **at least 26 weeks**;
- the application is made no later than two weeks before the **child's cut-off age**; and
- they have **not made another application** within the previous 12 months.

Once a request has been made the employer has to **arrange a meeting** within a specified timescale to hear the employee's reasons for the request. The employee has the right to bring along a companion (who gets the right to paid time off to attend). The employer must then write to the employee within 14 days, agreeing to the new work pattern or providing clear business grounds for rejecting it. There is a right to appeal but there is nothing specifically in the law to say that the same manager who turned down the request cannot also hear the appeal.

If the employer fails to comply with any of these requirements an employee can go to an employment tribunal or to **voluntary arbitration** (see chapter 1 – Binding arbitration), but only after all possible internal channels of appeal have been exhausted. If the case goes to a tribunal, it can award up to eight weeks' pay if the employer unreasonably turned down the request and up to an additional two weeks' pay if there was no meeting or if the employee was not allowed to bring a companion. Pay is capped at a maximum, currently £280 a week. This means that the most an employee can get is around £2,800.

Both the employee and companion have the right not to be victimised or dismissed, if the reason is to do with the exercise of the right to work flexibly.

The government has said that it is considering extending the right to request flexible work to all workers with caring responsibilities.

More information: LRD booklet *Working parents* (£4.25); LRD's *Workplace Report* has regular quarterly updates on discrimination law which cover the legal rules on pregnancy and maternity discrimination.

9. Industrial action

The legal position

The law relating to industrial action covers **not just strikes but lockouts, go slows, working to rule, refusing to cross picket lines** and **refusing to work with non-unionists**, regardless of whether or not industrial action is in breach of an agreed procedure. **Overtime bans** (even where overtime is voluntary), are normally considered as industrial action since the aim of those carrying it out is to put pressure on the employer to do, or not to do, something.

However, there are some rare circumstances where an overtime ban, called in response to an industrial dispute, nevertheless falls outside the definition of action in breach of contract. In one case the Privy Council (the highest appeal court for many Commonwealth countries) held that industrial action which involved the union refusing to make up overtime gangs to serve on the docks, could not be viewed as industrial action in breach of contract taken by the dockers themselves. The workers had played no role. They had not been asked to work and therefore could not be said to have refused *(Burgess v Stevedoring Services [2002] IRLR 810).*

In the UK there is **no positive legal right to strike**. Instead workers are protected by **"immunities"** if taking specific forms of industrial action that would otherwise be unlawful. How these immunities operate is explained below, although some workers — merchant seafarers, post office workers, the police, soldiers and some apprentices — may be excluded.

The *Employment Relations Act 2004* places a legal obligation on employers to seek to resolve disputes where conciliation or mediation has been agreed. A person who has authority to resolve the dispute must represent employers at such meetings.

The immunities

Section 219 of the *Trade Union and Labour Relations (Consolidation) Act 1992 (TULR(C)A 92)* establishes the "immunities". It says that an act done **"in contemplation or furtherance of a trade dispute"** is

not actionable in the courts just because it makes someone break a contract or interferes with a contract. For example, a union **leafleting campaign** aimed at persuading consumers not to buy a product, in the context of a dispute, does not fall within the definition of interference with a contract *(Middlebrook Mushrooms v TGWU [1993] IRLR 232).*

The first test is to establish whether or not a **"trade dispute"** exists. This is defined in *section 244 TULR(C)A 92* as a dispute that relates "wholly or mainly to": terms and conditions; recruitment, suspension or dismissal; work allocation; discipline; facilities for union officials; or the machinery of negotiation. A dispute over the impact of the national curriculum in schools on the working conditions of teachers, for example, falls within the definition *(LB Wandsworth v NASUWT [1993] IRLR 344).* So too does a dispute by teachers over the refusal to teach a disruptive pupil *(P v NASUWT [2003] IRLR 307).*

Where the industrial action is in furtherance of a "trade dispute" unions and members **do not risk civil legal action** provided that, if the action is authorised by the union, **a ballot** conforming to the requirements listed below has approved it.

The dispute has to be with an **employer in the UK**. And it must be a dispute **between workers and their employer**. The fact that the law refers to "workers" and not just "employees" (see chapter 2) means that it covers those employed under personal contracts. In 2001, Associated British Ports argued that "workers" could not take legitimate industrial action under UK law. The Court of Appeal rejected this, pointing out that the legislation applied to "workers", including the nominally self-employed on personal contracts.

The fact that industrial action has to involve a dispute with the workers' own employer has given employers the option of preventing industrial action by **reorganising** so that there is more than one employer. In a case taken in 1999, the train operating company Connex was able to get an injunction to stop industrial action by railworkers protesting about rail safety on the grounds that responsibility for safety lay with Railtrack, a separate company *(Connex SE v RMT [1999] IRLR 249).*

A dispute that is purely for **political ends** is not covered by the *section 244* definition and therefore cannot come within the *section 219* immunities.

A dispute over a **transfer to another employer** was a trade dispute, according to the Court of Appeal in the case of *Westminster City Council v UNISON [2001] IRLR 524*. It said that a dispute about the identity of a new employer was not a political dispute.

However, a dispute about the terms and conditions of **future workers** is not covered.

In 1999, the Court of Appeal held that employees calling for industrial action to win guarantees on the terms and conditions of future workers were not protected by *section 244*. The union took the claim to the European Court of Human Rights which, while accepting that a total ban on industrial action would be in breach, upheld the right of the state to impose limits on the right to take industrial action, provided these were proportionate *(UNISON v UK [2002] IRLR 497)*.

Under the *TULR(C)A 92*, **unions can be taken to court** for calling or endorsing unlawful action not covered by the immunities.

Overall the definition of a trade dispute is very **narrow**. There are good grounds for believing it violates international standards set by the **International Labour Organisation (ILO).**

The following forms of industrial action are **denied the protection of the immunities**: action that seeks to enforce union membership *(section 222)*; action in protest at a dismissal following earlier unofficial action *(section 223)*; secondary action (see below); and action intended to pressurise the employer to impose a union recognition requirement on a supplier or contractor *(section 225)*.

Under *section 235A TULR(C)A 92*, an individual who claims that the **supply of goods or services** has been affected by unlawful industrial action (for example, action carried out without a fully complying ballot) may apply to the High Court for an order against the union to discontinue its authorisation or endorsement of industrial action. Such individuals, who do not have to show that they would have been entitled to be supplied with the goods or services in question, can be assisted by the **Certification Officer** (see chapter 5 – Internal union matters).

Unions are not allowed to discipline workers who refuse to support industrial action.

Workplace reps

In theory, any **individual worker**, including a representative, can be sued by the employer for breaking a contract by taking industrial action. In practice, this is unlikely to happen since the employer can only claim **damages limited to the actual loss** caused by that employee and this is difficult to prove.

Workplace representatives can claim the *section 219* immunities. They **are protected** if they induce someone to break or interfere with a contract (not just a contract of employment), or threaten to do so, provided that they are acting "in contemplation or furtherance of a trade dispute" (see above). They can picket their workplace, persuade others to strike, and ask workers not to deliver goods.

A more likely response from the employer to industrial action is **dismissal** (see below – How the law aids employers), but even this is relatively rare. Furthermore, there is a **right to be protected** against unfair dismissal in at least the first 12 weeks of strike action. Any days when employees are "locked out" by their employers are excluded from the calculation of the 12 weeks (*Employment Relations Act 2004*).

Most employers want the dispute to end (to their satisfaction if at all possible) and work to resume, so use of the law by employers is not usually the main problem for representatives. The most important thing is to ensure that any action taken is **well organised** and that **union solidarity is maintained**. Experience also demonstrates that employers are more likely to use the law when they perceive workplace organisation to be weak.

However, this is not to say that representatives will never be threatened with legal action. Employers have threatened writs and in some cases issued injunctions (see below – How the law aids employers).

"Official" or "unofficial" action

The law describes a strike or any other kind of industrial action as "official" where the employee is a member of a trade union and the union has **authorised or endorsed the action** in question; or the employee is not a member of a trade union but there are among those taking part in the industrial action members of a trade union, which has authorised or endorsed that action.

Section 20 TULR(C)A 92 states that the action shall be taken to have been authorised or endorsed by a trade union where it was taken by:

- a person **empowered by the rules** to do, authorise or endorse acts of the kind in question;
- the **principal executive committee** or the president or general secretary; or
- **any other committee** of the union or any other official of the union (whether employed by it or not).

And where a **group of people organises** or co-ordinates the industrial action, any decision taken by the group or an individual of the group comes within the definition of "any other committee".

Section 21 also makes **unions legally responsible for all industrial action**, including that authorised by local representatives, even if the union views their action as unofficial because it is contrary to union rules. However, the union may **"repudiate"** (disown) the action. Once unofficial action has commenced, if the union wishes to make it official, it must first repudiate it and then hold the ballot. The union must, as soon as the action comes to its attention, do its best to give a copy of the repudiation, in writing, to every member taking part, or likely to take part in the action. A copy must also be given to the employer *(section 21 TULR(C)A 92)*.

If the union has not repudiated unlawful action, or if it itself has authorised action not in compliance with all the legal rules, it leaves itself open to legal action brought by the employer or a customer or supplier of the employer. This can be by way of an **injunction** (see below).

Employers may lawfully **victimise unofficial strikers** by dismissing selected individuals taking unofficial action (see below). Any subsequent strike action in support of an individual dismissed for taking part in unofficial action automatically loses the protection of the immunities, even if the later action is official and has been balloted on.

Balloting

Sections 226-235 TULR(C)A 92 **remove the immunities,** even where the action otherwise is not unlawful, where there has not been a ballot which complies with **all** of the following requirements:

- it must fulfil the **notice requirements to employers** (see below);
- it must be a **secret postal ballot**, with the ballot paper sent to the member's nominated address and specifying the address and date for return *(sections 227-230 TULR(C)A 92)*;
- **at least seven days** must be allowed for its return if first class (14 days if second class);
- **an independent scrutineer**, responsible for the eventual preparation of a report on the ballot arrangements, must be appointed and named on the ballot paper in all ballots of more than 50 workers *(section 226)*;
- the form must specify **who is authorised to call the action** *(section 229)*;
- **voters must be asked** whether they support strike action or action short of a strike. If being asked to vote on both this must be in the form of two separate questions *(section 229)*;
- if **action short of a full strike** (e.g. an overtime ban) is to be called, but may be **followed by full strike action**, workers must be asked **two separate questions**, one relating to the limited action and the other to the full strike action;
- members must be able to **indicate by "yes"/"no"** their views on the action proposed *(section 226)*;
- the forms must be **numbered consecutively**;
- the form must tell employees of their **rights not to be unfairly dismissed** (see below);
- the form must **contain the statement**: "If you take part in a strike or other industrial action, you may be in breach of your contract of employment", regardless of whether or not there would be a breach *(section 229)*;
- **only those that the union is calling on to take action** need to be balloted (*section 227)*;
- **separate ballots** must be held for **separate workplaces**, unless the dispute involves only common terms. Where there is at least one individual who is affected by the dispute in each of the workplaces, the ballots can be **aggregated** into a single ballot. Ballots can also be aggregated where linked by occupation and employer(s) *(section 228)*;
- where there have been separate ballots only those **workplaces with**

a majority for strike action can be called out;

- as soon as possible after the vote, members should be **informed of the number of votes cast**, those in favour, those against and those spoilt *(section 231);* and
- industrial action must **commence within four weeks** of the last day of voting, counting that day as day one *(RJB Mining v NUM [1995] IRLR 556).* Employers and unions can **agree to extend** this period by an additional **four weeks**. If the date when the action should have begun is delayed due to legal proceedings, it has to be called within an overall 12-week period *(section 234).*

Those being balloted must be told on the ballot paper that **any dismissal during an official, lawful dispute** "will be unfair if it takes place fewer than 12 weeks after you started taking part in the action". They will also be told that a dismissal outside the 12 weeks can still be unfair.

It is important that all these rules are complied with. It is particularly important that the union **ballots all those who should be included**, because they are likely to be called on to take industrial action. In the case of *RMT v Midland Mainline [2001] IRLR 813*, the Court of Appeal ruled that a ballot was invalid because not everyone had been balloted. The union was not aware that a group of workers was in the appropriate grade and had therefore not included them in the ballot.

The case of *London Underground v RMT [1995] IRLR 636,* also dealt with who should be balloted. The Court of Appeal held that the fact that the union had not balloted employees who were not its members prior to the ballot, but joined subsequently, did not invalidate the ballot.

Those being balloted are those whom the union considers will be called upon to take industrial action, but they do not all have to be directly affected by the issue over which the ballot is being called. In the case of *BT v CWU [2004] IRLR 58,* the High Court held that the union had not breached the law when, in a dispute over a new productivity scheme, some of the members it balloted would not have been party to the new scheme. There has to be a **dispute in existence**. The London Underground workers' union NUR (now RMT), by including in its strike ballot matters which were not yet the subject of an industrial dispute, was held by the High Court to have lost its protection (*London Underground v NUR [1989] IRLR 341).*

The ballot does not have to define every single issue of the dispute *(Associated British Ports v TGWU [1989] IRLR 399).*

Where the ballot paper contains two separate questions, a "yes" majority is determined in relation to the numbers voting "yes" to that question. The fact that they may not represent a majority of all those completing the ballot paper is not relevant *(West Midlands Travel v TGWU [1994] IRLR 578).*

A union is entitled to **campaign for a "yes" vote** in a ballot. This does not amount to an unlawful call for or endorsement of industrial action before the date of the ballot *(LB Newham v NALGO [1993] IRLR 83).*

Although the law states that the ballot paper must specify, in the event of a "yes" vote, **who can call action**, the courts have stressed that common sense permits a certain amount of delegation.

In a dispute called by the TGWU general union, the ballot paper indicated that the general secretary was the officer authorised to call the strike. However, the fact that the actual call was made by another official, after consultation with the general secretary, did not invalidate the ballot *(Tanks & Drums v TGWU [1991] IRLR 372).*

The High Court has ruled that a union is not expected to achieve 100% perfection in conducting ballots, so long as it has in place **structures which enable it to properly ballot** all the relevant workers *(RJB Mining v NUM [1997] IRLR 621).* Additionally, *section 232B TULR(C)A 92* says that where a union **makes "accidental mistakes"** in terms of those who are balloted, on a scale unlikely to affect the outcome, this will not invalidate the whole procedure.

The **"place of work"** for the purpose of ballots is not narrowly defined as the building occupied by the employee, according to the Court of Appeal in the case of *Intercity West Coast v RMT [1996] IRLR 583.* This meant that a single ballot covering all staff working at Manchester Piccadilly railway station was valid even though it covered two rail operating companies that had separate administrative buildings at the station.

The fact that **more than one employer** is involved does not mean that different ballots have to be organised, provided that all those being balloted share common terms and conditions *(University of Central England and Kingston University v NALGO [1993] IRLR 81).* This is also the case where they comply with the requirements regarding aggregated ballots (see above).

The four-week rule for commencing industrial action does not prevent a union **suspending action** and then re-imposing it *(Monsanto v TGWU [1986] IRLR 406)*. However, the gap between the suspension and re-imposition of the action should not be too long, or indicate a change in tactics by the union, otherwise it might find that the subsequent action is not covered by the ballot *(Post Office v UCW [1990] IRLR 143)*. Alternatively there can be **agreement over the length of any suspension of action**. Under *section 234A TULR(C)A 92*, unions can suspend industrial action for talks and then resume it without having to go through the balloting procedure again, provided there is agreement from the employer for this course of action, normally with the aim of trying to restart negotiations. Where this happens the union has to agree not to re-authorise industrial action before an agreed date.

Individual union members can, using *section 109 TULR(C)A 92*, take legal action against their own unions where ballots have not been held before official action. They can use the services of the Certification Officer to do this (see chapter 5 – Internal union matters).

Requirements to notify employers

To comply with the legislation a union must also **give notice to employers** at four key stages as set out below. Unions **do not have to name** those whom they intend to ballot. However, currently (May 2005) they must, under *section 226A TULR(C)A 92*, give information they possess to identify the types of workers being balloted. From 1 October 2005, the requirements to identify workers in this way will change. At that point in time it will be sufficient if the union gives notice of the categories of workers being called upon to take industrial action. The sort of information the union has to forward includes the number, category or workplace of the employees concerned. In the *Westminster* case (see above – The immunities) the Court of Appeal said that the union's notification to the council was sufficient. This said that the ballot would cover "all those staff who pay their subscription via the deduction of contributions at source system". It then stated the location of those to be balloted, what jobs they did and how many there were. However, merely stating that the union will ballot "all members of the union, employed in all categories at all workplaces" did not meet the requirements of *section 226A*, according to the following case.

In the case of *RMT v London Underground [2001] IRLR 228* the Court of Appeal held that the intention of the law remains that of ensuring that employers have as much information as unions can provide. The court said that employers were entitled to information that the union or any of its officers (including branch officers) held, which would enable employers to try and dissuade workers from taking action and, if unsuccessful, make plans to avoid or minimise disruption. The judges pointed out that the aim of the change to the law in 1999 (that meant unions no longer had to name those being balloted) was not to make things easier for unions. They could not argue that they had no obligation to provide the information because the new law actually imposed more of a burden on them.

This position was confirmed in the case of *Willerby Holiday Homes v UCATT, IDS Brief 749* where the High Court ruled that a ballot was unlawful because the union had balloted the wrong members, even though it had records which could have been used to rectify their mistake.

Provisions in the *Employment Relations Act 2004* (in force with effect from 1 October 2005) mean that unions will only have to provide the employer with a **list of the categories of worker** who are being balloted and a **list of their workplaces**, where an officer of the union holds the information. They will also have to give the total number of workers by category and by workplace, but without any requirement to name the workers.

Giving notice to employers

Stage 1 — when taking a decision to ballot for industrial action, a union must first **notify the employer in writing** at least seven days before the ballot that the union **intends to hold a ballot**, of **the date when it believes the ballot will begin**, and **describing employees entitled to vote**. (However, with effect from 1 October 2005, the requirement is only to give a list of the categories of worker and a list of their workplaces.)

Stage 2 — no later than **three days** before the ballot commences, the employer must have received a **sample copy of the ballot paper**.

Stage 3 — as soon as possible after the ballot result has been declared, the union has to **notify the employer of the outcome**.

Stage 4 — after the stage 3 notice, and at least seven days before the industrial action (which has been the subject of the ballot) begins, the union has again to **notify the employer in writing** giving information on the number, category or workplaces of the employees being called upon to take action; the date **when the action will begin**, or the date of each if planning a series of stoppages; and stating that it **gives notice under *section 234* of the 1992 Act**. The notice must also specify whether the action planned is **continuous** (giving the intended date when it will commence) or **discontinuous** (giving the intended dates when it will occur).

A Department of Trade and Industry (DTI) **code of practice**, *Industrial action ballots and notice to employers*, gives practical guidance on how the law should apply. In March 2005, the DTI published a consultation document aimed at revising the code of practice.

Picketing

Under *section 220 TULR(C)A 92* workers "in contemplation or furtherance of a trade dispute" (see above) can **lawfully picket** at or near their place of work, provided that the purpose is only peacefully to obtain or communicate information or persuade a person not to work. But, as is the case with industrial action, the **immunities** only protect them from being sued for breach of contract. They do not provide protection for activities like trespass, or from action under criminal law (see below).

If workers are not able to picket immediately in front of their workplace, the requirement that it is **"at or near"** allows some leeway.

Workers dismissed by a company sited on a trading estate were unable to picket their own workplace so they mounted a picket on the entrance to the estate. The Court of Appeal ruled that this was "at or near" their place of work *(Rayware v TGWU [1989] IRLR 134).*

Union officials representing members can picket their members' place of work. Those working from a number of different locations can lawfully picket any work location or alternatively their work headquarters, as long as they have actually worked from those different locations. If they were merely "occasional ports of call" they would not be regarded as the individual's place of work *(Union Traffic v TGWU [1989] IRLR 127)*. Workers **dismissed while on strike** have a continuing right to picket lawfully at their former place of work.

The law does not lay down the **number who can picket**. Often the police try to limit it to six, but they should issue a warning to this effect. This figure comes from the DTI *Code of practice on picketing* which says:

"Pickets and their organisers should ensure that in general the number of pickets does not exceed six at any entrance to a workplace; frequently a smaller number will be appropriate".

Although this code, like others, is only advisory, a 1985 case gave police additional support in attempts to reduce numbers to six.

During the 1984-85 miners' strike, pickets were posted at a pit in South Wales. Although six pickets stood outside the colliery gates, about 60 demonstrated across the road. The court ruled that the mass demonstration was a common law nuisance *(Thomas v South Wales NUM [1985] IRLR 136).*

Pickets are more likely to face the **criminal law** (see below) than have their picket declared outside the *section 220* protection. The criminal law is operated by the police and usually involves obstruction or breach of the peace offences. However, in the majority of cases pickets take place without the intervention of the law.

Supporting other workers

Solidarity has always played an important role for trade unionists, but this unity among workers has been undermined by the legislation introduced since 1980 and still in force. Under *section 224 TULR(C)A 92*, a person inducing or threatening another to break a contract of employment, which is not with the employer party to the dispute, is not protected by the immunities. If a union threatens to picket other places of work this will be unlawful.

The only form of secondary action permitted is where workers **picketing at or near** their place of work persuade other workers not employed there not to deliver goods or to enter the work premises.

How the law aids employers

The use of the courts by an employer is still uncommon and the success or failure of a dispute usually depends more on the level of workplace union organisation than on any legal threat from the employer. Nevertheless trade union reps need to understand how employers can use the law.

Injunctions

The injunction (interdict in Scotland) is the most popular legal remedy sought by employers. An injunction is a **court order to do or to refrain from doing something**. It may be granted where:

- there is an allegation of **unlawful action**;
- a **serious issue** is to be tried;
- the **employer alleges a harm greater** than that which the employees would suffer by having to call off their action; and
- where the employer alleges that **damages** awarded at a subsequent full trial would not adequately compensate for the harm suffered.

In employment matters an injunction is generally used to try to halt industrial action and is given in the form of an **"interlocutory injunction"** — that is an injunction intended as an interim measure until the case comes to trial. In practice, however, very few cases come to trial because the granting of the injunction itself serves the employer's purpose of stopping the action.

Failure to comply with injunctions can lead to **contempt of court** proceedings, and in some circumstances, to sequestration (seizing) of the union's assets. This can occur where a union has called, or not repudiated, unlawful action. If the union does repudiate the action, union funds are safeguarded but members are then at risk of selective dismissal.

Normally unions are the targets for injunctions, but they can be taken out against **one or more named individuals**, although failure to name an individual properly can result in the injunction failing.

If an injunction is served, those receiving it have to decide whether to comply or risk contempt of court. There have been few cases of contempt of court proceedings against individual union members and it should be noted that *section 236 TULR(C)A 92* says that no court can compel an individual employee to do any work or to attend work.

Section 221 TULR(C)A 92 puts some limitations on the granting of injunctions. It says that **where one party is not present**, and it could be argued that the action is in furtherance of a trade dispute, the court should give every opportunity for that party to attend before granting the injunction. In practice, however, the courts have sometimes ignored this principle and granted injunctions in the union's absence.

Dismissal

Section 238A TULR(C)A 92 gives employees **protection from dismissal during the first 12 weeks** of any lawful, balloted, official industrial action. During these 12 weeks the protection is absolute, provided that no other unlawful act, other than the employee's breach of contract, has occurred. Any dismissal, **regardless of how long the employee has worked, or their age, is automatically unfair** unless a tribunal decides that the dismissal was not to do with the industrial action. **Information** about these rights **must be included** on the industrial action ballot paper.

The 12-week period **can be extended** if employees are still taking action but, in the view of the tribunal, the employer has not taken reasonable procedural steps to seek to resolve the dispute. This could be, for example, where there was an offer to re-open negotiations, or of mediation or conciliation that was offered and unreasonably refused. For further information see chapter 10 – Dismissal while on strike.

Deducting pay

Employers may try to deduct pay, particularly when the action being taken is short of full strike action, such as a boycott of some work. A House of Lords decision in 1987 upholds their right to do this.

The law gives employers wide powers more generally to deduct pay in response to industrial action. A Court of Appeal decision in 1989 suggests that if the employer indicates that partial work is not satisfactory, the employee can have **all pay withheld**, including that for work done and accepted by the employer *(Wiluszynski v LB Tower Hamlets [1989] IRLR 259).*

The ruling in the case of *Ticehurst and Thompson v BT [1992] IRLR 219* took this interpretation one stage further. It stated that an employer could continue to refuse to pay employees ready and willing to carry out their full normal duties following a stoppage of work, so long as the employees continued to refuse to sign a statement disassociating them from their union's backing for industrial action.

There had been a practice (particularly in the education sector) of employers deducting 1/195th of annual pay for each day of strike action. However, in the case of *Smith v Kent High Court HQ03X00453*, the court ruled that this was unlawful and that the maximum lawful deduction is 1/365th of annual salary for each day of strike.

Pay deductions because of industrial action are not protected under *section 16* of the *Employment Rights Act (ERA 96)* (see chapter 4 – Deductions and underpayments) and regardless of whether a deduction is 'lawful', a tribunal cannot rule on deductions from wages resulting from industrial action. However, it can make a finding of fact as to whether what has taken place amounted to industrial action, rather than just relying on an allegation by the employer that industrial action did occur (*Gill v Ford Motor Co [2004] IRLR 840*).

Lockouts

Employers may try to anticipate a dispute by locking out workers. A lockout is defined in *section 235(4) ERA 96* to **include closures or suspensions** by the employer with a view to forcing workers to accept specific terms or conditions.

Establishing when a lockout has taken place can present difficulties, but it may be important where individuals are claiming **unfair dismissal**, as employees who have been locked out may have a slightly better chance of pursuing a claim successfully. The *Employment Relations Act 2004* extends the period of protection from unfair dismissal to include any time when employees are locked out. Thus if a group of workers want to return to work after being on strike for 12 weeks and their employer refuses to let them back they will still have dismissal protection.

Locked out workers are treated in exactly the same way as strikers as far as state benefits are concerned (see below).

Criminal law

There are a few instances where the criminal law can be used against workers taking industrial action. In these circumstances the police may instigate the actual prosecution.

Workers who are **picketing** may face **obstruction or breach of the peace** charges. These can include unreasonable obstruction of the highway and/or wilful obstruction of a police officer. Under the *Public Order Act 1986*, individuals may be charged with disorderly conduct, threatening behaviour, riot, violent disorder or affray. But the standard of proof required to convict on these charges is "beyond reasonable doubt", a much higher requirement than applies to civil law cases.

There are **four offences** that may be committed by people involved in picketing. They are: the use of violence; persistent following; hiding tools; and picketing a person's home. Although the law is rarely used, it was relevant in a 1984 "work in".

Laboratory staff employed by Fife Health Authority occupied their lab and began a "work in" as part of a long-running dispute. The "work in" ended when the police smashed down the door, arrested them and charged them. The court ruled that the workers were not protected by the immunities because these only applied to civil action *(Galt v Philp and Others [1984] IRLR 156).*

Section 15 TULR(C)A 92 furthermore makes it unlawful for the union to **pay an individual's fines** for criminal activity or contempt of court. *Section 16* gives individual members a right to go to court if union trustees permit the application of union funds for "unlawful purposes".

Conspiracy is another criminal charge available under the *Criminal Law Act 1977*. Conspiracy involves the agreement by two or more people to pursue a course of action which would necessarily involve the committing of an offence. The penalty for conspiracy cannot be higher than for the offence itself, and under *section 1*, unlawful civil action in the course of a dispute does not give rise to a conspiracy charge.

State benefits for strikers

Although strikers are **mostly excluded from claiming state benefits**, they should be able to continue to receive Working Tax Credit and Child Tax Credit.

For all other benefits, anyone taking industrial action loses entitlement to claim. This also applies to anyone **laid off** because of industrial action, unless it can be shown that they have no direct interest in the dispute at their place of work. If, by custom and practice, any pay increase obtained by those on strike would be given to those laid off, they too will be disqualified from benefits.

The **dependants of strikers** or those laid off and disqualified have an entitlement to claim benefit. However, in calculating their "personal allowances" for the purpose of assessing entitlement to means-tested benefits (for example Income Support), a **deduction of £30.80 a week** will be made (2005/06). This is supposed to represent the amount the striker would be receiving in union strike pay, but is deducted regardless of whether or not any strike pay is actually received. Any strike pay over that amount is classed as income and taken fully into account when assessing entitlement. The dependants of non-union members who are on strike have the same amount deducted.

More information: for full details of entitlement to benefits see the LRD booklet *State Benefits & Tax Credits 2005* (£5.45)

10. Dismissal

Every year thousands of people pursue unfair dismissal claims. It is the largest single category of claims coming before tribunals. However, the right to go to a tribunal was limited by changes in the *Employment Act 2002*, that came into force on 1 October 2004 (see chapter 1). These mean that claimants can no longer take their unfair dismissal claims to employment tribunals until they have followed the internal workplace disciplinary or grievance procedures.

An employer can only fairly dismiss an employee in accordance with section 98 ERA96, if they can show that:

- they had a **potentially fair reason** for the dismissal; and
- they **acted reasonably** in all the circumstances of the case.

For a dismissal to be reasonable the employer must have followed a fair procedure and show that dismissal was within a **reasonable range of responses.**

In cases to do with the employee's conduct, the employer must have carried out a reasonable investigation into the conduct. However, the need for an investigation is not limited to cases of misconduct. For example, investigation may also be necessary in cases of capability. A tribunal will only take into account facts known to the employer at the time of the dismissal.

What is a dismissal?

Section 95 of the *Employment Rights Act 1996 (ERA 96)* lays down the main circumstances that amount to a dismissal. An employee is dismissed if one of the following occurs:

- the **employment contract is terminated** with or without notice;
- a **fixed-term contract** is not renewed;
- the **employee leaves** but claims this is as a result of the employer's conduct (**constructive dismissal**);
- a **redundancy** takes place;
- a woman is not allowed to return to work after **maternity leave**;
- the employer claims there has been a **"self dismissal"**; or
- there is a refusal to re-employ after a **takeover**.

The first criterion therefore is that the **contract has to have ended**. It is still a dismissal even if the employee might have anticipated the contract would end, as in the case of a **fixed-term contract** (see below).

A **resignation by the employee** will bring the contract to an end, usually at the end of the period of contractual notice the employee had to give. In one case *(McLoughlin v Sutcliffe Catering EAT/0932/01)* the employee, on tendering her notice, was put on garden leave (told to stay at home with pay until the notice period ended) as allowed under the contract. She changed her mind and when she was not allowed to withdraw her notice she took an unfair dismissal claim. The EAT held that the employer had not dismissed her and therefore there was no right to claim. In the case of *Healey v Bridgend CBC [2004] ICR 561*, the Court of Appeal held that an employee who had **accepted early retirement** under an ill-health retirement scheme had no right to be paid during what would otherwise have been her notice period had she not resigned.

However, where a resignation is **given in haste** and appears to be the outcome of a personality clash, employers should exercise caution before acting upon it *(Kwik-Fit v Lineham [1992] IRLR 156).* In any case the resignation has to be communicated to the employer. An employee who has drafted a letter of resignation cannot be said to have resigned until the letter is sent *(Edwards v Surrey Police [1999] IRLR 456).*

Termination with/without notice

An employee on a permanent contract has a **right to notice** if the contract is terminated. The notice to end an employment contract must be stated in the contract and, under *section 86 ERA 96*, must be at least:

- **one week** — if you have worked between one month and two years; or
- **one week for each year** — if you have worked between two and 12 years.

It is important to establish what entitlement to notice your employer has to give you and also what **notice you have to give** if you want to leave. The minimum notice an employee has to give is **one week**, unless the contract provides for longer notice. If an employee fails to give proper notice this too amounts to a breach of contract. However, that does not mean that the employer can **refuse to pay** money due.

Mrs Sands-Ellison failed to give proper notice when she decided to resign. As a result her employer refused to pay her holiday pay which she was due. The EAT held that this amounted to an unlawful deduction from her wages. Even though her contract only guaranteed her holiday pay if she gave notice, the EAT said that her employer still did not have a right to deduct pay *(Sands-Ellison v One Call Insurance EAT/0002/02).*

While everyone has the right to the minimum statutory notice, there will often be a better contractual entitlement. However, it is important that the **contract makes it clear** that during the period of notice the employee will have the right to be paid, or employees may lose out, as the following case shows.

Mr Budd was off work on long-term sickness absence and had exhausted his contractual entitlement to sick pay. After being off for more than two years the employer gave him contractual notice of termination, which amounted to a week more than under the statutory scheme. He was not paid during the notice period. Budd claimed the right to payment for all of the contractual notice period, or at least for the statutory notice period. The EAT held that statutory rights, including the right to payment, are "disapplied" where contractual notice is at least one week more than statutory notice. Budd had the right to longer notice but since there was nothing in his contract that said he would be paid during that notice, he had no entitlement to pay *(Scotts Co v Budd [2003] IRLR 145).*

If the employer has **not given proper notice** a claim can be taken to an employment tribunal. If the contract does not specify the notice period, the courts can imply "reasonable" notice, taking account of the employee's length of service and seniority. However, if an employee waives the right to notice there is no breach of contract *(Baldwin v British Coal [1995] IRLR 139)*. A contract may state that the employer can dismiss without notice. This does not of itself mean that there is a right to dismiss without pay in lieu, according to the Court of Appeal in the case of *T&K Home Improvements v Skilton [2000] IRLR 595.*

If employees are dismissed without notice they must **mitigate** (lessen) the amount that would be claimed in damages for not receiving contractual notice. This applies where there is a term in the contract that gives the employer, but not the employee, the option of **pay in lieu of notice** *(Cerberus Software v Rowley [2001] IRLR 160)*. Furthermore, if the contract allows for pay in lieu of notice, the employer choosing this option can pay wages without any commission that would have been earned had the employee worked *(Marshall Cambridge v Hamblin [1994] IRLR 260)*. Pay in lieu of notice is taxable.

Non-renewal of a fixed-term contract

When a temporary (fixed-term) contract comes to an end in law this is **still regarded as a dismissal**. Whether or not it is unfair depends on the reasons for the termination and whether the employee qualifies for unfair dismissal protection. This normally requires continuous employment of a year or more. It is unlawful to ask fixed-term contract employees to agree to **waive their rights** to unfair dismissal protection (see chapter 2 – Temporary employees).

Constructive dismissal

A constructive dismissal is one where the **employee resigns** but claims that the **employer's conduct left no alternative**. The conduct must amount to a **serious breach of an express or implied contract term** (see chapter 3 – Contract changes). Additionally, the resignation must be on account of the breach.

To claim constructive dismissal **three elements** must be present:

- the employer must have **breached the contract**;
- the employee must have **left as a consequence** of that breach; and
- there has to have been **no significant delay** between the breach and the employee's departure.

These three tests have been laid down in the case of *Rofique v The Governing Body of Turves Green Girls' School EAT/569/02* when it held that an employee who resigned because she had been offered a new job could not pursue a constructive dismissal claim. Her resignation was not on account of her employer's breach of contract.

If an employee does delay this could mean a loss of the right to claim constructive dismissal. In the case of *El Hoshi v Pizza Express Restaurants EAT/0857/03*, the EAT held that a delay in resigning *could* mean loss of constructive dismissal rights although in this case it did not because the reason for the delay was due to the employee being off sick at the time.

The employer **needs to know** why the employee has resigned. Failing to tell the employer the reason for the resignation makes it more difficult to claim constructive dismissal.

Where the employer **threatens to dismiss** and as a consequence the employee resigns, this too can be a constructive dismissal. And, according to the case of *Jones v Mid Glamorgan CC [1997] IRLR 685,* this is so where the dismissal threat was **not the sole reason** the employee resigned. In the *Greenaway* case (see chapter 3 – Contract changes), the employer's conduct in trying to alter the shift arrangements was held to be an **anticipatory breach** of contract, entitling her to resign and claim constructive dismissal.

An employee resigned following the removal of some of his duties in breach of his contract. The tribunal upheld his claim of constructive dismissal, even though the decision to remove the duties had been carried out in breach of the club's own rules and therefore was invalid in any case *(Warnes v Trustees of Cheriton Oddfellows Social Club [1993] IRLR 58).*

A constructive dismissal does not rely on there having been just one serious action by the employer. The EAT has held that the employee can rely on a **cumulative effect**, such as in a case of an employee walking out after an argument with the supervisor which was the "last straw" in a whole series of incidents. It does not matter even if **none of the incidents in themselves would amount to a serious breach**, if together they would amount to a breach or even if there is a **gap in time** between the previous action by the employer and the "last straw" action. In one case, the EAT held that even a gap of as much as 18 months could be counted. An employer's action in **appointing someone else to an employee's job**, where in good faith they believe that the employee will not be returning to work, can still amount to constructive dismissal *(Brown v JBD Engineering [1993] IRLR 568).* So too can action by the employer which leaves the employee with no alternative but to leave, even if it was **not the employer's intention** to get rid of the employee. Inviting an employee to attend a disciplinary hearing where it is clear that a decision has already been made, and that the employee's presence is only to see if there are any mitigating circumstances, can also amount to a constructive dismissal. However, to amount to a "last straw" constructive dismissal, while the final action causing the employee to resign does not have itself to amount to a breach of contract, it is unlikely to be something "reasonable" or "justifiable" (*LB Waltham Forest v Omilaju [2005] IRLR 35*).

An employee can still request reinstatement or re-engagement without jeopardising a constructive dismissal claim. The request does not imply that trust and confidence has not been broken.

The failure to pursue a grievance bars the employee from taking a constructive dismissal claim to a tribunal.

Other types of dismissal

A dismissal for **redundancy**, even when fair and lawful, is still a dismissal by the employer (see chapter 11).

Deborah Lassman felt she had no alternative but to take redundancy after the arrival of a new manager. The hotel tried to argue that by accepting redundancy she had not been dismissed. The EAT held that even where a redundancy is voluntary it still amounts to a dismissal *(Lassman v De Vere University Arms Hotel [2003] ICR 44)*.

A refusal to allow a woman the right to return to work after maternity leave is also a dismissal (see chapter 8 – Returning to work).

In most circumstances a **"self dismissal"** can still be a dismissal by an employer. For example, some contracts suggest that where a worker goes on leave and fails to return on a given day, the employment contract is automatically terminated — in effect, a "self dismissal". However, in most cases tribunals will view this as a dismissal by the employer *(Igbo v Johnson Matthey Chemicals [1986] IRLR 215)*.

In dismissals following a **transfer under TUPE** (see chapter 12), claims should be brought against the **new employer** *(Thompson v Walon [1997] IRLR 343)*. An employee cannot take an unfair dismissal claim against a **third party** for inducing the dismissal *(Wilson v Housing Corporation [1997] IRLR 346)*.

Fair dismissal

It is unlawful for employees to be dismissed for an **automatically unfair reason** (see below). Additionally, if they have worked for their employer for at least a year, employees can only be dismissed for a **"fair" reason**. The grounds for a fair dismissal under s*ection 98 ERA 96* relate to:

- **capability** or **qualifications** to perform the work;
- **conduct**;
- **redundancy**;
- complying with **legislation** (e.g.. *Health and Safety at Work Act*); or
- "some other **substantial reason**".

Dismissal for all other reasons is **unfair**.

Capability

A **"capability"** dismissal normally relates to **"skill, aptitude, health or any other physical or mental quality"**. In law a worker can be fairly dismissed due to a **poor sickness record**. However, in such circumstances an employer will usually have to show that attempts were made to establish the employee's medical condition and that alternatives to dismissal were examined (see chapter 7 – Dismissal while sick). If the worker is disabled, within the meaning of the *Disability Discrimination Act 1995*, there is additional protection (see chapter 6 – Disability discrimination).

The employee's capabilities are **assessed at the date of the dismissal**. The employer does not have an obligation to monitor the decision to dismiss by taking account of a change in circumstances between that date and the date of the appeal *(Two Shires Ambulance NHS Trust v Brooks EAT/0330/02)*.

If a dismissal is on the grounds of skill or aptitude the employer would be expected to have **given warnings** and stated the standards of work required and the consequences of failing to meet them. There would also be a requirement to show that alternatives, such as a transfer to another job, had been considered.

Conduct

A conduct dismissal is one based on the employee's conduct or, more accurately, **misconduct**. Employers should **make clear** to employees what they would **regard as misconduct**. A failure to do this could make an otherwise fair dismissal unfair.

Ms Goudie was dismissed for unacceptable misuse of her employer's computer facilities. Her employer had never made it clear that there was such a policy against personal use. The dismissal was therefore unfair (*Royal Bank of Scotland v Goudie EAT/0693/03).*

Whatever disciplinary rules an employer seeks to impose, they should be **clear, well known and applied consistently**. In other words, the employer must deal in the same way with the same disciplinary offence, although the outcome can be different. In the case of *LB Harrow v Cunningham [1996] IRLR 256,* the EAT confirmed that employers could take factors like the employee's record into account and impose different penalties for the same offence. Where the disciplinary procedure can impose **warnings that expire after a period of time**, employers should not use the previous warning as a grounds for dismissal for a further offence, if the warning has expired.

One situation when it would be lawful for an employer to treat two employees differently would be where **different managers** dealt with the cases and one was not aware of the decision of the other.

Dismissal for a **single act of misconduct** will usually only be regarded as fair in very serious cases. But the Court of Appeal has held that it was fair for the employers to dismiss an employee whom they suspected was intending to breach a works rule, even though he had not done so at the time when he was apprehended *(BRB v Jackson [1994] IRLR 235).*

Dismissal of an employee for **refusing to obey an instruction** can be fair, even if the instruction is outside the scope of the employee's duties, provided that it was issued in the genuinely mistaken belief that the employee was contractually obliged to obey *(Farrant v Woodroffe School [1998] IRLR 176).*

Employers also reserve a right to dismiss without warning for offences deemed to be **"gross misconduct"** — where an employer is justified in not tolerating the continued presence at the place of work of the employee who has committee the offence. However, they have to show that they **believed the employee to be guilty**, that there were **reasonable grounds** for the belief and that they had carried out a **reasonable investigation** *(Scottish Daily Record v Laird [1996] IRLR 665).* An employer can still carry out a proper investigation even where not all the evidence has been examined, if as a whole the tribunal finds that the investigation was fair and that the employer acted reasonably in dismissing the employee *(Abbey National v Morgan EAT/0403/03).*

Even where there is a clear rule that prohibits certain conduct, employers should take care before dismissing an employee.

In the case of *John Lewis v Coyne [2001] IRLR 139,* the EAT said that although there was a rule which prohibited employees from making private telephone calls, this did not make every dismissal under the rule fair. A tribunal could consider whether, according to the ordinary standards of reasonable and honest people, what the employee did was considered dishonest and also whether the employee herself realised that what she was doing was dishonest.

A dismissal related to **drink and/or drugs** could be fair, although again it is important that the employer's policy on the issue has been communicated to employees. Before any dismissal for this reason the employer should have: carried out an **investigation**; made it **clear** that there was a **rule** barring substance use at work; **acted consistently**; and **consulted** with the employee on any dependency problem. However, once there is a policy in place a dismissal is likely to be fair. In one case the employee's defence was that his food had been "spiked" and he did not know he had taken drugs. The EAT upheld his dismissal as the policy clearly said that any employee found with traces of illegal drugs would be dismissed *(SW Trains v Ireland EAT/0873/01).* If there is a separate **alcohol or drugs policy**, the employee should be dealt with under it rather than the disciplinary policy.

The fact that the employer might be willing to consider **offering alternative employment** to someone dismissed for gross misconduct does not invalidate the dismissal. There can be circumstances where an employer could not trust the employee to perform one job properly while believing they were able to undertake less responsible work *(Hamilton v Argyll & Clyde Health Board [1993] IRLR 99).*

Employers may also dismiss fairly for the **conduct of the employee outside work**, but only if it is in some way related to work. The mere fact that an employee has been charged with an offence is not justification for dismissal without an investigation *(Securicor Guarding v R [1994] IRLR 633).*

The rules on how **disciplinary proceedings** should be conducted before any dismissal are explained below – Disciplinary procedures.

Redundancy

Although dismissals for **redundancy** will normally be regarded as fair, there are circumstances that could make them unfair. The law relating to redundancy is explained in detail in chapter 11.

A redundancy dismissal may be unfair if the selection procedure was not clear or if there was a failure to consult with the employee. However, dismissal law cannot be used to determine whether the employer acted reasonably in **deciding to make the redundancies**.

Anyone who is unsure whether their claim is one of unfair dismissal or redundancy should always, when filling in the tribunal claim form, state that termination of employment is "redundancy and/or unfair dismissal". Failing to do this means that it may not be possible to change from one to the other later. It may well be the case that, in the course of putting together the evidence for the claim, or of discovering the employer's response to it, you find that what appeared to be a redundancy claim is really one for unfair dismissal.

Complying with legislation

It is fair to dismiss an employee for whom continued employment would be "contravention of duty or restriction" — in other words **where the employer would be breaking the law** by continuing to employ them. This could include, for example, a lorry driver who no longer had a driving licence and for whom there was no alternative employment.

Other reasons

The law also says that it is fair to dismiss for **"some other substantial reason"**. These can include business efficiency, economic necessity, a breakdown of trust and confidence caused by the employee or the interests of the organisation. It could even include third party pressure where, for example, the third party was the employer's only or main client (*Martin v JFX Press EATS/0010/04*). But if this type of reason is used the employers must produce **evidence** to prove their case. The EAT said that the dismissal of employees who refused to accept a **reduction in their Christmas bonus** was not a "substantial reason".

However, in one possibly inconsistent ruling, the EAT said that dismissing an employee because he had earlier intimated he intended to resign could come within the "some other substantial reason" justification *(Ely v YKK Fasteners [1993] IRLR 500).*

Disciplinary procedures

With effect from 1 October 2004, all employers must have a disciplinary and grievance procedure. There are two types of disciplinary procedure — a **standard procedure** covering all types of dismissal other than collective dismissals (including dismissals for redundancy) and a **modified** procedure for cases of gross misconduct.

It is an **automatically unfair dismissal** if the employer does not follow the correct procedures, giving the tribunals the power to award increased compensation. However, if an employee "unreasonably" **refuses to attend a meeting** over disciplinary or grievance matters called by their employer, the tribunal can reduce compensation.

Employees claiming constructive dismissal must use the grievance procedure before they are able to submit a tribunal claim — although this can be done after the employment has terminated in appropriate circumstances.

Employees who **fail to use the procedures** are barred from pursuing tribunal claims. And even in cases where they have gone through the appropriate procedure, employees have **to wait at least 28 days** for the employer's reply before they can lodge a tribunal claim.

The statutory procedures are the **minimum** that must be followed — if an employer has more extensive procedures these should be followed.

Case law rulings suggest that employees facing disciplinary action should be given **adequate time to prepare a defence** and have the opportunity to give and **call evidence** and to **call witnesses** *(R v Securities and Futures Authority [2001] IRLR 764).* However, there is no absolute right to **cross-examine any of the employer's witnesses**, although the EAT has held there might be specific circumstances in which it would be unreasonable for the employer to refuse a request to cross-examine *(Santamera v Express Cargo Forwarding [2003] IRLR 273).* In some cases the employer may be basing the case on evidence based on allegations from other unidentified employees. In such cases the tribunals will assess the fairness of the employer's approach by looking at the reasons for giving anonymity.

Disciplinary procedures will normally specify a **series of warnings** leading eventually to dismissal. Usually the warnings will expire after a period of time set out in the procedure. **Fixed-term employees** whose contracts end and are then offered a new contract should note that any unexpired disciplinary warning can transfer to the new contract. Dispute resolution procedures, effective from 1 October 2004, state that where an employer issues a **warning** (whether informal or formal) this does not amount to a disciplinary action and thus there is no statutory right to a disciplinary hearing.

The fact that the employer has failed to consider lesser penalties could make the dismissal unfair. Additionally, failing to hold a proper disciplinary hearing can affect the **amount of compensation** a tribunal awards against the employer *(Charles Robertson v White [1995] ICR 349).*

In cases of **dismissal during pregnancy** or while on maternity leave, the right to be heard is absolute. A pregnant employee dismissed after a disciplinary hearing which took place while she was absent due to a pregnancy-related illness, was unlawfully dismissed.

The **established procedures** should be followed and the employee should be told that what is taking place is a disciplinary hearing.

There are a number of **procedural matters** that could still mean that a "conduct" dismissal is unfair. They include:

- a refusal to take account of **new evidence** presented at the appeal;
- a **delay** in fixing a date for the disciplinary appeal;
- disciplinary hearings not carried out in accordance with the **rules of natural justice** (*Campion v Harmsworthy Engineering [1987] ICR 966)*;
- failing to ensure that, where possible, **witnesses to a disciplinary offence** are not involved in hearing the case *(Moyes v Hylton Castle Working Men's Club [1986] IRLR 482)*;
- a **failure to obtain sufficient proof** of the charge and an inadequate investigation *(ILEA v Gravett [1988] IRLR 497)*; and
- giving **only one hour's notice** of a disciplinary hearing *(R v BBC ex parte Lavelle [1982] IRLR 404).*

A dismissal is **automatically unfair** if the employer has **failed to**

follow the standard or modified dismissal procedure. However, if the contractual disciplinary procedure is more generous and a dismissal takes place without reference to the procedures, the dismissal could still be unfair. A defective disciplinary hearing, for example one where the employee has not had the opportunity to prepare a case, can be put right on **appeal**, but would require that the person hearing the appeal was not involved in the earlier stage (*Byrne v BOC [1992] IRLR 505*). Additionally, the appeal must be a **re-hearing** and not just a review of the earlier decision. Reducing a disciplinary penalty on appeal from dismissal to a lesser penalty means that the employee cannot continue to pursue an unfair dismissal claim

Mr Roberts was dismissed and lodged an unfair dismissal claim. However, on appeal the dismissal was reduced to demotion. Roberts argued that he still could pursue the unfair dismissal claim since his reinstatement did not mean that he had not been dismissed. The Court of Appeal held that in these cases the effect of the appeal was to revive retrospectively the contract of employment, in such a way as if he had never been dismissed (*Roberts v West Coast Trains [2004] IRLR 788*).

In some circumstances disciplinary hearings would need to be conducted in accordance with the standards of a **fair trial**, laid down under *Article 6* of the *European Convention on Human Rights* and the *Human Rights Act 1998*. This would be the case where the hearing was capable of deciding whether or not someone could continue to practice in their chosen profession *(Tehrani v UK Central Council for Nursing, Midwifery and Health Visiting [2001] IRLR 208)*. Outside of these circumstances, however, it is unlikely that disciplinary hearings would need to meet these high standards. The *Human Rights Act 1998* also guarantees a right to privacy and is relevant in relation to the public sector where tribunals are considering unfair dismissal claims. The Court of Appeal, in the case of *X v Y [2004] IRLR 625*, set out the following guidelines:

- whether the circumstances of the dismissal would come within the areas covered by human rights legislation; if so
- whether the state has a positive obligation to secure enjoyment of the right; if so
- is interference with the right justified; or, if not
- was there a fair reason for the dismissal.

Every employee has the **right to have a grievance dealt with**. This is a fundamental right implied in every contract (*W A Goold (Pearmak) v McConnell [1995] IRLR 516).*

The right to be accompanied

Under *section 10* of the *Employment Relations Act 1999 (ERA 99)* a worker who is **required or invited by an employer** to attend a disciplinary or grievance hearing has the right to make a reasonable request to bring a **companion**. The companion is **chosen by the worker** and can be: a **full-time union official**, whether or not the union is recognised; a **certified lay official** (someone whom the union has trained to accompany individuals to hearings); or a **co-worker.**

To qualify for this right, the disciplinary hearing has to be one that could **result in a warning** or some other action provided that this is held on the employee's file and represents a stage in a disciplinary procedure *(LU v Ferenc-Batchelor [2003] IRLR 252).*

The **grievance hearing** has to concern "the performance of a duty by an employer in relation to a worker". This would cover existing implied and express terms, but not a grievance over future terms.

The worker and the companion have **protection against any detrimental act or dismissal** in connection with exercising their *section 10* rights and can take a claim to a tribunal within three months. If working for the **same employer**, both the companion and the worker have the **right to be paid**. A lay official working for a different employer would be protected from detrimental action by that employer, but has no right to be paid by that employer for any time taken to deal with the hearing.

If a worker's chosen companion is not available on the date fixed for the hearing it has to be **postponed,** provided the new date is reasonable and within five days of the original hearing.

These rights are regardless of **length of service** or the **upper age limit**.

The companion has the legal right to put the worker's case, confer with the worker, sum up the case and respond on the worker's behalf, to any views expressed at the hearing.

An Advisory, Conciliation and Arbitration Service (Acas) **code of practice** on disciplinary and grievance hearings, effective from 1 October 2004, lays down the essential features of a disciplinary procedure and how it should operate in practice. It recommends that disciplinary rules and procedures should: be in writing; specify to whom they apply; provide for matters to be dealt with quickly; indicate the disciplinary penalties and provide for opportunities for the case to be heard. The code provides examples of gross misconduct and emphasises that even in cases of summary dismissal an employee should have the right to appeal at a hearing. In the case of *Spence v Manchester United EAT/0285/04,* the EAT said that tribunals have a statutory obligation to consider the code in deciding whether a dismissal is fair.

Qualifying for unfair dismissal rights

Section 94 ERA 96 gives all employees, regardless of the hours they work, the right not to be unfairly dismissed. To qualify to make a claim they must:

- have been **dismissed**;
- not be above the **"normal retirement age"** for their work or, where there is none, over 65 *(section 109 ERA 96)*;
- have been working for the employer for **at least one year**; and
- present the application to a tribunal **within three months** of the date of dismissal.

The qualifying conditions relating to length of service and age may not necessarily apply in **automatically unfair dismissals** (see below).

The **"normal retirement age"** is the age at which workers in the workplace usually retire and must be the same age for men and women. This may be ascertained by looking at the reasonable expectations of retirement in the relevant group. Employers attempting to **change the normal retirement age** should only do so by agreement. However, in the absence of clear evidence to suggest otherwise, the **retirement age specified in the contract** establishes the normal retirement age. There can be a normal retirement age even if the employee's grade is unique *(Wall v British Compressed Air Society Case [2004] IRLR 147).* If there is no normal retirement age, the state retirement age of 65 applies.

There can also be a normal retirement age even if in practice employees are permitted to work beyond it. An employer's decision to revert to it would not give the employee the right to pursue an unfair dismissal claim *(Barclays Bank v O'Brian [1994] IRLR 580)*.

Continuity of employment

Workers with broken or irregular service with the same or an "associated" employer may have difficulty in proving they have the necessary continuity of employment to establish their right to claim. A gap of less than a week does not break continuity even if, within that week, the employee goes to work for another employer and then returns to the old employer. Under *section 210 ERA 96* **continuity is presumed** in such cases, unless the contrary is shown, for example, where it was clearly intended that a series of temporary contracts would not be regarded as continuous *(Booth v USA [1999] IRLR 16)*.

Under *section 212 ERA 96* a "temporary cessation of work" does not break continuity. In a case of an employee who was unemployed for a few days between two contracts with the same employer, the EAT said that it was not up to the employee to prove continuity.

In the case of *Carrington v Harwich Dock Co [1998] IRLR 567,* the employee agreed to resign, breaking his continuity, so that he could take advantage of a favourable early retirement package. He immediately returned to a new job with the same employer. The EAT said that his continuity was not broken because he could not sign away his statutory rights.

Employees cannot contract out of rights to claim continuity merely because they have earlier entered into a settlement agreed by Acas, according to the EAT in the case of *Collison v BBC [1998] IRLR 238*.

Where the gap between contracts is longer, the employee will need to show that there continues to be a **mutuality of obligations** between employer and employee. In one case, the EAT held that the fact that there were no formal guarantees of re-employment and no obligation on the employee to accept new work indicated the absence of mutual obligations. This meant there could be no continuity *(Reed v The Royal Highland & Agricultural Society of Scotland EAT/0020/02)*.

This is particularly important in the light of a ruling of the Court of Appeal, in the case of *Curr v Marks & Spencer [2003] IRLR 74*.

Cheryl Curr had worked for Marks & Spencer for 20 years when she took a career break. She returned to work at the end of it and worked for another five years before being made redundant. Curr had assumed her redundancy pay would take account of all of her service, but the Court of Appeal ruled it did not. There was no agreement or custom by which she could have been regarded as an employee during the period of her career break and therefore her continuity was broken.

The *Curr* ruling makes it essential that representatives examine any **career break schemes** to ensure that individuals taking advantage of them do not then forfeit future employment rights. There is a similar ruling from the European Court of Justice, in the case of *Mau v Bundesanstalt fur Arbeit C-160/01* and also in the case of *Osterreichischer Gewerkshaftsbund, Gerwerkshaftskammer Osterreich C-220/02,* where the court held that it was not necessary to take account of an employee's parental leave in calculating service, just because there was a rule that took account of time on leave for military service.

However, in the case of *Unwin v Barclays Bank EAT/0273/02*, the EAT held that an employee on a career break did have continuity of employment, so that when she was made redundant a year after returning to work, her service prior to her career break was included. There was, according to the EAT, a continuing employment relationship.

The following examples show the circumstances when the rules operate to **preserve continuity**:

- employment on a series of **fixed-term contracts** *(Pfaffinger v City of Liverpool Community College [1996] IRLR 508)*;
- **dismissing and then reinstating** an employee *(Ingram v Foxon [1985] IRLR 5)*;
- gaps between employment which are **relatively short** in comparison to the period of employment *(Sillars v Charringtons Fuels [1989] IRLR 152)*;
- **two contracts**, one following on from the other *(Tipper v Roofdec [1989] IRLR 419)*;
- a period of **work abroad** followed by one in the UK with the same employer *(Weston v Viga Space Systems [1989] IRLR 429)*;
- where a **transfer of undertakings** has occurred *(Macer v Abafast [1990] IRLR 137)* (see chapter 12);

- a **break for sickness** of fewer than 26 weeks even if the employee worked elsewhere in that period *(Donnelly v Kelvin International Services [1992] IRLR 496)*;
- a two-week gap during which the **employee continued to work for the old employer** before being transferred to the new employer under the TUPE regulations *(Tuck A & G v Bartlett [1994] IRLR 162)*; and
- a week during which the employee **received unemployment benefit** in the period between his employment shutting down and reopening *(Justfern v D'Ingerthorpe [1994] IRLR 164)*.

If an employee is **on strike** for any part of a week, continuity is not broken. However, that week does not count in calculating continuous length of service.

Women on **ordinary maternity leave** preserve their continuity of employment and the period of the leave itself is counted.

Employers' reasons for dismissal

Under *section 92 ERA 96*, workers with at least one year's continuous service, regardless of the hours they work, have the right to get a **written statement** from their employers within 14 days, giving the reason/s for dismissal.

If an employer **refuses to give a statement**, the employee can complain to an employment tribunal. But there is no basis for such a claim unless the employee has asked for the statement and it has been refused.

If an employer **dismisses without giving any reasons**, the dismissal will almost certainly be unfair *(Adams v Derby City Council [1986] IRLR 163)*. **Changing the reasons** for dismissal at a later date could also make the dismissal unfair *(Hotson v Wisbech Conservative Club [1984] IRLR 422)*.

It is up to the employer to show that the reason for the dismissal comes within the list of fair reasons. Even if this is done, the tribunal has to be convinced that an employer acted reasonably in treating this as grounds for dismissal. The Court of Appeal has ruled on how to judge whether an **employer has acted reasonably**.

In the case of *HSBC Bank v Madden [2000] IRLR 827,* the Court confirmed that the tribunal should not substitute its own view of what is reasonable for that of the employer. The task for the tribunal is to establish whether the decision to dismiss the employee fell within the **band of reasonable responses** that a reasonable employer might have adopted.

This test equally applies to the **investigation** itself. Where the same individual acts as the investigating, disciplining and dismissing officer the tribunal is likely to find that the investigation is unreasonable. One judge has stated that this practice "if possible should be avoided".

While an inadequate investigation might lead to a finding that the dismissal was unfair, the tribunal cannot substitute its own views of what would be a reasonable investigation. If it would meet the objective standards of a reasonable employer, it cannot be challenged as unreasonable. The EAT has laid down criteria which an employer, acting reasonably, should follow:

In a case involving the dismissal of an employee for taking a milkshake without permission, the EAT noted that the offence was minor; there was an absence of deceit on the part of the employee; and the incident was isolated. Taking these factors into account the employer's decision to dismiss was unreasonable *(Rentokil v Mackin [1989] IRLR 286).*

However, in another case, the EAT held that dismissing someone for stealing an item valued at just £1.50 could be reasonable where the employee, whose overall disciplinary record was poor, had lied about the theft when confronted. It was also fair to dismiss two employees for fighting even though the conduct of one of the employees, viewed objectively, was worse than that of the other. In contrast, in another case the EAT ruled that a tribunal could decide that an employer had acted unreasonably and had not applied proper principles of industrial relations when dismissing a worker with very **long service** because of one incident of dishonesty. Equally, according to the Court of Appeal, in the case of *Strouthos v London Underground [2004] IRLR 636,* tribunals should also take length of service and previous record into account, when deciding whether a dismissal was reasonable.

Failing to allow an employee the **right to an internal appeal** could make a dismissal unfair.

Mr Tipton, a Co-op milk worker, was denied the right of appeal when dismissed for absenteeism. The House of Lords said that this denial made the dismissal unfair because facts might have come out of the appeal which would have made a difference to the decision to dismiss *(West Midlands Co-op Society v Tipton [1986] IRLR 112).*

Indeed, failing to follow all stages of an appeal procedure could also make a dismissal unfair (*Stoker v Lancashire CC [1992] IRLR 75).*

Dismissal while on strike

Employees have the right not to be dismissed in the first 12 weeks of taking **lawful, official action** (see chapter 9 – How the law aids employers). This is the **protected period**, but beyond this period there may still be a measure of protection from dismissal. In a case taken to a tribunal by workers at automotive company **Friction Dynamics**, who were dismissed after eight weeks had expired (prior to the coming into force of the *Employment Relations Act 2004*, the protected period was eight weeks only) the tribunal ruled that the workforce still had protection. It gave two reasons for this:

- threatening letters to workers were sent within the protection period. These made it clear that the **employer had already taken a decision to dismiss** the workforce; and
- the employer's refusal to take any steps to resolve the dispute after the protection period had expired was in breach of the legal **obligation to take reasonable procedural steps** to resolve a dispute.

The *Employment Relations Act 2004* has also extended the protected period to include any time when employees are locked out.

After the 12 weeks, if employers want to dismiss some strikers they have to **dismiss all** of them and cannot pick and choose.

After **three months from the date of dismissal** employers can take back who they want without the risk of unfair dismissal claims.

The House of Lords in the case of *Crosville Wales v Tracey [1997] IRLR 691*, said that where all the employees had taken industrial action, it would not be possible to judge whether one employee was to blame without referring to the conduct of the other employees. This meant, in practice, that all had the right to damages for unfair dismissal.

Whether or not an individual is taking part in a strike is **decided objectively**. The test is what the employee did, not why it was done.

Mr Britton was instructed to drive a van without a heater. He refused and was dismissed. At the end of the day's work another employee (Mr Lewis) attempted to intervene on Britton's behalf and informed the employer that no one would work unless the dismissal was reversed. All the other drivers were then dismissed. On application to the tribunal the EAT upheld a finding that they had been "taking part in strike action" and that the tribunal had no jurisdiction to hear their case *(Lewis v E. Mason and Sons [1994] IRLR 4).*

In one case an employee only took part in a strike to enable him to report back to the company on what the strikers were up to. When everyone else was dismissed he was not and the company tried to argue that he had not really been taking part in the strike. The EAT disagreed, saying his motive for taking part was irrelevant.

Workers must actually be taking industrial action when dismissed. If they have already **returned to work** and are then dismissed, they are not barred from taking unfair dismissal claims. Whether or not they were taking the action is a question for the tribunal, not the employer, to decide *(Jenkins v P & O Ferries [1991] ICR 652).*

In cases of **unofficial action** there is no protection against dismissal, even if it is selective.

The **International Labour Organisation (ILO)**, the body responsible for regulating employment law worldwide, has repeatedly condemned UK law for allowing the dismissal of strikers, saying that it breaches international standards.

Automatically unfair dismissals

There are some dismissals that are automatically unfair no matter what reasons the employer gives. In these cases it is, however, for the **employee to prove** that the reason for the dismissal fell within one of the automatically unfair categories. In the case of *Povey v Dorset CC EAT/209/01,* the employee claimed his dismissal was due to his **health and safety activities**. However, he could not prove this. His employers successfully argued that he had been dismissed for refusing to obey a legitimate order.

The list of automatically unfair dismissals continues to grow, as new employment rights impose greater limitations on employers' rights to dismiss. The different types of automatically unfair dismissals are described below.

From October 2004, when the relevant provisions of the *Employment Act 2002* came into force, a dismissal following the **failure of an employer to comply with the terms of the statutory dispute**

resolution procedure is also **automatically unfair**. In addition, where this procedure has not been followed, dismissed employees will have a guarantee of minimum compensation of four weeks' pay.

Except for dismissals relating to business transfers and after failure to comply with a statutory dispute resolution procedure, there is **no service qualification** for the following unfair dismissal rights, nor does the **maximum age** qualifying condition apply (see above – Qualifying for unfair dismissal rights).

Pregnancy and parental rights

Dismissing a woman because she is pregnant or on maternity leave, or for any reason connected with her pregnancy, is contrary to both the *Sex Discrimination Act 1975 (SDA 75)* and *section 99 ERA 96*. The dismissal of an employee due to a pregnancy-related illness is unlawful *(Brown v Rentokil [1998] IRLR 445)*. Dismissal of employees for exercising their parental, paternity or adoption leave rights is also automatically unfair (see chapter 8).

Statutory dismissal procedures

The failure by an employer to comply with the statutory disciplinary procedures makes a dismissal for that reason automatically unfair. However, to qualify for the right the employee needs to have worked for at least a year for the same employer.

Sale of business

If the employer sells the business, including the goodwill, employees have the right to continue in work with the new employer under the *Transfer of Undertakings Regulations 1981* (see chapter 12).

Trade union membership

Section 152 of the *Trade Union and Labour Relations (Consolidation) Act 1992 (TULR(C)A 92)*, protects those dismissed either because they are, or propose to become, a member of an **independent trade union** or take part in its activities at an "appropriate time", i.e. outside working hours or inside those hours with the employer's consent. In the case of *Britool v Roberts [1993] IRLR 481* individuals dismissed because of their trade union activities, including their involvement in the preliminary planning stage of a strike, were protected under *section*

152. A management-grade employee, who was also a rep and was dismissed for advising new employees that their only safeguard lay with the union, was also held to have been unfairly dismissed.

Employees are protected by *section 152* if they are dismissed for invoking the assistance of the union in relation to their employment *(Speciality Care v Pachela [1996] IRLR 248)*. However, an employee dismissed for **organising or taking part in industrial action** cannot use the protection contained in *section 152*.

Anyone dismissed for trade union reasons should immediately use the **interim relief procedures** in *section 161 TULR(C)A 92*. This must be done within seven days of the dismissal and the application must include a certificate, signed by a union official, which says that the dismissal is on account of union membership. The tribunal will, if it believes there are grounds for the claim, make a continuation order which means that the employer must continue paying the employee pending the full tribunal hearing.

The *Employment Relations Act 2004* increased the protection against dismissal for trade union reasons where the dismissal is related to the use of union services.

Representation rights

Employees have protection from dismissal where they are exercising their right to be accompanied or are acting as a companion in disciplinary and grievance hearings (see above – The right to be accompanied).

Protected industrial action

During the period of protected industrial action (see above – Dismissal while on strike) employers are barred from dismissing employees taking industrial action.

Enforcing a statutory right

It is automatically unfair to dismiss someone because they have attempted to enforce a statutory right, such as a claim in respect of working time or protection of wages, irrespective of whether or not in law they have such a right, provided they acted in good faith *(section 104 ERA 96)*. In the case of *Mennell v Newell and Wright [1997] IRLR*

519, the Court of Appeal held that there could be a claim based on dismissal for asserting a statutory right, even where there was no evidence of the statutory right being breached. Part-time workers and fixed-term employees are also covered if dismissed for exercising their rights to no less favourable treatment. In the case of *Pearce and Pearce v Dyer EAT/0465/04*, the EAT held that the dismissal of employees because they had alleged their employer had made **unlawful deductions** from their wages was a dismissal for enforcing a statutory right and therefore automatically unfair.

Health and safety reasons

Under *section 100 ERA 96*, if an employee who is acting as a safety rep is dismissed for carrying out their health and safety duties, the dismissal is automatically unfair. So too would be the dismissal of any worker leaving or proposing to leave work in circumstances where they believed there to be a **"serious and imminent"** danger. However, in the case of *Balfour Kilpatrick v Acheson [2003] IRLR 683* staff who walked out over being made to wear damp clothing were not able to show that there was an imminent risk justifying their action without a prior ballot.

An employee who leaves work due to **threats from another employee** may be able to claim protection if dismissed *(Harvest Press v McCaffrey [1999] IRLR 778)*. This even extends to an employee leaving a kitchen where he works because he believes that health standards are putting customers at risk *(Masiak v City Restaurants [1999] IRLR 780)*.

Refusal to work on Sundays

A **"protected worker"** (see chapter 4 – Working hours and breaks) may claim unfair dismissal if this occurs due to their refusal to work on Sundays.

Employee representatives and pension fund trustees

Under *section 103 ERA 96* an employee representative, or a candidate for such a position, who is dismissed because they have performed, or proposed to perform, functions of such a representative will be regarded as having been unfairly dismissed. Similar protection applies to trustees of occupational pension funds under *section 102 ERA 96*.

The dismissal of an employee for activities as a member of a European Works Council (EWC) is also automatically unfair.

Whistleblowing

Under the *Public Interest Disclosure Act 1998 (PIDA 98)*, an employee who "blows the whistle" on their employer's fraudulent or criminal activities has **protection against victimisation**. They have the right not to be subjected to any detriment, not to be victimised short of dismissal and not to be dismissed. Even if it turns out that the allegation was wrong, provided that the employee had a reasonable belief and made the disclosure in good faith, the law will protect them from detrimental treatment *(Darnton v University of Surrey [2003] IRLR 133)*. However, the employee's reasons for making the disclosure **must be motivated entirely by the public interest** and not by personal antagonism.

Frances Street made a number of allegations against her manager. An investigation revealed that her motivation for making the allegations was malicious and Street was dismissed. She took an unfair dismissal claim. The Court of Appeal dismissed the claim. It held that even if an employee believes the disclosure to be true, they would not be acting in good faith unless motivated entirely by public interest (*Street v Derbyshire Unemployed Workers' Centre [2004] IRLR 687*).

Employees are protected even if the whistleblowing relates to something that happened before the 1998 Act came into force, provided that the victimisation itself occurred after the law came into force *(Miklaszewicz v Stolt [2001] IRLR 656)*.

The EAT has held that the Act also covers workers who complain about breaches of **any legal obligations** their employers have under their individual employment contracts. In the case of *Parkins v Sodexho [2002] IRLR 109*, an employee used the Act successfully to complain about lack of adequate supervision, amounting to a breach of the health and safety obligations.

Compensation in whistleblowing cases can include an award for **injury to feelings**.

Minimum pay and working time

The regulations guaranteeing minimum pay and imposing working time restrictions for health reasons (see chapter 4) provide protection for anyone dismissed for trying to pursue their rights to pay, hours or holidays in accordance with the law.

Union recognition

Dismissing employees for seeking rights to trade union recognition comes within the definition of automatically unfair dismissals.

Successful claims

Most workers taking unfair dismissal cases want their jobs back. However, in the vast majority of cases tribunals **do not award reinstatement** or re-engagement. Most get financial compensation while less than 1% of those who win are reinstated or re-engaged.

Reinstatement or re-engagement

Under *sections 113* and *114 ERA 96* tribunals can order an employer to **reinstate** (give back the old job on existing terms, with full back pay and continuity) or **re-engage** (rehire under a new contract without continuity). But they cannot be ordered to give an employee a **better job** than the one held prior to the unfair dismissal (*Rank Xerox v Stryczek [1995] IRLR 568).* A reinstatement restores the original contract and preserves continuity.

Mr Kirkpatrick was dismissed and two months later re-instated after an internal appeal. A month later his employers reneged on the decision to re-instate and restored the original decision. They then argued that Kirkpatrick could not bring an unfair dismissal claim because his continuity of service had been broken by the original dismissal. The EAT rejected the employer's submission. The decision to re-instate meant that as a matter of contract Kirkpatrick was regarded as not having been dismissed. To hold otherwise would allow employers to dismiss employees (for example prior to a redundancy), re-instate them and then claim they had no service upon which their redundancy pay could be based (*London Probation Board v Kirkpatrick EAT/0544/04*).

Employers cannot avoid their obligations to reinstate or re-engage simply by showing that they have already hired a replacement.

When deciding whether to order the re-employment of unfairly dismissed employees, the tribunal has to make a provisional assessment of the practicability of the employer complying with the order. A final decision is only made if the employer refuses to comply *(Port of London Authority v Payne and Others [1994] IRLR 9).*

The usual test is whether, despite the dismissal, the fundamental relationship of **trust and confidence has broken down**. In the case of *Cruikshank v LB Richmond [1999] (unreported)*, the fact that the employee had made allegations about the employer while presenting his tribunal claim was not enough to show that this fundamental relationship had been destroyed. However, if a tribunal has already found that the employee was partly responsible for the dismissal it is very unlikely to order re-engagement.

Compensation

Compensation has two main elements — a **basic award** and a **compensatory award**.

The **basic award** depends on length of employment and age prior to dismissal. It is calculated as the number of "weeks' pay" according to age and length of service, as follows:

- **age under 22** — half a week's pay for each complete year worked under this age;
- **age 22 to 40** — one week's pay for each complete year worked between these ages; and
- **age 41-65** — one and a half weeks' pay for each complete year worked between these ages.

When calculating the **"week's pay"** there is a **maximum of £280** (2005/06). It is based on **gross pay** and, where earnings are **irregular**, is averaged over a **12-week period**. However, where **overtime** is worked only the basic hourly rate is taken into account *(British Coal v Cheesbough [1990] IRLR 148)*. The "week's pay" also cannot be calculated at less than the national minimum wage, even if the employee was not receiving it *(Paggetti v Cobb [2002] IRLR 861)*.

The **maximum number of years** of work that can be taken into account is **20**. So a worker aged 45 with 25 years' service earning more than £280 a week would still only be entitled to a basic award of 22 x £280 = £6,160. In cases of dismissal for **trade union duties and activities**, for carrying out the duties of a health and safety rep, of a trustee of a pension scheme or an employee rep, the minimum basic award is £3,800 (2005/06). There may also be an entitlement to an additional award (see below).

Anyone **aged 64** will have their basic award **reduced** by 1/12th for every month past their 64th birthday. The basic award can be reduced if the employee is offered reinstatement or re-engagement and unreasonably refuses it *(section 119 ERA 96).*

The formula for calculating the **compensatory award** is laid down in *section 123 ERA 96.* It is based on any loss sustained as a result of the dismissal to include:

- expenses incurred by reason of the dismissal;
- loss of wages — current and future;
- loss of pension rights;
- loss of accrued statutory protection;
- cost to employee of time and effort in seeking new work; and
- future loss.

Loss of **pension rights** amounts to more than just the money the employer would have paid into the pension fund. It is the amount of pension an individual would have been entitled to had it not been for the unfair dismissal *(Clancy v Cannock Chase Technical College [2001] IRLR 331).* Losses of wages do not include any separate earnings from **self-employment**. A claimant can only recover losses that are attributable to the employer's actions. A hospital consultant was not entitled to recover earnings from private work he took on externally because these were not earnings he was entitled to under his contract with the NHS Trust. The EAT, in the case of *Schlesinger v Swindon & Marlborough NHS Trust EAT/0072/04*, held that even if the dismissed employee could establish that his additional earnings were dependent on the existence of his substantive post, he could not claim for the loss.

An employee can be found to have been unfairly dismissed but still not get any compensation for loss of wages, if the tribunal finds that the reason why the employee was unemployed was not as a consequence of the dismissal but due to incapacity (illness).

It is not possible to claim for **injury to feelings** in unfair dismissal cases. In the case of *Dunnachie v Kingston upon Hull City Council [2004] IRLR 727*, the House of Lords, reversing a previous decision of the Court of Appeal, held that compensation in unfair dismissal cases does not include amounts for injury to feelings, unlike the situation in discrimination claims (see chapter 6 – Taking a discrimination claim) when the manner of dismissal has resulted in an injury (for example, psychiatric illness) to the employee.

An example of a **future unanticipated loss** comes from a case taken against Strathclyde Buses.

Unfairly dismissed employees who were required to sell shares allocated under a share-option scheme were able to claim for the fact that the value of the shares rose after their dismissal but prior to the tribunal hearing *(Leonard v Strathclyde Buses [1998] IRLR 693).*

There is no right to claim damages for the loss of a right to claim unfair dismissal *(Harper v Virgin Net [2004] IRLR 390).* Leave to appeal to the House of Lords has been granted in this case and the court is likely to give its ruling in October 2005.

Employees have an obligation to **"mitigate** (lessen) **their losses**" by, for example, looking for alternative work. Of course, this means that if they successfully obtain new employment, their overall compensation entitlement will decline. When looking for alternative work an employee should try to replicate their earnings in their previous job. However, they will not lose compensation if they were unable to achieve these earnings or could not get the **same level of employment** benefits, for example, a comparable pension scheme. The tribunal will take account of any earnings they have achieved. However, it will not look at **earnings in a second job** an employee already had prior to the dismissal. An employee may be able to show mitigation in other ways. For example, in the case of *Orthet v Vince-Cain [2004] IRLR 857*, the EAT ruled that a dismissed employee had mitigated her loss by attending a university course, since it was unlikely that she would get a comparable new job to the one she had lost without further qualifications

The burden of proof that the employee has failed to mitigate their losses rests with the employer *(Fyfe v Scientific Furnishings [1989] IRLR 331).* An unreasonable refusal of an offer of re-employment can amount to a failure to mitigate. The tribunal will consider whether the employee acted unreasonably in refusing the offer, not whether the employee could reasonably have refused the offer *(Wilding v BT [2002] IRLR 524).*

Any earnings in the period between the dismissal and the tribunal hearing can be taken into account in assessing the compensatory loss *(Justfern v D'Ingerthorpe [1994] IRLR 164)*. This means that if the employee gains higher paid work, there is no claim for loss of earnings. However, if the individual gets and then loses a better-paid job, before the date of the tribunal hearing, the loss of wages can be taken into account. What cannot be claimed is for any period of unemployment that the tribunal assesses is due to the employee's incapacity rather than due to the dismissal. Where an employee is paid in lieu of notice any earnings in a new job, during the period which would have been notice in the old job, are not taken into account in assessing compensation *(Voith Turbo v Stowe [2005] IRLR 228)*. An ex-employee can also claim compensation for the "time and effort" used in securing new work, with one EAT awarding an additional £500 under that heading.

In the case of an employee who had been unable to work due to ill-health as a result of an unfair dismissal, the tribunal was entitled to award compensation for whatever period it decided the employee was out of work as a consequence of the dismissal *(Devine v Designer Flowers [1993] IRLR 517)*.

There is **no overall maximum** for compensation in cases of dismissal based on discrimination, for health and safety reasons or in whistleblowing cases. In all other cases the **maximum compensatory award** that can be made is £56,800 (2005/06). An attempt to argue that the ceiling on the compensatory award breached rights to property under the *Human Rights Act 1998* was rejected by the EAT. It held that the *European Convention on Human Rights* gave neither the right to a job nor to a remedy for unfair dismissal *(Yorkshire Rider v Neckles EAT/0089/02)*.

If the tribunal thinks the employee's **conduct** contributed to the unfair dismissal it can **reduce the award** by a percentage to reflect this. However, to justify a reduction in compensation, the conduct has either to be a breach of contract or conduct properly capable of being described as "perverse, foolish, bloody-minded or unreasonable in all the circumstances" (*Ceesay v Sercuricor Security EAT/0105/04*). The tribunal cannot take account of any **conduct** of the employees **after the dismissal**. In the case of *Soros v Davison [1994] IRLR 264*, the fact that the employees, after their dismissal, sold their story to a newspaper was not grounds for reducing the award. If the employee has already received some money from the employer (for example an ex-gratia payment) paid as a consequence of the dismissal, the amount already paid would be deducted from any calculation of compensation. If money has been paid by a permanent health scheme, where only the employer had made contributions, they too can be taken into account in assessing the compensation (*Altos Origin IT Services UK v Haddock [2005] IRLR 20*). Incapacity benefit paid to the employee can also be taken into account (*Morgans v Alpha Plus Security EAT/0438/04*).

Compensation can also be reduced to reflect a finding on the facts that there was a chance that, even if a fair procedure had been followed, the employee would have been dismissed *(Rao v Civil Aviation Authority [1994] IRLR 240)*. The £56,800 maximum is applied after any such reduction *(Walter Braund v Murray [1991] IRLR 100)*.

Compensation cannot be reduced to take account of things like the size of the employer. Small employers cannot use the argument that they have fewer resources to avoid paying the level of compensation that reflects the employee's loss.

Social security benefits are offset against the compensatory award, as are any **redundancy payments** *(Digital Equipment v Clements [1998] IRLR 134)*, but only if the tribunal finds that there was a redundancy.

In the case of *Boorman v Allmakes [1995] IRLR 553,* the employers terminated Boorman's employment, paying him an ex-gratia payment, which was said to incorporate statutory redundancy pay. However, the tribunal found there had been no redundancy. Therefore the ex-gratia payment was not offset.

An **additional award** applies in trade union membership (or non-membership) cases and in cases of unlawful discrimination and dismissal for health and safety reasons where the employee asked for reinstatement or re-engagement but the employer refused to comply with the tribunal order. It gives between 26 weeks' and 52 weeks' pay.

Section 160 TULR(C)A 92 gives the tribunal power to order that the compensation award be **paid by the union** instead of the employer in cases where the tribunal decides that the union induced the employer to dismiss.

If the **sum awarded remains unpaid** 42 days after the tribunal decision, interest is payable on amounts outstanding.

In cases where the employer is **insolvent** and unable to pay compensation, the secretary of state for trade and industry assumes responsibility, but only for some of the money due. The right to payment from the secretary of state covers basic awards for unfair dismissal, arrears of pay (to a maximum of eight weeks) and holiday pay (six weeks' maximum). But in these cases a "week's pay" is calculated as for the basic award for unfair dismissal with a maximum of £280 (2005/06). The employee receives a net sum after tax and other deductions *(Titchener v Secretary of State for Trade and Industry [2002] IRLR 195).* Contractual lay off pay is not payable by the secretary of state as it does not come under the definition of pay, according to the case of *Benson v Secretary of State [2003] IRLR 748.*

A payment made by the secretary of state **breaks continuity**. Even if employees subsequently transfer to a new employer, they will have lost their right to count previous service.

If the secretary of state fails to make any payment a claim should be submitted to a tribunal **within three months**. If any other money is due from the employer it is dealt with either as a **priority debt** or an **unsecured debt**.

An important ruling by the European Court of Justice may mean that the current system for dealing with money due to employees in insolvency is unlawful and may need to be changed. Although the case is based on Spanish law, the basic rules are the same. Under Spanish law, like UK law, employees can only claim partial compensation when their employer is insolvent. The ECJ held that this rule is in breach of equal treatment laws *(Rodriguez Caballero v Fondo de Garantia Salarial [2003] IRLR 115).*

Payment made under a **protective award** (see chapter 11 – Remedies for failure to consult) can be offset against that due from the secretary of state *(Mann v Secretary of State for Employment [1999] IRLR 566).*

A payment received as compensation for unfair dismissal under a compromise agreement is not taxable (as long as it doesn't exceed £30,000) even if the employee is reinstated (*HM Inspector of Taxes v Clayton [2005] IRLR 115*).

Wrongful dismissal

Workers who do not meet the qualifying conditions for unfair dismissal rights, usually because they have not worked for at least a year and whose dismissal is not "automatically unfair", may be able to claim wrongful dismissal or seek an injunction. As a minimum, a person who shows that they have been wrongfully dismissed will receive compensation at least equal to the pay they would have received had the employer lawfully dismissed them.

A wrongful dismissal is one in **breach of a contract** and can include dismissal without **proper notice**. Usually the contract will specify the notice that the employer and the employee must give to end the contract. Employees who are wrongfully dismissed without proper notice can take a claim for any rights they would have had during the period of the notice, according to the Court of Appeal in the case of *Silvey v Pendragon [2001] IRLR 685.*

Where employees have the benefit of a contractual entitlement to a disciplinary or appraisal procedure they will be entitled to be paid for the time it would have taken to operate the procedure where the employer, in breach of contract, had not done this.

For **employees on high earnings** there could be circumstances where claims for wrongful dismissal would yield a higher level of compensation because, unlike claims for unfair dismissal, there is no maximum limit. Additionally, if a worker has a fixed-term contract they may be able to claim damages equivalent to the pay they would have received to the end of the contract.

Employees who have a contract clause stating that **their pay will be reviewed annually** may have their damages assessed to take account of future pay increases they might have had, if they had not been wrongfully dismissed *(Clark v BET [1997] IRLR 348).*

Injunction

In some cases it may be possible to seek an **injunction** to stop the employer dismissing. Anyone contemplating this course of action would need to seek **expert advice** before proceeding. The general rule is that the court will grant an injunction to order the employer to revoke a dismissal where it is believed that there is continued mutual trust and confidence between employer and employee and monetary damages would not be an adequate remedy.

Date of dismissal

It is important to be clear about the date on which a dismissal takes place, as the **three-month time limit** for applications to employment tribunals runs from that date *(section 111 ERA 96)*. However, there is an exception if the employee can show that it was "not reasonably practicable" to present the claim in time. This is quite difficult to show, but an example might be where the employer had acted fraudulently, hiding from the employee the real reason for the dismissal.

In one case the fact that the employee did not find out until some time later that the reason given for her dismissal — redundancy — was a sham made it "not reasonably practicable" to present the claim within the three-month limit.

In the case of *Marley v Anderson [1996] IRLR 163*, the Court of Appeal held that, where the facts emerge over time, an employee is not automatically time barred in making a second claim just because the first claim was out of time. It is up to the tribunal to determine what is a reasonable time within which the employee should have presented a claim, having discovered the relevant information that formed the basis for the claim.

There are some **basic rules** used to calculate the date of dismissal:

- a dismissal cannot take effect until it is communicated to the employee;
- a notification to an employee to return to work or face dismissal is not a notice of a future dismissal but only an indication of the date when the dismissal will occur *(Rai v Somerfield [2004] IRLR 124)*;
- where an employee communicates an immediate resignation by fax, the effective date of termination (EDT) is the date of receipt of the fax. If a letter is sent by post, it is the date when the letter is received, even if the employer does not immediately read it;
- if a contract is ended with notice, the EDT is the date when the notice expires;
- the EDT depends not on what the parties might agree should happen but on what has actually happened *(Fitzgerald v University of Kent and Canterbury [2004] IRLR 300)*;
- if ended lawfully without notice (summary dismissal for gross misconduct), the EDT is the day of the dismissal itself;

- where an employee is told that there is no need to work a notice period the EDT remains the date when notice expires;
- where an employee appeals against dismissal but the appeal is unsuccessful, the EDT is the date of the original dismissal;
- if an employee entitled to statutory notice is dismissed without it, the EDT is the date when the notice would have ended, unless the employer was justified in dismissing summarily for gross misconduct (here the tribunal must decide, on evidence, whether there was gross misconduct or not);
- if an employee waives notice for payment in lieu, then the EDT does not take account of the notice period; and
- if an employee is dismissed orally then the EDT is not earlier than the day after it is given.

One of the most important points to note is the effect of **internal appeals** on the EDT. Where an appeal upholds a dismissal, it is the **original date** of dismissal which stands, not the date of the appeal. This is the case unless the employee can show that the employment continued until the appeal hearing, by virtue of a contractual term, or because, for instance, the employer continued to pay the employee. This ruling was confirmed in the House of Lords case of *West Midland Co-op v Tipton [1986] IRLR 112* (see above – Employers' reasons for dismissal). For **teachers** however, the date of dismissal cannot be earlier than the date of the appeal.

A **P45** is **not proof of a dismissal**. Employees who wait until they get their P45 and so fall outside the three-month time limit will lose the right to pursue a claim *(LB Newham v Ward [1985] IRLR 509)*.

More information: LRD booklets *Disciplinary and grievance procedures* (£4.20) and *Dismissal – a legal guide* (£3.50); LRD's *Workplace Report* has quarterly updates on dismissal law.

11. Redundancy

What is redundancy?

An employee is dismissed for redundancy, and may be entitled to redundancy pay, if either of the following occurs:

- the employer has ceased, or intends to cease, carrying on the business; or
- the requirements for employees to carry out work of a particular kind, or to carry it out in the place in which they are employed, have **ceased or diminished**.

For **consultation purposes only** there is a different definition of "redundancy" (see below).

A redundancy can therefore occur where the workforce is reorganised and there is **less work**; when changes in conditions mean that the **old job is quite different** from the new one; and when an employer decides to **put work out to contract**. The test for redundancy is whether the employer **requires fewer** (or no) **workers** to do work of a particular kind and not just whether the work itself has ceased or diminished.

The hospital where Mr Shawkat was employed carried out a reorganisation. As a result he was asked to undertake different duties from those he had carried out before. He argued that he had been made redundant, but the Court of Appeal disagreed. The fact that he was asked to carry out other duties, as well as his existing ones, was not conclusive proof that there had been a redundancy. There had been no cessation or diminution of the work overall *(Shawkat v Nottingham City Hospital [2001] IRLR 555).*

The employer does not have to show that there is any **economic justification** for the decision to make redundancies or that there are financial problems that have led to the reduction of work.

Section 139 of the *Employment Relations Act 1996 (ERA 96)*, which defines rights to redundancy pay, makes specific reference to the individual's **"place of employment"** as the test for whether or not the dismissal is for redundancy. This point has been clarified in the case of *Bass Leisure v Thomas [1994] IRLR 104.*

Ms Thomas was employed for 10 years as a travelling collector. Her job allowed her to arrange her hours to tie in with her domestic responsibilities.

The depot from which she worked was closed and she was offered relocation. She tried the new job but found the additional travelling too inconvenient and resigned, claiming redundancy. Her employer refused, arguing that her contract contained a mobility clause. The EAT, however, held that work at her "place of employment" had ended and this was the sole test for determining whether there had been a redundancy. She was therefore entitled to redundancy pay.

The fact that the employees' contracts could require them to **work elsewhere** does not mean that they cannot be made redundant when their own work ceases *(Murray v Foyle [1999] IRLR 562)*. Thus, where employees work at one location they can claim redundancy pay when that work goes, even in cases where their contract specifies that they can be required to work at other locations *(High Table v Horst [1997] IRLR 513)*.

A dismissal for redundancy purposes is defined in *section 136 ERA 96* in a broadly similar way to that for unfair dismissal (see chapter 10 – What is a dismissal?), but it does not matter whether workers have **volunteered or been selected**. The tribunal will treat either as dismissal for redundancy reasons.

The EAT held *(Langston v Cranfield University [1998] IRLR 172)* that tribunals should **consider all aspects of redundancy**, including whether there was an unfair selection, lack of consultation or failure to seek alternative employment, in cases of unfair dismissal on grounds of redundancy.

Some collective agreements contain a "**no compulsory redundancy**" clause. Under these the employer "guarantees" not to make redundancies, other than from volunteers. However, the Court of Appeal, in the case of *Kaur v MG Rover [2005] IRLR 40*, has held that such clauses are "aspirational" only and are not enforceable by employees threatened with compulsory redundancies.

Consultation

The *Collective Redundancies and Transfer of Undertakings (Protection of Employment) (Amendment) Regulations 1995*, place a legal obligation on employers to consult whenever they are **proposing** to dismiss as redundant **20 or more employees at one establishment** within a 90-day period. It does not matter if in the end fewer than 20 employees will be made redundant, because some employees would be offered alternative employment, the obligation to consult exists if the **proposal** was to make 20 or more redundancies (*Hardy v Tourism SE EAT/0631/04*).

To calculate whether or not the number of redundancies is 20 or more, you can only take account of the numbers employed in the establishment. The term "**establishment**" is defined narrowly as the location where the employee works, according to the case of *Rockfon v Specialarbejderforbundet [1996] IRLR 168.*

The definition of redundancy for the purposes of consultation differs from that given above. It is **"a dismissal for a reason not related to the individual concerned"**. "Unless the contrary is proved" an employee must be presumed to have been dismissed for redundancy.

Employers should **not make redundancy dismissals without having first completed the statutory consultation**, according to the case of *Junk v Kuhnel C-188/03.*

Irmtrauud Junk was employed as a care assistant. The home where she worked was insolvent and as a result she was made redundant. Junk challenged the redundancy on the grounds that it had occurred before the consultation period had ended. The European Court of Justice held that a contract could only be terminated after conclusion of the consultation procedure. The effectiveness of rights to be consulted would be compromised, if an employer were entitled to terminate contracts of employment during the course of the consultation procedure. It would also make it more difficult for workers' representatives to achieve withdrawal of a decision to make the redundancies.

Who is consulted?

Regulation 3 says that the employer **must consult** "all persons who are **appropriate representatives**" of any employees likely to be made redundant. Where the union is recognised the "appropriate representatives" are defined as representatives from the **recognised unions**. Trade union representatives have the right to paid time off to take part in consultation.

Where there is no recognised union the employer must invite employees likely to be made redundant to **elect employee representatives** "long enough before the time when the consultation is required". The law is silent on what happens if employees do not accept the invitation. They may lose the right to be consulted, although this appears to go against the requirements of a European directive. Employee representatives need to be **suitably elected and independent**. There are clear rules governing the arrangements for election, numbers to be elected and terms of office. Where there is no recognised union, the employer can consult with members of a standing body with which it consults on a regular basis.

Employee representatives elected for the purposes of redundancy consultation have **statutory protection against dismissal**. The protection from any detrimental action extends to representatives and **candidates for election**. Employee representatives are also entitled to **reasonable time off** to perform their functions as reps or candidates. They must be allowed **access to employees** and must be provided with accommodation and other appropriate facilities.

Employers have an implied duty to **consult with individual employees**, even where there is no obligation in law to consult with the union or employee representatives due to the small numbers involved. If the employer wishes to avoid an unfair dismissal claim, consultation has to be more than a mere notification of the intention to declare redundancies. There should be consultation even if at the end of the day the employee would almost certainly be made redundant.

Without warning Mr Derry was told his job was at risk. Within a week he was given his redundancy notice. The EAT ruled that his employers should have consulted with him. Even though the likelihood was that he would be made redundant, the EAT awarded him an additional three weeks' pay over and above his redundancy pay. This represented a reasonable consultation period and Derry should not have been given notice until after that period had passed *(Derry v BHC Aerovox EAT/0558/01).*

A **failure to consult** can make what might otherwise have been a fair dismissal into an unfair one.

Thomas Oakley was told his job was redundant. He applied unsuccessfully to be redeployed to different posts, on lower grades. He was rejected and made redundant. He later discovered that the employer had a private policy against the redeployment of redundant staff to lower graded posts. Had he or the union known of this during the consultation, they would have been able to make representations for his redeployment. The EAT held that the consultation was therefore "tainted with unfairness" and that Oakley's dismissal was unfair *(Oakley v Merseyside Magistrates Court Committee EAT/379/02).*

In one case the EAT said that an employer's failure to **warn an employee** about a likely redundancy several months in advance made the eventual dismissal unfair.

The consultation process

If 100 or more employees at one establishment (workplace) are to be dismissed **consultation must begin at least 90 days before the redundancies take effect**. If the numbers involved are more than 20 but less than 100 the minimum consultation period is reduced to **30 days**. Although these are the minimum periods laid down by law, in practice employers should **consult as soon as possible** and not wait until the statutory time clock starts ticking *(Elkouil v Coney Island [2002] IRLR 174)*.

Consultation must begin once the employer has **adopted a specific proposal** involving redundancies *(Hough v Leyland [1991] IRLR 194)*. A "proposal" to make redundancies occurs once it has been submitted to the management board for ratification *(Dewhirst v GMB EAT/0486/03)*. Employers should not wait until the proposals reach the stage where they could be implemented. However, the EAT in the case of *MSF v Refuge Assurance [2002] IRLR 324* said that while the European directive on collective redundancies referred to consultation beginning when redundancies were "contemplated", the UK law appeared to require consultation at a later stage. Although this did not seem to meet the standards set by EU law, the EAT was not able to go beyond what the UK legislation clearly said. However, even where the employer is looking at two options, only one of which involves redundancies, there is still an obligation to consult *(Scotch Premier Meat v Burns [2000] IRLR 639)*.

Consultation is not linked to whether or not the recognised union has members who will be affected. The employer must **consult with all recognised unions** *(Governing Body NI Hotel and Catering College v NATFHE [1995] IRLR 83)*.

Consultation must begin "**in good time**". Just giving the employee rep or union a copy of the notice which goes to the secretary of state (see below) is unlikely to be sufficient to initiate the redundancy consultation period *(MSF v GEC Ferranti Defence Systems [1994] IRLR 113)*.

Employers are also obliged by law to consult on:

- ways of **avoiding dismissals**;
- **reducing the number** of employees to be dismissed; and
- **mitigating the consequences** of dismissal.

In the course of consultation the employer must consider representations and reply to them. And this consultation should be undertaken **"with a view to reaching agreement".**

Consultation must be real and not a "sham", according to an EAT decision which said that issuing redundancy notices by letter half an hour after a meeting with the unions had ended suggested that the consultation was not **meaningful**. The representatives consulted must have time to consider properly any proposals put to them *(TGWU v Ledbury Preserves [1985] IRLR 412)*. If an employer has already **decided to make redundancies** before consulting with reps and is not prepared to consider other options, this would not amount to genuine meaningful consultation *(Middlesborough BC v T&G [2002] IRLR 332)*.

The Court of Session in Scotland, in the case of *King v Eaton [1996] IRLR 199*, held that the mere fact that the employer had **meetings with the reps** was not sufficient to establish that there had been fair consultation.

The employer must also **notify the secretary of state** (in practice the local Department of Trade and Industry office) of all proposed redundancies of 20 or more employees.

In the case of *Ferguson v Prestwick Circuits [1992] IRLR 266*, the employer said that previous experience suggested **employees did not like consultation**. This did not, according to the tribunal, absolve the employer of the obligation to consult.

The fact that an employer reasonably believes there is **no alternative to redundancy** is not sufficient to avoid the obligation to consult, since it could have been the case that the employee, unknown to the employer, was in possession of facts which altered the situation *(Heron v Citylink [1993] IRLR 372)*.

In the case of *R v British Coal ex parte Price [1994] IRLR 72*, the High Court held that a fair consultation must include giving the person being consulted the proper **opportunity to fully understand the**

issues. They also need to be able to express their views on them, and for these to be given genuine consideration. But the High Court also noted that the fact that voluntary redundancies are occurring while the consultation is in process does not, in itself, invalidate the consultation.

Remedies for failure to consult

If employers fail or refuse to consult, a complaint can be made to a tribunal. This must be done by whoever should have been consulted — either the union or the employee representative. The tribunal can make a **protective award**, which is a sum of money paid to each affected employee. The purpose of the award is not to compensate the employee for the loss they have suffered, but to provide a **sanction against the employer** for the failure to consult, according to the Court of Appeal in the case of *Susie Radin v GMB and others [2004] IRLR 400.* In the case of *Smith and Moore v Cherry Lewis [2005] IRLR 86*, the EAT held that the sanction of a **protective award is meant to be punitive**. The award can be up to 90 days' pay and the EAT has said that the tribunals should use this as a starting point and then decide whether there are circumstances to justify reducing it *(T&G v Morgan Platts EAT/0646/02)*. A tribunal will grant this unless the employer can show that there were **special circumstances** making it not reasonably practicable to consult, but that all reasonably practicable steps to comply were taken. In a recent case where the question of what these special circumstances might amount to was examined, the EAT held that an employer could not escape the obligation to consult in good time by claiming that not all the necessary information was available. If some information is available it must be consulted over *(GMB and Amicus v Beloit Walmsley [2004] IRLR 18)*. **Insolvency of itself does not constitute special circumstances**. For these circumstances to apply there has to be something out of the ordinary and insolvency does not come into that category, according to the EAT in the case of *Iron and Steel Trades Confederation v ASW Holdings [2004] IRLR 926)*.

But the employer will still be liable to pay the protective award even if its view was that consultation would have **made no difference** to the redundancies *(Sovereign Distribution Services v TGWU [1989] IRLR 334)*. Even if the company goes into receivership this does not bring the award period to an end (*AEEU/GMB v Clydesdale Group [1995] IRLR 527)* nor does it allow for the award to be offset against any redundancy pay due.

In one case, the EAT reduced the compensation award by 50% to take account of the fact that, even if the correct procedures had been followed, the employees still had a 50% chance of losing their jobs because there were four employees, but only two available posts.

But the tribunal can still make an award to cover an additional period when the employee would have worked had proper consultation occurred *(Mining Supplies v Baker [1988] IRLR 417).* If the employer fails to consult it is therefore worth claiming both redundancy and unfair dismissal.

The claim for the award must normally be made within three months of the dismissal. If an employer fails to pay the award, individuals covered by it can go back to a tribunal to claim it. There is a **three-month time limit** within which to present this further claim.

Although the government announced in early 2001 that it intended to review the law on consultation in redundancies, by April 2005 it still had not published any firm proposals.

Selection for redundancy

Usually the employer will operate a formula for selecting employees for redundancy. Selection criteria will rarely be regarded as having been **incorporated into an employee's contract** of employment. This means that the fact that an employer decides to change the selection procedures will not normally give rise to a breach of contract claim. When examining selection criteria the tribunal will merely ask whether a reasonable employer could have adopted the criteria chosen. As long as the criteria are fairly and reasonably applied and are **not discriminatory** on the grounds of **sex, race, disability, gender reassignment, trade union membership**, **sexual orientation or religion or belief** and are not for any of the reasons connected with automatically unfair dismissal (see chapter 10), they cannot be challenged. An employer cannot directly discriminate in selection, but may be able to indirectly discriminate, although they must objectively justify this choice, according to the ECJ in the case of

Kachelmann v Bankhaus Hermann Lampe [2001] IRLR 49.

You may be able to succeed in claiming unfair dismissal if selected for redundancy without consultation. The *Employment Act 2002 (effective from 1 October 2004)* requires there to be a hearing prior to a dismissal and without this the dismissal can be automatically unfair. Where the same manager makes the selection and also hears the appeals, again it may be open to the tribunal to find that the selection is unfair for procedural reasons.

The selection of two employees because they had been **leading strike activists** comes within the definition of an unfair dismissal *(Britool v Roberts [1993] IRLR 481).* Selecting someone for redundancy because they spent **too much time on union activities** is automatically unfair, even in cases where the employer has no malice or intent to get rid of the employee because of trade union activities *(Dundon v GPT [1995] IRLR 403).* Equally, an employer cannot assess an employee based on skills demonstrated while carrying out their work as a **safety rep** *(Smiths Industries v Rawlings [1996] IRLR 656).* An employee's duties as a trade union or safety rep should **neither prejudice nor advantage** a redundancy selection.

However, union representatives need to exercise care if switched to alternative work to allow them to **accommodate their trade union duties**. The Court of Appeal ruled that it was fair to select the rep for redundancy when the company no longer needed the alternative work he was doing, even though there was still the need for work in his substantive post *(O'Dea v ISC Chemicals [1995] IRLR 599).*

A proposal not to select an employee for redundancy only if they nominate an alternative candidate has also been held to be an unfair dismissal *(Boulton & Paul v Arnold [1994] IRLR 532).*

There is currently no law outlawing discrimination based on **age**, although the *Rutherford* case (see chapter 6 – Types of unlawful discrimination) is due to be heard at the House of Lords later this year. Some selection procedures use age as a criterion and this has, on occasion, been challenged as potentially discriminatory.

Employers may use criteria like **absenteeism** to select, so long as the impact is not to discriminate against disabled workers (see above).

Where sickness absence is used as a criterion for selection (other than in relation to disabled workers) the employer is not obliged to take account of the employee's reasons for having been off sick.

Tribunals will usually look to see whether employers have followed previously adopted criteria. Most organised workplaces will have an agreed procedure for redundancy selection, but the *Deregulation and Contracting Out Act 1994* removed the presumption that a dismissal is unfair where the employer ignores the agreed selection procedure.

In the case of *British Aerospace v Green [1995] IRLR 433*, the Court of Appeal held that there was no legal obligation on employers to disclose the assessments of employees not selected.

The EAT has said that whilst an element of subjectivity in deciding on redundancy selection is not in itself grounds for a challenge, the **complete elimination of criteria** like length of service should be avoided.

Employers do have duties in relation to selection. For example, a decision to make a long-standing employee redundant when a job he was temporarily attached to ended, was held by the EAT to amount to an unfair selection, in so far as the employer should have considered selecting other similarly graded employees with less experience or qualifications *(Balfour Beatty Construction v Baird EAT/120/00).*

Asking for **volunteers first** is not part of a selection procedure itself and is therefore not bound by the rules of the selection procedure. At the same time the refusal of a company to call for volunteers before implementing its selection procedure would not give grounds for a claim *(Rogers and others v Vosper Thornycroft [1989] IRLR 82).*

Alternative work

An employer is obliged to consider offering suitable alternative work if it is available and this might include considering whether employment was available in other companies within the same group. Employers **must offer** alternative work, if available, to women who are **pregnant or on maternity leave**. There is no obligation to offer alternative work on a higher grade than that of the redundant post. If the employer does not consider offering alternative employment, the tribunal will take this into account in deciding whether the redundancy was fair. However, if the employer considers the employee not suited to the job there is no obligation to offer the alternative.

Offers of suitable alternative employment are covered by *section 141 ERA 96*. This lays down that any such offer must be made before the old contract ends and must be for such work to begin **within four weeks** of the date of the end of the original employment.

It must be the **same as, or a suitable alternative** to, the previous work and must be **suitable for that particular employee**. But the EAT has said that the issue of whether work is suitable is to be considered separately from whether an employee is acting reasonably in refusing it. Whether or not work is **suitable depends upon subjective factors personal to the employee.**

Mr Ruse was made redundant and offered suitable alternative work at the same grade but in a post which he saw as of lower status. The EAT accepted this gave him the right to reject the offer and seek redundancy pay *(Cambridge Co-op v Ruse [1993] IRLR 156).*

Mr Denton was offered an alternative job that would have required him to work in a dusty environment. Even though the work was suitable, he had an obsession with the potential health hazards of air borne dust since close relatives had died from respiratory infections. The tribunal said that even though his fears were groundless, they were genuine and made the refusal reasonable *(Denton v Neepsend [1976] IRLR 164).*

Work would normally be considered unsuitable if it involved changes in pay, travelling time, skill requirements or status.

If employees **refuse an offer of suitable alternative work** they will lose the right to redundancy pay.

Employees have the right to a **trial period** of four weeks in the new job. These four weeks are defined as calendar, not working weeks *(Benton v Sanderson Kayser [1989] IRLR 19)*. The employer should give the worker a **written copy** of the agreement specifying the terms and conditions of the new work and the date of termination of the trial period *(138 ERA 96)*. If an employer refuses a trial period the employee can claim unfair dismissal *(Elliot v Richard Stump [1987] IRLR 215)*. If an employee agrees to accept the offer of a new job for a trial period there will still be the right to redundancy pay if the post proves not to be suitable due to the employer not giving the employee the support that was promised. Working beyond the four weeks is likely to bar the employee's right to claim redundancy pay, if the alternative does not work out.

Mr O'Hara accepted an offer of alternative work. He then decided it was unsuitable and wrote to his employer to that effect. However, he continued working. The EAT held that his letter did not amount to a notice to terminate his employment and since he had worked beyond the four weeks he had no right to redundancy pay (*Reality (White Arrow Express) v O'Hara EAT/0447/03*).

Looking for work

While under notice of redundancy, employees have the right **to reasonable time off with pay** during working hours to look for alternative work, provided that they meet the qualifying conditions (see below). There is no fixed amount of time off that employers should give.

If an employer refuses time off, or payment for the time off, employees can make a claim to a tribunal that can order the employer to pay *(section 52 ERA 96)*. However the maximum an employer can be required to pay by a tribunal is 40% of weekly earnings. The complaint must be made **within three months** of the employer's refusal.

Qualifying for redundancy pay

To qualify for statutory redundancy pay employees must be employed for **two years** by the date of dismissal, **regardless of their hours of work**. The one-year service qualification in unfair dismissal claims **does not apply** to redundancy claims.

Employees **do not qualify** for statutory redundancy pay if:

- offered **suitable alternative employment** (see above);
- **aged under 20 or over their "normal retirement age"** (or 65 if there is none);
- guilty of **misconduct** *(section 140 ERA 96)*;
- working under a **fixed-term contract** entered into before 1 October 2002 and have waived redundancy rights; or
- **industrial action** is taking place and redundancy notice is given *(section 140 ERA 96)*.

Employees on a series of **fixed-term contracts** may be entitled to redundancy pay at the expiry of each contract *(Pfaffinger v City of*

Liverpool Community College) [1996] IRLR 508). Employers can no longer get temporary employees to sign waiver clauses and so avoid paying them redundancy pay, although they will still have to have worked for the employer for at least two years to qualify.

Employees will lose the right to claim statutory redundancy pay if they **leave work before the actual issue of the redundancy notice**. But employees under notice of redundancy can mutually agree with their employers to **extend the notice**, for example, in the hope of work picking up, without jeopardising redundancy entitlement *(Mowlem Northern v Watson [1990] IRLR 500)*. However, if employees do **agree to an earlier termination** date you need to bear in mind that by bringing forward the date of dismissal, if later they find that there is the basis for an unfair dismissal claim, it must be lodged within three months of the new date of dismissal (*Palfrey v Transco [2004] IRLR 916*).

The **time limit** for making a claim for redundancy pay is **six months** from the date when the contract ends.

Compensation for redundancy

Contrary to widely held beliefs there is **no European Union scheme** to pay workers made redundant, nor are there plans for one. Redundancy pay depends entirely on what is in the employment contract or, if it is silent on the issue, on the statutory scheme.

Statutory redundancy pay is calculated by taking account of **the worker's age and length of employment** and then working out how many "weeks' pay" they have the right to. It is **uprated annually**, taking account of the increase in the RPI each September. The new rate usually comes into effect the following February. The method of calculation is based on age and length of service, and is similar to that for the unfair dismissal basic award (see chapter 10 – Compensation).

For the purposes of the calculation, a week's pay cannot be more than £280 (in 2005/06) and the **maximum** number of years of employment that can be taken into account is 20. This means that the maximum statutory redundancy pay in 2005/06, where the worker is aged 61 or over, is £8,400.

Employment before age 18 is not included in the calculation. Employees who have moved from full-time to **part-time work** cannot credit their years of full-time earnings to calculate redundancy pay *(Barry v Midland Bank [1999] IRLR 581).*

Redundancy pay (both statutory and contractual) is tax free up to £30,000. However, **negotiated settlements** reached in the absence of an alleged breach of contract are **taxable**.

Mr Delaney had a contractual right to 18 months' notice. His employers told him that they wanted to end his contract and, following negotiations, they agreed to pay him a lump sum of £75,000 "in compensation for the termination of his employment and loss of office". Delaney thought that this amounted to a redundancy and that the whole of the first £30,000 would be tax free. The Inland Revenue won a ruling in the High Court that it had the right to tax him on the whole amount *(Richardson (Inspector of Taxes) v Delaney [2001] IRLR 663).*

The employer must give the employee a **written statement** saying how **redundancy pay is calculated** *(section 165 ERA 96)* and must also **inform the representative**. Employers can be fined a small amount for failure to comply with this requirement.

Employers can offer **contractual redundancy pay** that is better than the statutory scheme. However, according to the Court of Appeal decision in the case of *Albion Automotive v Walker [[2002] EWCA Civ 946*, employees will only have a contractual right to the occupational scheme if all of the following apply:

- the terms have been **drawn to the employees' attention** and are **well-known**;
- the terms have been **followed for a substantial period of time**;
- these have been followed on a **number of occasions**;
- payments were made **more or less automatically**;
- the policy as **communicated** to staff indicated that management intended to be bound by it;
- it was **adopted by agreement** with workplace representatives;
- its **terms were incorporated** into a written agreement;
- its terms were **consistently applied**; and
- employees had a **reasonable expectation** that they would be applied.

Where an employer has on previous occasions paid redundancy at an enhanced rate, but never included it in the terms of their contracts, there is no custom and practice to guarantee the right to the payment in a later round of redundancy (*Quinn v Calder Industrial Materials [1996] IRLR 126).* It is also the case that where a redundancy pay scheme requires a decision on each occasion, it is not an incorporated term in the employee's contract. However, where there is an enhanced redundancy scheme, the case of *Powermarque v Sykes EAT/0954/03* may be relevant. In that case, the EAT held that once an employee had been accepted for redundancy they gained entitlement to the enhanced scheme. Any discretionary element within the scheme only related to the right to apply for redundancy.

Employers cannot try to **avoid paying contractual redundancy pay** by dismissing employees instead.

Mr Jenvey was dismissed for asserting his statutory right to ask for the reasons for his dismissal. His employers argued that because they had unfairly dismissed him he had no right to his contractual redundancy pay. The High Court rejected the argument. The employer could not use the unfair reason for dismissal as a way of getting round having to pay contractual redundancy pay *(Jenvey v Australian Broadcasting Corp [2002] IRLR 520).*

In determining entitlement to redundancy pay, employers cannot impose criteria that **discriminate on unlawful grounds**. A contractual redundancy scheme that excludes employees over state retirement age, and therefore currently excludes women over 60, is unenforceable and the EAT has ruled that such a scheme must apply equally to women workers up to the age of 65 *(McKechnie v UBM [1991] IRLR 283).*

In certain circumstances workers may also have redundancy **pay offset against periodic occupational pension** entitlement *(section 158 ERA 96).*

The pay rights of employees on **annual hours' contracts** are sometimes called into question when the contract ends during the year of calculation.

In the case of *Ali v Christian Salvesen [1997] IRLR 17,* the Court of Appeal ruled that employees on annualised hours could not have their salary, for redundancy pay purposes, calculated to take account of the fact that they would have averaged more than 40 hours a week had their employment lasted the full year.

If the employer pays **more generous** redundancy pay this can be fully credited against any compensatory award for unfair dismissal *(Digital Equipment v Clements [1998] IRLR 134).*

For **local government employees** a separate statutory scheme allows for a maximum of 66 weeks' pay for those under age 50 but is discretionary for the over 50s. A "week's pay" is calculated on actual earnings and not subject to the £280 maximum.

Employees who have been unfairly selected for redundancy or who have been made redundant in breach of procedure can claim compensation for unfair dismissal, in addition to their statutory redundancy pay (see chapter 10 – Compensation).

If the employer cannot pay redundancy compensation because of **insolvency**, it becomes payable, under *section 182 ERA 96*, by the secretary of state (see chapter 10 – Compensation). However, the basic award will be set off against the redundancy payment.

In the case of *Crawford v Secretary of State for Employment [1995] IRLR 523*, the employee, along with the receivers, presumed that he had been transferred under TUPE to the new employers and that his continuity was preserved (see chapter 12 – Protecting employment rights). He later discovered that the transfer was not under TUPE and lodged an application for redundancy pay. The EAT ruled that he was outside the three-month time limit. The fact that he was unaware of his true legal position was not relevant.

State benefits

Workers who have lost work either through unfair dismissal or redundancy will normally be entitled to the **Jobseeker's Allowance**. If a worker is dismissed without notice and notice pay is awarded by a tribunal, any state benefit already received will be offset *(Westwood v Secretary of State for Employment [1984] IRLR 209).*

Workers cannot claim **Income Support**, however, if personal resources (including redundancy pay or unfair dismissal compensation) exceed £8,000.

More information: LRD booklets *Redundancy law* (£3.50); *State Benefits & Tax Credits 2004* (£5.50); LRD's *Workplace Report* has regular quarterly ,updates on redundancy law.

12. Business transfers and contracting out

If a company is sold (other than through a share transfer) or if a service is privatised or contracted out, the *Transfer of Undertakings (Protection of Employment) Regulations 1981 (TUPE)*, give some protection to employees who are transferred.

There is **no time limit** after which TUPE protection no longer applies. In one case the EAT held that an employee who was dismissed **two years after a transfer** could still claim protection under TUPE. His employers wanted him to agree to have his protected terms and conditions harmonised with those of other workers who had not transferred. He refused and was dismissed. The EAT ruled that this was a dismissal for an automatically unfair reason.

The TUPE regulations were introduced to give effect to the European *Acquired Rights Directive* 1977. It says that existing terms remain the same until the termination, or entry into force, of a new collective agreement, with a proviso that existing terms may be observed for no less than a year.

However, the one-year minimum does not apply to UK law because it is the employment contract that governs employment relations, and any unilateral change to it, at any time, may give rise to a breach (see chapter 3 – Contract changes).

In March 2003, the government announced it would introduce amendments to the TUPE regulations with the aim of:

- applying TUPE **more comprehensively** when the business transferred or contracted out is labour intensive;
- placing legal obligations on the old employer to give the new employer **proper information on the pay and benefits** of staff likely to transfer;
- limiting the **powers of employers to dismiss** for economic reasons following a transfer; and
- changing the law to **assist in business rescues**, where companies are insolvent.

In March 2005, the government finally published the draft revised TUPE regulations, which were expected to come into force in October

2005. Public consultation on the legal effect of the draft regulations was due to end on 7 June 2005, after this booklet went to press.

Relevant transfers

The directive and the TUPE regulations protect employees affected by a **relevant transfer**. This is defined as a transfer:

- from **one person to another** of an entity or undertaking;
- effected by **sale or some other disposition**; and
- which may be effected by **two or more transactions**.

In the *Allen* case (see below) the European Court of Justice (ECJ) refines this definition to state that a relevant transfer includes:

"a change in the natural or legal person responsible for carrying on the business, who by virtue of this acquires the obligations of an employer vis-a-vis employees of the undertaking, regardless of whether or not ownership is transferred".

Transfers of **franchises and leases** and sales of subsidiaries therefore also come within the definition, as do transfers to a wholly owned subsidiary *(Allen v Amalgamated Construction [2000] IRLR 119)*. This means that companies cannot restructure in advance to **hive off** sections of the company and thus avoid TUPE. In the case of *In re Maxwell Fleet [2000] IRLR 368* the employer tried to avoid TUPE through a series of transfers prior to the eventual transfer. The High Court said that the series of transfers should be seen as one.

Entity or undertaking

For TUPE to apply, something has to be transferred from one employer to another. The business transferred is normally referred to as an **entity** or **undertaking**, defined by the ECJ as:

"an organised grouping of persons or assets facilitating the exercise of an economic activity which pursues a specific objective".

The entity or undertaking can be **identified** by: its workforce; its management; the way in which work is organised; its operating methods; or its operational resources. The entity should be: **stable**; **identifiable**; and **not limited to performing one specific contract**.

Even if **no staff** or significant assets have been transferred there could still be a relevant transfer, according to the Court of Appeal. In the case of *RCO Support Services v UNISON [2002] IRLR 401*, the new employer was prepared to rehire the old workforce as long as they resigned and accepted new but inferior terms. The court said that this showed there was still an identifiable entity and that not transferring staff was primarily aimed at avoiding TUPE protection. As a result, staff were protected by TUPE. In June 2004, an appeal against this ruling will be heard by the House of Lords.

Similarly, in the case of *Abler v Sodexho [2004] IRLR 168*, the ECJ held that a catering activity could not be assessed solely on its workforce and the fact that workers had not transferred did not mean that there was no relevant transfer. The court held that since the assets (premises, water, energy, customers and so forth) had transferred, there was a TUPE transfer. This, in turn, meant that the workers should also have transferred with TUPE protection.

The **workforce** itself can make up an economic entity, if no assets other than the workforce transfer.

It is not necessary that there is a **contractual link** between the transferor (the old employer) and the transferee (the new employer).

Until 1994, the cleaning contract for Volkswagen in Belgium was subcontracted to BMV, which in turn subcontracted the work to a subsidiary, GMC. Volkswagen terminated this contract and awarded a new contract to Temco. GMC dismissed all the staff but, under the terms of a collective agreement, Temco then hired 75% of the old workforce. Four workers who had not been hired took their claim to the ECJ for the right to transfer with the work. It held that so long as the staff taken on were essential, in terms of their number and skills, to the performance of the new contract, they were covered by the directive *(Temco Service Industries v Imzilyen [2002] IRLR 214)*.

The workers in the *Temco* case succeeded because they were an economic entity with identifiable tasks. Just being a group of workers hired under similar circumstances, but not identifiable as a single unit in any other way, would not be sufficient to qualify. In the case of *Wynnwith Engineering v Bennett [2002] IRLR 170*, the EAT ruled that the mere fact that some retired ex-employees had been rehired to cover jobs which would otherwise not have been filled did not make them an identifiable economic entity.

Examples of relevant transfers

A **"relevant transfer"** has been held to include:

- where **no staff transferred** but where other assets (like the transfer of client telephone numbers on payment of goodwill) did transfer *(McLeod v Ingram EAT/1344/01)*;
- the crew of an oil rig, when the company that employed the crew lost the contract to a new company, which did not take on the existing crew (*Dolphin Drilling v Gordon and others EATS/0101/03*).
- where **two unions amalgamate** staff contracts transfer to the new union body *(Godrich v PCS HC/02C01433)*;
- an **asset reliant service** (in this case providing lorries) where assets did not transfer *(P&O Trains European v Initial Transport [2003] IRLR 128)*;
- the transfer to a **local authority** of work previously carried out by a non-profit-making association, provided its identity is maintained *(Mayeur v Association Promotion de L'Information Messine [2000] IRLR 783)*;
- the transfer of a **public function** to a state-owned company *(Collino v Telecom Italia [2000] IRLR 788)*;
- the transfer of a **subcontracted business** to the contracting company;
- the transfer of a **single employee** from an existing employer to a new contractor *(Schmidt v Spar und Leihkasse [1994] IRLR 302)*;
- the transfer of all or part of the assets of a company in **voluntary liquidation** to another company that manages the transferred employees but where their work is subject to the orders of the company in liquidation (*Europieces SA v Sanders C-339/96*); and
- the transfer of an economic entity which consisted of the **workforce itself** *(Francisco Hernandez* case *[1999] IRLR 132)*.

No relevant transfer

In contrast, there are situations where **TUPE will not apply** because the courts rule that there is no relevant transfer. For example, where **neither physical assets nor most staff** transfer *(Whitewater Leisure Management v Barnes [2000] IRLR 456)*. The case of *Oy Liikenne Ab v Liskojarvi [2001] IRLR 171* is important here.

The ECJ considered whether the transfer of a contract from one contractor to another was capable of coming within the terms of the transfer regulations. The

ECJ ruled that although tenders for contracts could be covered, whether or not they were in practice depended on whether there was a relevant transfer. In looking at the transfer of a contract to provide a bus service, the ECJ held that the fact that the service provided by the old and new contractors was similar was not in itself indicative of a relevant transfer. The assets of a bus company amounted to more than its employees. This meant that where there was no transfer of "significant" assets, such as equipment, there was unlikely to be a relevant transfer. The ECJ also held that the contract itself, which was only for three years, was not a significant intangible asset.

Other situations held not to amount to a relevant transfer include:

- an internal reorganisation where a group manages its business through a number of different entities with different names *(McChrystal v Wimpey Homes EAT/0046/03)*;
- in cases of **insolvency** where there is an irretrievable cessation of the business. The EAT, in the case of *Perth & Kinross Council v Donaldson [2004] IRLR 121,* held that an operation that depends for its existence on a day-to-day handout of work cannot be a stable economic entity;
- the award of a contract where the new company made it clear that it did not want any of the old workforce and where the **individual did not want to transfer**. The fact that there was no transfer of assets or employees and the business was labour intensive indicated that there was not a relevant transfer *(Williams v Lockhart Security Services EAT/1395/01);*
- the award of a new contract which required a **different level of supervision and different working hours**. No assets or employees were transferred and this meant that there was no identifiable economic entity and therefore no TUPE transfer *(Initial Contract Services v Harrison EAT/64/01)*;
- where the entity itself, although identifiable as a separate undertaking before the transfer, does **not maintain a separate identity after the transfer**;
- where a new firm takes over a contract but **does not take on any staff**, provided that the reason is not to avoid TUPE. The Court of Appeal held that "the mere loss of a service contract to a competitor cannot itself indicate the existence of a transfer" *(ADI (UK) v Willer [2001] IRLR 542)*;
- the transfer of an employee to a new contractor only to **complete a contract** commenced by the old employer *(Ledernes Hovedorganisation v Dansk [1996] IRLR 51)*;

- the transfer of a **purely administrative function** from one administrative authority to another *(Henke v Gemeinde [1996] IRLR 701)*; and
- where **no significant** buildings, moveable property or intangible **assets transfer**, or if only a minority of employees are taken on *(Suzen v Zehnacker [1997] IRLR 255)*.

In all of these situations the **old employer is liable** for any dismissal or redundancy claims, as there has been no relevant transfer.

Collective agreements and consultation

The TUPE regulations affect collective organisation in two ways. Under *regulation 6* the terms of **collective and procedural agreements** automatically transfer, as do any **recognition** agreements that the old employer has accorded to the union. *Regulations 10* and *11*, as amended, state that prior to the transfer the old employer is under a duty to **consult in good time** and to inform representatives of:

- the fact that the transfer is taking place;
- its legal, economic and social implications; and
- measures to be taken in relation to employees.

As with redundancy (see chapter 11 – Consultation), the employer **must consult with the representatives of any recognised union**. Where there is no union, consultation takes place with specially elected **employee representatives**. The representatives should be allowed access to employees and appropriate facilities. If no representatives are appointed, the employer should take steps to inform employees directly of the proposed transfer.

The information to be given must cover "any employees who may be affected". Consultation must be "with a view to seeking their agreement to measures being taken". According to the EAT in the case of *South Durham HA v UNISON [1995] ICR 495*, there is no start date for the consultation and therefore no grounds for the employer to contest a complaint over lack of consultation by stating that it is premature. If there is no recognised union the employer must arrange for elections for employee representatives to create a consultation body. And if no representative is elected within a reasonable time, the employer must give relevant information to the affected employees.

Otherwise there is a failure to consult (*Howard v Millrise [2005] IRLR 84*).

If the employer fails to consult in accordance with *regulation 10*, under *regulation 11* the union or employee representatives may, **within three months**, make a complaint to an employment tribunal which can **award up to 13 weeks'** pay. This claim has to be made against the old employer *(TGWU v James McKinnon Haulage [2001] IRLR 597)*. The amount will not be offset against any payment under a protective award (see chapter 11 – Consultation).

Identifying employees who transfer

There is a presumption that employees do transfer and, unless there is evidence to show that this has not occurred, they will be taken to be employed by the new employer *(Sunley Turriff v Thompson [1995] IRLR 184)*. Where employees are assigned to work at **more than one location** it may be difficult to decide who is transferred and who is not when part of the business is sold off. In the case of *Duncan Web Offset v Cooper [1995] IRLR 633*, the EAT ruled, that since TUPE should be interpreted to give employee protection, tribunals should go beyond the declared terms of the contract to discover how, in practice, work is carried out.

In the case of *Securicor Guarding v Fraser Security Services [1996] IRLR 552*, the EAT held that security guards were identified with the **site to which they were assigned**. In the case of *Buchanan-Smith v Schleicher [1996] IRLR 547*, an employee located in one part of an organisation, but whose duties took her to another branch, was identified with that branch for TUPE purposes.

The individual must be employed at the date of the transfer. The case of *Dowling v ME Ilic Haulage and Berkeley Logistics EAT/0836/03*, a trade union victimisation case, showed that an individual not employed at the date of the transfer loses TUPE protection.

Mr Dowling was dismissed and claimed this was for trade union reasons. He applied for interim relief (see Chapter 10 – Trade union membership) and won a continuation order which meant that his employer had to continue paying him until his claim was heard at a tribunal. Before this could happen the place where he worked was transferred under TUPE. He sought to pursue his claim against the new company, but the EAT held that he was not an employee at the date of the transfer. The continuation order was only an order to continue paying him wages, it did not mean that his employment contract was still in existence.

There is often a problem identifying who transfers where **some work is transferred** while the rest remains in house. Where an employee has been engaged in both work that is being transferred and that which is not, the tribunal will make an assessment of the amount of time spent on each. The employee will be said to be attached to the work that takes up the majority of their time *(CLP Distribution v Todd [2003] IRLR 28)*. A worker **temporarily transferred** to an assignment at a different work location is not identified with that workplace in the event of a TUPE transfer. In the case of *Birmingham City Council v Gaston EAT/0508/03*, the EAT held that an employee, who was on 100% facility time as a union representative, could not be identified with a particular section of the workforce and was not therefore transferred under TUPE, when the part of the business in which he would have been working, had he not been on full-time trade union duties, was transferred.

There may also be a **breach of contract** claim where the employer fails to give the employee assurances about the work with the new employer. This, according to the case of *Euro-Die v Skidmore* EAT/1158/98, can amount to a breach of trust and confidence.

The transfer takes place when the undertaking is transferred, regardless of whether employees were given notice of the change, or whether they knew the identity of the new employer *(Secretary of State for Trade and Industry v Cook [1997] IRLR 150)*.

An employee may **object to a transfer** to another employer, but this may mean that the contract of employment is terminated without being treated as an unfair dismissal. In other words, employees can refuse to transfer, but cannot then claim redundancy or unfair dismissal. However, employees may be able to claim **wrongful dismissal** (see chapter 10 – Wrongful dismissal) where a change in terms and conditions would be substantial and detrimental *(University of Oxford v Humphreys [2000] IRLR 183)*.

Protecting employment rights

Contracts of employment existing at the date of the transfer **automatically transfer**, regardless of the intentions of the old or new employer *(Rotsart de Hertaing v J Benoidt SA [1997] IRLR 127)*. This means that employees **keep their existing terms and conditions**.

Regulation 5 of TUPE states that any employee in employment immediately before the transfer, and transferred as the result of a relevant transfer, has the right to **continued employment on existing terms and conditions**, including profit-related pay. The right applies only to the **contractual terms that employees had at the date of the transfer**.

In the case of *Ackinclose and others v Gateshead MBC [2005] IRLR 79*, the EAT ruled against a group of school meals workers, who had been contracted-out under TUPE and then contracted back in. They argued that on their return to the contracted-in service they should have the right to the terms and conditions they would have had if they had never been contracted-out. The EAT held that the right under TUPE applied only to terms at the date of the transfer.

The definition of **"immediately before"** includes employees, who would have been employed immediately before the transfer, had their old employer not unfairly dismissed them. In some cases it is difficult to identify the actual moment when the transfer occurred.

In the case of *Astley v Celtec [2002] IRLR 629*, the Court of Appeal, reversing an earlier EAT ruling, held that it is essentially **for the tribunals to decide** on the moment of the transfer. The new owner does not have to be in actual occupation and control before there can be said to have been a transfer. The employer appealed against this ruling and in November 2003, the House of Lords decided to **refer the case to the ECJ**. The Advocate General, the ECJ's chief legal officer, has suggested that unless the law is interpreted to take account of a transfer in stages, it would make it impossible for workers, whose workplace is being progressively transferred, to have TUPE protection. The ECJ will give its judgement later in 2005.

The rights to keep existing terms and conditions include, according to the case of *Whent v T Cartledge [1997] IRLR 153*, maintaining pay rates (including future rates) as set out in the **national agreement**. This is the case where the employee's contract states that pay is as is set down in the national agreement, regardless of whether or not the new employer is a party to that agreement *(Glendale Managed Services v Graham [2003] IRLR 465).*

Other employment rights that transfer include: claims regarding pay arrears; equal pay claims; outstanding legal claims (other than criminal claims); personal injury claims; disciplinary records; and any contractual requirements regarding confidentiality, patents and so on. If the employees claim that their old employer failed to consult over the forthcoming TUPE transfer, a claim can be brought against the new employer *(Alamo Group v Tucker [2003] IRLR 266).*

The ECJ, in the case of *Boor v Ministre de la Fonction Publique et de la Reforme administrative [2005] IRLR 61*, held that an individual's length of service also transfers for the purpose of calculating pay, where length of service was used to calculate pay.

Redundancy pay terms can also transfer.

Mr Spiers was transferred under TUPE but was then offered inferior redundancy terms. The EAT ruled that his new employer could not ignore TUPE rights. Indeed it went further and held that Spiers himself could not agree to vary his contract terms, if the sole reason for doing so was the TUPE transfer *(Lansing Linde Severside v Spiers EAT/1490/01).*

Even if, after the transfer, the employer offers those accepting voluntary redundancy different terms, which they accept, this does not affect contractual redundancy pay rights *(Solectron Scotland v Roper and others [2004] IRLR 4).* There may, however, be circumstances where the employee will have an **"equivalent"** employment right as opposed to an identical right — for example, where it is not in the new employer's power to offer the identical term.

In the case of *MITIE Managed Services v French [2002] IRLR 52,* employees had benefited from a **share option scheme** with their old employer. The EAT held that it was sufficient for the new employer to offer a similar entitlement. In another case the EAT went further and held that a share option scheme was not remuneration at all since the only money paid into it comes from the employee. This meant that it was not covered by TUPE *(Keiller v Lothian Borders EAT/199/02).*

The contract transfers **in its entirety**. The employee cannot decide that there are terms unfavourable to her/him that should not be transferred.

It is **not the case that employment terms can never be changed**. In the course of any employment terms and conditions do change, usually by agreement. In the case of *Norris v Brown & Root EAT/386/00,* the EAT held that a change to the employee's terms, two years after the transfer, as a result of funding difficulties, was not covered by TUPE. However, where there is no agreement, any changes to the contract could potentially be a breach of contract (see chapter 3 – Contract changes).

Employees may also lose TUPE rights if they **agree to contract changes**, for example on promotion.

Mr Barry transferred with TUPE protection. He was then offered promotion and a new contract. Although it was never pointed out to him, the new contract did not give him the redundancy pay terms he had under TUPE. The EAT held that by accepting the new contract he had lost his TUPE rights *(Barry v Bateman Catering EAT/1515/00).*

The right to maintain existing conditions applies even if the new employer could have chosen to dismiss the employee for reasons unconnected with the transfer, but chose not to.

Mr Lutak had a medical condition that affected his work performance. His old employer had ignored this but the new employer decided to move him to another job that he could do, but which involved a pay loss. The EAT held that the change happened only because of the transfer. As a result Lutak's terms and conditions were protected *(Lutak v William West EAT/0032/01).*

The new employer also becomes liable for any **acts of discrimination** that occurred prior to the transfer *(DJM International v Nicholas [1996] IRLR 76).* Workers cannot currently claim rights to terms and conditions that might be **negotiated in the future** between the old employer and the union, in the absence of a contractual entitlement. Nor can they claim rights that they would not have had under the old contract.

College lecturers on fixed-term contracts had always had these contracts renewed under standard terms (known as the "silver book"). However, after the transfer they were offered new contracts when their existing contracts ended, but not on the same terms. The EAT held that they could not use TUPE to claim the terms they might have been offered if there had been no transfer *(Ralton v Havering FE College [2001] IRLR 738).*

In the case of *Wilson v St Helens BC [1998] IRLR 706,* the House of Lords ruled that employers could offer **worse conditions** where employees were made redundant before the transfer then re-hired.

According to the Court of Appeal in *Cornwall County Care v Brightman [1998] IRLR 228*, where there has been a dismissal and an offer of new employment on inferior conditions, the employer is obliged to pay compensation, but it is not the case that the original contracts continue in operation.

In cases where a company is **insolvent** and being wound up, but it nevertheless continues to trade, employees unlawfully dismissed shortly before the transfer can claim against the new employer *(Jules Dethier v Dassy [1998] IRLR 266).* This ECJ ruling contradicts a UK ruling in the case of *Warner v Adnet [1998] IRLR 394* in which the Court of Appeal ruled that TUPE dismissal rights did not apply.

The only employment entitlement that does not automatically transfer in its entirety is **pension rights**. *Regulation 7* excludes rights to preserve pensions on transfer *(Adams v Lancashire CC [1997] IRLR 436).* In the case of *Powerhouse Retail v Burroughs [2004] IRLR 979,* the Court of Appeal held that claims relating to pension rights must be brought against the transferor within six months of the date of the transfer. The case (previously known as *Preston v Wolverhampton Healthcare NHS Trust (No.3) [2004] IRLR 96)* was brought by UNISON on behalf of around 60,000 part time workers who had been denied the right to join the pension scheme. UNISON has appealed the decision and the appeal is due to be heard by the House of Lords in February 2006.

However, the ECJ held, in the case of *Beckham v Dynamoc [2002] IRLR 578*, that the local authority contractual pension scheme for the over 50s is a **substitute redundancy pay scheme** and therefore transfers under TUPE. It held that early retirement schemes, including pensions and lump sums, are covered by the *Acquired Rights Directive* because they are not strictly speaking "old-age benefits".

In the case of *Martin and others v South Bank University [2004] IRLR 74,* the ECJ made an important new ruling on pension rights.

The Redwood College of Health Studies transferred to the South Bank University. Staff were offered a new contract, which they did not have to accept. However, they were told that they would not be able to remain in the NHS pension scheme. Some time later there were redundancies and employees were offered early retirement but without the benefits that would have been available to them under the NHS scheme. The ECJ ruled that those transferred with TUPE protection must get the same early retirement benefits as they would have had prior to the transfer. Furthermore, even if they agree to accept lower benefits in return for early retirement, this will be invalid and the employer will still be legally obliged to pay the full benefits. While workers can agree to changes to their contracts after a transfer, they cannot do so if the changes have only been brought about as a result of the transfer, for example to harmonise their conditions with those of existing staff.

Changes to the law in 2000 allow **local authority employees** whose jobs are contracted out to choose to remain in the local authority pension scheme. They can do so provided their employer has included an **admission agreement** in the contract with the new contractor. This provides for the right of existing and future staff to remain within the local government pension scheme. If no such agreement is reached, transferred staff only have the right to a "broadly comparable" pension and there is no provision for new staff.

Under the *Pensions Act 2004,* employees who had access to an occupational pension scheme or a money purchase scheme that the employer contributed to prior to a transfer have the right to transfer to an occupational scheme operated by the new employer or to a stakeholder or money purchase scheme into which the new employer must make "relevant contributions" matching those of the old employer, but only up to a maximum of 6%.

However, the legislation still allows the parties after a transfer to opt out of the pension provision. Unlike other TUPE protection, pension rights would not be permanently guaranteed. *The Transfer of Employment (Pension Protection) Regulations 2005* set out the mechanics of pension protection following a TUPE transfer and establish the standards that the new pension scheme for TUPE transferred employees must maintain.

Protection against dismissal

Where the reason for dismissal is a transfer or impending transfer it will be **automatically unfair** (see chapter 10 – Automatically unfair dismissals). Employees dismissed before a transfer to make the business look more attractive, or where terms and conditions have been changed to standardise arrangements, have successfully pursued unfair dismissal claims. Because the regulations cover those employed "immediately before the transfer", certain employees can be excluded from protection if dismissed earlier. In the case of *Ibex Trading v*

Walton [1994] IRLR 564, the EAT held that employees dismissed after an administrator was appointed, who had proposed a substantial reduction in their wages, were not covered because at the time of their dismissal there was no identified purchaser for the company. In the case of *Meade and Baxendale v British Fuels [1996] IRLR 541* a dismissal prior to a transfer, even if unfair, was an actual dismissal and fresh contracts offered after the dismissal did not guarantee TUPE protection.

The one situation where a dismissal would not be automatically unfair is where the employer can show it is for an **"economic, technical or organisational" (ETO)** reason which involves **changes in the workforce** and is **reasonable** under *section 98 ERA 96*. According to the EAT, *regulation 8* of TUPE, which permits dismissals for economic reasons, is not limited to those redundancy dismissals which would have occurred even if there had not been a transfer *(Trafford v Sharpe & Fisher [1994] IRLR 325)*.

The tribunal, therefore, will **first consider if the transfer is a reason for the dismissal**. If it decides it was, then it will consider whether it is an ETO dismissal, which must involve changes in the workforce. This could be either a change in the numbers employed or a real change in a substantial or key area of the workforce. If either is the case, the dismissal will be for a fair reason (redundancy). Qualifying employees (see chapter 11 – Qualifying for redundancy pay) would be entitled to redundancy pay.

Even if dismissals are for an ETO reason, the employer still has to have **acted reasonably** and complied with the normal standards for unfair dismissal and redundancy.

If dismissals occur before or at the time of the transfer, the claim should be brought against the employer to whom the work has been transferred (*Stirling v Allan [1995] IRLR 301*). However, if they take place before a purchaser has been identified, the dismissals are not covered by TUPE.

Employees whose contracts have been breached may be able to resign and claim constructive dismissal. But, according to the Court of Appeal in the case of *Rossiter v Pendragon [2002] IRLR 483*, the contract must have been fundamentally breached (see chapter 3 – Contract changes).

Employees dismissed for **genuine redundancy** reasons prior to a transfer are not regarded as having transferred to the new employer. Their claims for redundancy pay and any other compensation due under the contract must be pursued against the old employer *(Thompson v SCS Consulting [2001] IRLR 801)*.

Contracting out of public services

The *1981 TUPE Regulations*, as initially drafted, had specifically sought to exclude the contracting out of public services by stating that the regulations only applied to transfers of a commercial nature. In 1993, the government was forced to change TUPE to reflect the intent of the EU directives that such transfers were to be included.

The case of *Wren v Eastbourne Borough Council [1993] IRLR 425*, involved a claim from cleansing workers who were made redundant when an outside contractor won a tender to do their work. The EAT ruled that a relevant transfer had occurred, despite the fact that nothing concrete was transferred, nor any goodwill, nor outstanding contracts.

This position was further strengthened after the ruling of the Court of Appeal in *Dines v Initial Healthcare Services [1994] IRLR 336*. This held that the dismissal of employees as redundant, when the **contractor they worked for lost the contract**, was covered by TUPE, so that the new contractor had to offer them the same terms and conditions as enjoyed under the old contractor.

A number of cases have examined the consequences of TUPE for public sector employment. They have ruled that there would only be "genuinely exceptional circumstances" where TUPE did not apply, for example, where the activity was new, there was no group of staff specifically or permanently assigned to the task, or where the features of the new service were significantly different. The courts have ruled that:

- the transfer of a **contracted-out service back into local authority** control was covered under TUPE *(Council of the Isles of Scilly v Brintel Helicopters [1995] IRLR 6)*;
- a district health authority's decision to switch a paediatric services **contract from one hospital to an NHS trust** was covered by TUPE *(Porter & Nanayakkara v Queens Medical Centre [1993] IRLR 486)*;

- the transfer of a housing maintenance contract which was to be carried out by **self-employed workers** was a relevant transfer *(BSG Property Services v Tuck [1996] IRLR 134)*;
- contracting out of a **Home Office education service** was a relevant transfer obliging the further education corporation that won the contract to honour the terms and conditions of existing staff *(Kenny and others v S. Manchester College [1993] IRLR 265)*; and
- transfers of ground maintenance work to an outside contract or the transfer of a street lighting maintenance contract are covered, although in both cases **no assets were transferred**.

However, with an increasingly complex series of interpretations of the regulations, there are also situations which appear similar and yet where a TUPE transfer has not been accepted. For example, a case in 1999 of a contractor who took over a refuse collection contract, together with only a minority of staff, was held not to be a TUPE transfer.

Representatives should **always attempt to claim TUPE protection** and seek from the existing employer a statement saying that the transfer is under TUPE. If the council decides to **reduce the wages** of staff to win the contract in-house, this may provide the grounds for an equal pay challenge (see chapter 4 – Equal pay).

One particular area of difficulty for unions organising in sectors where work has been transferred out has been the creation of a two-tier workforce of those with TUPE protection and those taken on after the transfer with no rights to the same terms and conditions. Following a determined trade union campaign on the issue, in early 2003 the government published a **statutory code** to protect the terms and conditions of newly employed staff. This does not give them the right to be employed on the same terms, but on "no less favourable terms" overall than those of transferred staff. New staff must also be offered "reasonable pension provision".

More information: LRD booklet *Transfers – an LRD guide to the TUPE regulations* (£3.50); LRD's *Workplace Report* has regular updates on TUPE.

Further information

Legal sources and publications

Throughout the booklet references have been made to the relevant **statutes**. Copies of these can be obtained directly from The Stationery Office (tel: 0870 600 5522) or from its website at: www.tso.co.uk.

Full text of the cases referred to in this booklet is contained in the monthly *Industrial Relations Law Reports (IRLR)* or in the *Industrial Cases Reports (ICR)*. Recent cases are also published on the web. EAT cases are found at: www.employmentappeals.gov.uk; Court of Appeal decisions are at: www.courtservice.gov.uk; House of Lords decisions are at: www.publications.parliament.uk

The following **books** may also be of use if you are taking a legal case:

Employment Handbook, Slade (Tolleys) (18th edition);

Discrimination Law Handbook, Ed: Aileen McColgan (Legal Action Group); and

Employment Tribunal Procedure, McMullen, Eady and Tuck (Legal Action Group).

Your **local library** may have copies of the statutes and can obtain the books and law reports. When using law books always check the date of publication to make sure that the book actually deals with the current law. Books published before 2004, for example, will omit many important legal developments in employment rights, for example the new requirements regarding tribunal claims.

The **Labour Research Department** also publishes booklets on specific legal issues. Relevant titles have been referred to in the "More information" box at the end of each chapter of this booklet. To order any of these titles see the tear-out order form overleaf.

LRD's monthly magazine *Workplace Report* provides up-to-date coverage of all legal developments with quarterly updates on contracts, termination of employment, discrimination, TUPE and tribunal procedures. To subscribe, see advertisement on inside back cover.

For LRD publications, tel: 020 7928 3649, see website: www.lrd.org.uk or contact LRD, 78 Blackfriars Road, London SE1 8HF.

Useful organisations

Organisations publishing codes of practice and guidance referred to in the booklet include the:

Central Arbitration Committee (CAC), which makes awards of statutory recognition of trade unions and deals with union requests for disclosure of information (see chapter 5). The CAC is at Third Floor, Discovery House, 28-42 Banner St, London EC1Y 8QE, tel: 020 7251 9747, www.cac.gov.uk

Department of Trade and Industry (DTI), 1 Victoria Street, London, SW1H 0ET, Enquiry Unit tel: 020 7215 5000, www.dti.gov.uk

Advisory, Conciliation and Arbitration Service (ACAS), Brandon House, 180 Borough High Street, London SE1 1LW, helpline: 08457 474747, textphone: 08456 061600, publications: 08702 429090, www.acas.org.uk

Equal Opportunities Commission (EOC), Arndale House, Arndale Centre, Manchester M4 3EQ, tel: 0845 601 5901, www.eoc.org.uk

Commission for Racial Equality (CRE), St Dunstan's House, 201-211 Borough High Street, London SE1 1GZ tel: 020 7939 0000, www.cre.gov.uk

Disability Rights Commission (DRC) can be contacted at DRC Helpline, Freepost MID02164, Stratford-upon-Avon, CV37 9BR, tel: 08457 622633, textphone: 08457 622644, www.drc-gb.org

Equality Commission for Northern Ireland (EOCNI), Equality House, 7-9 Shaftesbury Square, Belfast, BT2 7DP, tel: 028 90 500600, textphone: 028 90 500589, www.equalityni.org

The address of the regional **employment tribunal** offices can be obtained from the Bury St Edmunds Office of the Employment Tribunals Service, Southgate Street, Bury St Edmunds, Suffolk, IP33 2AQ, tel: 01284 762300, www.employmenttribunals.gov.uk

The Information Commissioner runs a data protection helpline, tel: 01625 545 745, email: mail@ico.gsi.gov.uk, www.information commissioner.gov.uk

The website also contains information on data protection and privacy and electronic communications.